International Office
WRITTLE COLLEGE
Chelmsford Essex CM1 3RR UK

D0532996

Landmark

ADVANCED | Student's Book

Simon Haines

OXFORD
UNIVERSITY PRESS

1.1 20th century people

Lead in

Time magazine marked the end of the 20th century by profiling 100 'remarkable people', who most influenced the last hundred years. They put these people into five categories.

- Leaders and Revolutionaries
- Artists and Entertainers
- Builders and Titans
- Scientists and Thinkers
- Heroes and Icons

1 The people in the photos were all included in the list. Which categories do you think they belong to?

2 Who do you think was *Time* magazine's *Person of the Century*?

Mohandas Gandhi

Oprah Winfrey

Albert Einstein

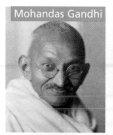

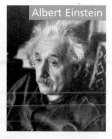

Sigmund Freud

Marilyn Monroe

Pelé

Bill Gates

Pope John Paul II

Pablo Picasso

Reading

1 You are going to read one person's reaction to the *Time* magazine list. As you read, tick or underline any ideas that you agree with.

I am the teacher of a third year English class in a school in Geneva. I discovered a web-site that fascinated me. *Time* magazine had chosen their one hundred most important people of the twentieth century. Their site had lots of interesting things to read,

5 look at, listen to. But I had one big disagreement with *Time*: of their hundred people, about fifty-six were Americans. It gave me the impression that you have to be American in order to be important. Nevertheless, I enjoyed their site, began making my own choices, discussed them with friends.

10 I have now completed my own list on which I tried to include more representatives of the Third World, more from the beginning of this century, fewer figures from contemporary American pop culture. I soon realized how little I know - about some places (China or Africa?), about certain subjects (medicine or

15 economics?), about the early part of this century.
Here are some of the problems I encountered in making my list:
- I too am ethnocentric, i.e. I tend to consider the people of my culture more important than those whom I don't know.
- I am fifty-three years old and I know the people who lived in
20 the second half of this century a lot better than those of my parents' generation.
- I tend to consider the people I like more important than those whom I don't.

Cliff Ruesch

2 Complete these sentences.

a The writer objected to *Time* magazine's list because …
b He thought he could write a better list by …
c The writer's personal limitations when he tried to make a list were that …

Language focus: discourse markers

1 What is the purpose of the words in **bold** in these extracts from the article? Which marker introduces examples, and which introduces a contrast?

  a *It gave me the impression that you have to be American in order to be important.* **Nevertheless,** *I enjoyed their site, …*

  b **Here are** *some of the problems I encountered …*

2 Here are some categories of discourse markers. Add the examples from the list to the chart below, and any more you know.

another thing is as well as that despite this firstly
for instance frankly I mean in short incidentally
lastly on top of that quite honestly so
what I mean is what's more while

Purpose of words or phrases	Examples
Adding information	*in addition*
Balancing contrasting ideas	*whereas*
Changing the subject	*anyway*
Concluding / summing up	*to sum up*
Pointing out a contrast	*however*
Giving examples	*for example*
Logical consequence	*therefore*
Making something clear	*in other words*
Showing your attitude	*to be honest*
Structuring and sequencing	*to start with*

3 Which of the discourse markers in your list would you use in informal conversation? Are there any you would only use in very formal writing?

Close up

l.12 What does *figures* mean here? What other meanings does it have?

l.16 Which less formal word could be used instead of *encountered*?

l.17 *ethnocentric* means making judgements about another race using the standards of your own. What do these related words mean: *ethnic minority*? / *ethnic cleansing*? / *ethnology*?

l.22 What would be a less formal way of phrasing *more important than those whom I don't*?

Henry Ford

Exploitation

1 Add the discourse markers in **bold** in this list to the chart.

actually anyway **as a matter of fact** **at first** despite this
eventually for instance however **in the end** quite honestly
so **then** to start with what I mean is whereas

2 Complete this article with appropriate discourse markers from the list in **1**.

………¹ when I saw *Time* magazine's list of a hundred influential people, I thought what an unusual idea. ………², as I worked my way through the list, I found myself disagreeing with more and more of the magazine's choices. ………³, I found it interesting reading. ………⁴, I've always been fascinated by lists of any kind. ………⁵, when I'd finished, I thought it would be fun to write my own list, ………⁶ I got some paper and began to write down names. ………⁷ it was easy, I wrote 20 or more names in less than a minute. ………⁸ it got more difficult and I slowed down. ………⁹ I just sat there staring at the paper. I had only thought of 45 names.

………¹⁰ I decided to ask other people for their ideas. One of my house mates came up with some good names, ………¹¹ Nelson Mandela and Steven Spielberg, ………¹² the others couldn't think of anyone I hadn't already got on my list. I asked several other people but ………¹³ they had hardly any ideas at all.

………¹⁴, I've discovered that it's not easy to think of people who have had a real influence of international importance. ………¹⁵, it's easy to think of people who are famous in their own country in their own time, but impossible to know how long their influence will last.

Speaking

Time also compiled other '100' lists.

1 **1.1** Read these examples and listen to some people giving their own ideas. Note down what they suggest.

100 Events of the century – a selection
- Elvis teaches American teens to rock 'n' roll
- First landing on the moon
- World War II
- US civil rights movement

100 Worst ideas of the century – a selection
- Prohibition
- Suntans
- Message T-shirts
- Videophones

2 Think of things you would include in the two lists.

3 Compare your ideas in groups. Try to agree on a 'Top 5' for each list.

4 Finally, present your lists to the rest of the class.

1.2 My influences

Lead in

Discuss these questions.

1 What groups of people can have an influence on children and teenagers as they are growing up? Think of people inside and outside the family.

2 What is it about these people that makes them influential?

3 Is there a difference between someone who influences you and a 'role model'?

Listening

1 **1.2** You are going to hear three speakers talking about people who influenced them.

a Who does each speaker talk about?

b What do the three people you hear about have in common?

2 Answer these questions.

a What kind of feelings did the first speaker have for the person who influenced him?

b What special circumstances led to the relationship this speaker describes?

c What personality differences are there between the second speaker and his role model?

d What does he admire especially in the person he describes?

e In what way did the third speaker's role model stand out?

f What did seeing this person's situation make her realize?

Exploring natural speech

1 Which words are missing from these extracts from the recording? Complete the sentences.

   a I'd say one person .... really influenced me when I .... growing up was erm .... teacher. Now I'd moved schools at a time when not many children .... moving across to .... new school …

   b … Wow if she .... do it then, then I .... definitely do it .... er I just always loved watching her stories .... the questions .... she would ask and .... me she .... just .... smart woman …

   c … she .... a real inspiration and made me feel like as a woman as a young girl I could really do whatever I wanted .... do …

   d … so she was a role model for me in .... way.

2 **1.3** Listen and check. What sound do the words you have added to **a–c** have in common? How is the added word in **d** different? Why?

Vocabulary: two-part adjectives

Barbara Walters presented *hard-hitting news.* It is common to form new adjectives from an adjective + *-ing* form like this.

1 Match the adjectives from **A** with an *-ing* form from **B** to make new two-part adjectives.

A hard   easy   long   fast   slow   clean   low   loose

B fitting   flying   going   growing   hitting   living   moving   suffering

2 Match the two-part adjectives you have found with appropriate nouns from this list.

business   company   documentary   family   film   jacket   jeans   patient   plane politician   speech   story   student   teacher   traffic   wife

3 Make some more two-part adjectives. How would you describe the following?

   a a play which runs for a long time
   b a flower which smells sweet
   c a river which flows fast
   d a letter which looks important
   e a person who talks in a smooth way

Speaking

1 Think about a particular individual who has been your role model. What influence has this person had on your personality? Your ideas and beliefs? Your career or education?

2 Compare memories and experiences with other students. Tell each other:

   • who your role models are
   • what they are like
   • their influences on you.

Writing

You are going to write a profile of the person you have just talked about.

1 Plan your profile, paragraph by paragraph. Here's a possible plan.

   Paragraph 1   Background
   Who is the person? How did you meet? What is your relationship with them?

   Paragraph 2   Qualities
   What are their influential qualities? Give examples of actions or behaviour which illustrate these qualities.

   Paragraph 3   Their influence on you
   Summarize the concrete ways in which this person has influenced you. What would you have been like now without this influence? Is this person still an influence? Do you expect them to influence you in the future?

2 Write the first draft of your profile in 150–175 words.

3 Exchange profiles with a partner. Read what your partner has written and suggest improvements.

   • Do you get a clear picture of the person and their influence on your partner?
   • Are there enough real-life examples of the person's qualities?

4 Discuss your ideas for improvements, then write your final profile.

▶ **Writing guidelines p.150**

1.3 -isms

Lead in

Work in groups.

1 How many words can you think of that end with the suffix *-ism*, for example, *socialism, heroism, nationalism*?

2 Put the *-ism* words on your list into these meaning groups.

- Political or religious beliefs
- Attitudes and abstract qualities
- Creative movements

Reading

1 Which *-isms* do paragraphs A–F describe? Choose the right words from this list. (You do not need to use one of the words.)

Pacifism Nihilism Materialism Buddhism Racism Behaviourism Anarchism

2 Which *-ism*, A–F

- **a** says that life is pointless or absurd?
- **b** says that people's actions are learnt and not influenced by thinking processes?
- **c** says that there should be no formal organization of society?
- **d** says that war and conflict must be avoided?
- **e** says that only physical (not spiritual) things exist?
- **f** is an important world religion?

3 What do you personally associate with the *-isms* you have read about? What's your opinion of them?

A .... -ism

.... is the idea that the only thing that really exists in the world is matter in its various states and movements. Thus .... is the opposite of idealism. .... considers any talk of, say, the soul, to be complete nonsense.

B .... -ism

.... was an influential movement among psychologists, founded by John D. Watson in
5 1913, made famous by B.F. Skinner, and continually popular throughout the twentieth century. .... amounts to a reduction of human and animal activity to simple stimulus and response, excluding any functional role for consciousness.

C .... -ism

.... is an individualistic religious and philosophical tradition that originated in India and spread throughout the Orient. ...., in fact, is quite similar to Taoism: both stress the belief
10 that we cannot trust in the world of appearances and that there is an underlying unity to the universe. Both emphasize a certain level of detachment from worldly affairs.

D .... -ism

.... takes its name from the Latin word for 'nothing' and is an extreme form of pessimism which holds that life has no meaning and that even if you try to achieve your values, in the end your life must necessarily come to nothing – thus .... is similar to fatalism. In
15 fact, however, ... is worse than fatalism because ....* don't usually say that life comes to zero but to less than zero, since they hold that life really just consists of one thing: pain.

* This word refers to the people who believe in this idea.

E .... -ism

.... was a sometimes violent political movement around the turn of the century, but the word also describes a moral-political ideal of a society untouched by relations of power and domination among human beings. This moral ideal has most often expressed itself in
20 what is the technical meaning of the term, namely the total absence of government.

F .... -ism

.... holds that the highest political or social value is peace, which must be sought at all costs. Another meaning of .... – connected with the actions and views of reformers like Gandhi, and Martin Luther King – is the ideal of non-violence in human affairs.

Peter Saint-André, *The Ism Book*

Close up

l.2	What is the word for a person whose philosophy is *idealism*?
l.3	What does *say* mean here?
l.4	What is the infinitive of *founded*?
l.13	What would be a less formal alternative to *holds* in this context?
l.17	When is the *turn of the century*?
l.21	What is the infinitive of *sought*?

Language focus: *all, both, either, neither, none*

1 Paragraph C mentions some of the similarities between Buddhism and Taoism.

  a Which of these words is used to show similarity?

all	both	either	neither	none

  b Which words in the list above refer to

    1 one person or thing?
    2 two people or things?
    3 more than two people or things?

2 Which of the words are followed by plural verbs?

3 Complete these sentences about numbers with the best word from the list above. Choose the correct verbs.

> Here are four numbers: 13 – 23 – 35 – 40. .... **1** of them *is / are* below fifty, but .... **2** of them *is / are* under ten. Two numbers are less than thirty. .... **3** of these *ends / end* in three, but .... **4** *is / are* higher than twenty-five.

Exploitation

1 **a** Compare these sets in as many ways as you can.

    Example
    Paris and London are both European capital cities.
    Neither of them is on the coast.

    1 Paris and London
    2 buses, trains, and planes
    3 cats and dogs
    4 letters, telephone calls, and e-mails
    5 swimming, running, and weight-training

  b Write some sets of your own like this and exchange them with a partner. Your partner has to compare the items in your sets.

2 Find out about some of the similarities and differences between you and other students in the class. Use *both, neither,* etc. and expressions from the box.

  a First work in pairs. Talk about some of these subjects.

    • Yourself (*Marina and I have both got blond hair, but whereas my hair is short, hers is long.*)
    • Family (*In comparison with Nhan, I come from a large family.*)
    • The place you live
    • Your taste in clothes, food and drink, holidays, music, TV

  b Then work with another pair. Try to find out what you all have in common.

    We all like cheese but none of us likes mushrooms.
    We're all completely different …

Speaking

1 Which *-isms* are important in your country or your family? Are they important to you? Exchange ideas with a partner.

2 Work in groups.

You are going to make up a new *-ism* of your own. Your *-ism* can be serious or humorous, and should appeal to people of your own age.

Me -ism – everybody should do what I say.

  a Start by noting down some key ideas.
    Example
    Bright colours should replace dull colours. Black should be abolished in public places.
    People who make other people laugh should be the most highly-paid people in society.

  b Give your *-ism* a name. It could be the name of a person, like *Thatcherism*, or a more descriptive name, like *Colourism*.

  c Finally present the key features of your *-ism* to the rest of the class.

Comparison language

- in comparison with / to
- I'm .... , whereas he's ....
- (exactly) the same as
- we're (complete) opposites
- (completely) different from
- more / less .... than
- (quite) similar to

Exploring words

Why we are like we are

1 a What's the difference in meaning between these words?

character   mood   nature   temperament

b **1.4** You are going to hear some people discussing the questions below. Make a note of any useful expressions you hear.

c Answer the questions about yourself, then tell a partner. Compare the words you and your partner have chosen. How different are you from each other?

Your personality

1 Which of these words describe your character? (Choose one word from each pair.)

a strong* / weak*
b independent* / self-centred*
c dependable / unreliable

2 How would you describe your temperament? (Choose one word from each pair.)

a calm* / excitable*
b difficult / easy-going
c cautious* / passionate

3 How would you describe your nature? (Choose one word from each pair.)

a assertive* / timid*
b gloomy / sunny
c agreeable / moody*

4 What sort of mood are you in at the moment? (Choose one word from each pair.)

a good / bad
b carefree / thoughtful*
c optimistic* / pessimistic*

d What are the nouns related to the personality adjectives marked * in the questionnaire?

Example
strong / strength

e Here are some more adjectives to describe personality. In your opinion do they represent positive, negative, or neutral qualities? Write **P**, **N**, or **Ne**.

affectionate ....   aggressive ....   ambitious ....
determined ....   emotional ....   energetic ....
frank ....   hypocritical ....   logical ....   loyal ....
malicious ....   modest ....   narrow-minded ....
obstinate ....   possessive ....   practical ....
protective ....   rational ....   reserved ....   selfish ....
sensitive ....   truthful ....

Compare ideas with your partner.

2 a What's the difference in meaning between these pairs of words?

affect / effect   open to / prone to   mood / temper

b Choose the right words to complete this text.

Things going wrong have a terrible *affect / effect* [1] on him. Ever since I've known him, he's been *open / prone* [2] to violent mood *swings / turns* [3]. If anyone annoys him, he just can't *hold / keep* [4] his temper. We were driving through London once when the car in front stopped suddenly and we bumped into it. Jack completely lost his *mood / temper* [5] and started shouting at the other driver. We had to *constrain / restrain* [6] him before a fight broke out. After a few minutes he managed to *regain / reclaim* [7] his *composure / calmness* [8].

c How can these factors affect your mood? Discuss your ideas.

colours   food or drinks   music   people   places
time of day   time of year   weather

Are there any other factors you could include in this list?

3 Work in pairs.

a Decide on five qualities you would look for in each of the following people.

- Someone you will have to work closely with
- Someone you are going to share an apartment or go on holiday with
- A close personal friend

b Compare ideas with another pair. How far do you agree?

Language commentary

1 Discourse markers

Introduction

Discourse markers link one idea to another in speech or writing. They clarify the relationship between these ideas for listeners or readers.

I'm fed up with this dreadful weather, **so** I can't wait for the summer. **Having said that,** I'm not keen on very hot weather.

a Adding information

as well as that   as if that wasn't enough   another thing is furthermore*   in addition (to that)   moreover* on top of that   what's more   (* very formal)

Liz must have gone out in a hurry. She didn't wash up, left the light on and, **on top of that,** she forgot to lock the door.

In any case and *besides* add a final conclusive argument.

It's got a horrible taste and it's expensive and **in any case / besides** you're too young to drink alcohol.

b Balancing contrasting (not contradictory) ideas

I really like action films full of adventure and drama, **whereas / while** my boyfriend prefers romantic films.

On the other hand is used between sentences.

We could take our American friends to London. **On the other hand** it could take ages to get there.

c Changing the subject

By the way and *incidentally* introduce something new.

By the way / Incidentally, your CD arrived this morning.

Anyway and *anyhow* are used to end one idea and show that the next idea is more important.

I've had a bad time since the accident. I was off work for three months and for most of that time I watched TV. **Anyway,** that's all over now – I'm going back to work on Monday.

d Concluding / summing up

In conclusion   In short   To sum up

To sum up, I'd say that this has been a very useful experience.

e Pointing out a contrast

All the same   Despite this   Even so   However In spite of this   Mind you   Still

She said she'd be in all day. **However,** when I tried to phone her there was no reply.

She said she was feeling fine. When I saw her, **however,** she looked dreadful. I can't say I really enjoyed my last job. **Still / All the same,** I'll miss the people I worked with.

The price of cars has gone up recently. **Mind you,** it doesn't matter to me – I've got a company car.

I realize I haven't got much chance of getting the job. **Even so,** I'm not going to give up hope yet.

f Giving examples

There are lots of ways of keeping fit like, **for example / for instance,** running, swimming, or cycling.

g Logical consequence

As a result   Consequently   Therefore   So

My new shoes fell apart the first time I wore them. **So** I took them straight back to the shop.

h Making something clear

I mean   That's to say   What I mean is …   What I'm trying to say is …   In other words

I'm afraid we're going to have to let you go. **In other words** you've lost your job.

i Showing your attitude

Frankly   To be frank   Quite honestly   To be honest

I'm fed up with politicians. **To be honest** I don't think it's worth voting any more.

j Structuring and sequencing

First of all   Firstly (Thirdly, etc.)   In the first place   Lastly Finally   To start / begin with   For one (another) thing

There are a number of points I'd like to make. **To begin with,** I don't understand why we need another supermarket in the town – we've got three already. **For another thing,** what effect is the new shop going to have on the traffic situation?

2 all, both, either, neither, none

a all, both

All and *both* are followed by plural verbs.

All / Both the children are going swimming this afternoon.
All / Both of the children are going swimming this afternoon.
The children / They are **all / both** going swimming this afternoon.
All / Both of them are going swimming this afternoon.

b either, neither

Either and *neither* refer to one of two people.

A Have you seen **either** of my parents?
B No, I haven't seen **either of them.** / No, I've seen **neither of them.**
A Have you thought of being a postman or a bus driver?
B Yes, **either job** would suit me. / No, **neither job** appeals to me.

There's room for **either** Jo **or** you, but not for both of you.
Neither my uncle **nor** my aunt could read.

▶ Note Although *either* and *neither* are singular words, in everyday speech they are often used with plural verbs.
Is / Are either of you coming to my party on Friday?
Neither of my brothers **is / are** married.
Do / Does either of you two **want** another coffee?

c none

None means *not one.*
None of my friends **likes / like** football.
A Where's the coffee? / Have you got any apples?
B **There's none** left. / **There are none** left.

▶ Note *None* can be used with a singular or a plural verb.

2 Infernal machines

2.1 Computers and cars

Lead in

Which of the things in the photographs do you use? Which do you consider to be essentials, which are luxuries, and which are irrelevant? Compare ideas with a partner.

Reading

1 You are going to read an article about the kinds of things that can go wrong with computers. In pairs, make your own list of possible computer faults.

2 Now read the article comparing cars with computers. Complete each point 1–10 with one of these phrases.

a encourage the buying of more cars
b force you to restart your journey
c to the company that sold the petrol
d use the radio
e would go no faster and work no better

f know if there was still a fault
g to get spares in a bundle
h the same engine
i work any more
j zero within two years

If only everything in life was as reliable as a computer

Bill Gates allegedly once said: 'If General Motors had kept up with technology in the way the computer industry has, we would all be driving $25 cars that got 1,000 miles to the gallon.' To which GM is reported to have asked who would want a car that crashed twice a day.

10 Just think of it, if a car was really like a PC, then …

❶ The car would regularly stop for no reason when performing a common manoeuvre. When you restarted it, it would appear to work normally, but would sometimes ……… .

❷ If you fitted a new wing mirror, the car might not ……… .

❸ If you wanted new tyres, you would have to buy new seats and windscreen wipers too, because it would only be possible ……… .

❹ When you turned on the radio, the car might tell you the battery was low and that you must turn off another device (such as the headlights) if you wanted to ……… .

❺ Every brand of car would have virtually ……… and a sticker on the side showing where the maker got it.

❻ All the warning lights for oil, petrol, electricity, brakes and airbags would be installed as a single message which would flash: 'Something is wrong, please stop the car.' When you started up again, you wouldn't ……… .

❼ When you called for help, you would have to ring a freephone helpline and select the number for the repair you wished to have done. An automated voice would talk you through repairing the car yourself, and when that didn't work would refer you ……… .

❽ Every time you bought a new car, it would have a bigger engine, but ……… . It would also have extra features that were of no use whatever.

❾ The re-sale value would drop 75 per cent as soon as you drove out of the showroom, and would be ……… .

❿ The man whose company made the carburettor would travel round the globe advising world leaders that their economies would fail if they didn't ……… .

Cover Magazine

Language focus: the conditional

1 Without looking back at the article, complete these *if* sentences with the appropriate forms of the verbs in brackets. Then check.

   a If a car .... (be) really like a PC, then the car .... (regularly stop) for no reason. (l.10)

   b If you .... (fit) a new wing mirror, the car .... (not work) any more. (l.17)

2 a Which conditional sentence pattern is used more than any other in the article?

   b Why is this pattern used? Choose one description. The writer is thinking about:

     A something possible in the future
     B something imaginary in the past
     C something unreal or hypothetical
     D something improbable in the future.

3 Which description **A**, **B**, **C**, or **D** fits these sentences?

   a *If I'd known what I know now, I'd have bought a more expensive computer.*

   b *If I get a new computer, I'll give you my old one.*

   c *If I had children, I'd make sure they were computer literate.*

   d *If I had the chance, I'd probably choose a career in computers.*

4 What times are referred to in the two parts of these sentences? What are conditional sentences like this called?

   a *If General Motors had kept up with technology in the way the computer industry has, we would all be driving $25 cars that got 1,000 miles to the gallon.*

   b *If you're so good with computers, you would have remembered to save all your work.*

   c *I'd probably have a really good job now if I'd had basic computer training at school.*

Close up

1.14 A *manoeuvre* is an action or movement. How do you pronounce it? What are *army manoeuvres*?

1.26 What follows the phrase *such as*? What other words or phrases could be used instead of *such as*?

1.28 What *brands* of computers do you know? Which word with the same meaning as *brand* is used to describe cars?

5 Rewrite these *if* sentences using these conjunctions.

as long as   provided (that) / providing (that)   unless

   a You can borrow my new digital camera if you look after it.

   b If I don't get my computer fixed, I won't be able to finish the job I'm doing.

   c You wouldn't be able to use this programme if you hadn't done the training course.

   d If you've got the right kind of scanner, you can turn a text into a computer file.

Exploitation

1 Complete these sentences in different ways.

   a If you don't want to lose your job, …

   b I wouldn't have ended up in hospital …

   c I wouldn't be spending so much time on the phone if …

   d If you had been taught how to use a computer properly, …

   e Unless the company pays us more, …

   f You can borrow my car as long as …

   g I'll lend you some money for a new computer provided / providing (that) …

2 Work in pairs. Use your imagination to compare other things with computers.

   • If children were like computers, …

   • If the government was like a computer, …

   • If planes were like computers, …

Discussion

1 What are the implications of the developments suggested by these future newspaper headlines?

NEW GENERATION OF COMPUTERS CAN THINK – IT'S OFFICIAL!

Pollution kills three – London, Paris, and New York decide to ban cars

Early exposure to computer games can cause mental illness in middle age

2 What do you think the consequences will be if cars and computers continue to develop at the rate they have been developing over the past 25 years? Make a list of brief predictions, then write some of your ideas as newspaper headlines.

2.2 Computers and you

Lead in

Complete this questionnaire, then compare answers in pairs or groups.

You and Computers

1 What proportion of people in these groups regularly use a computer? Make a rough estimate.

* your family   ...... %
* your friends   ...... %
* your school / college ...... %
* your street   ...... %
* your city or country ...... %

2 Which of these things do you (or would you) use a computer for?

* work   ......
* word-processing   ......
* e-mail   ......
* games   ......
* the Internet   ......
* listening to music / MP3 ......
* art / design   ......

* other uses (Please specify)
  ....
  ....
  ....
  ....
  ....

Listening

1 **2.1** You are going to hear five people talking about computers in their lives. Where and why does each person use computers?

2 Listen again. Which speaker, 1–5

a feels that their life is dominated by computers?

b is not very good at playing computer games?

c has a computer at home but has not used it for a long time?

d would quite like to go back to traditional ways of communicating with people?

e is not sure whether it is a good idea to have a computer at home?

Exploring natural speech

1 Look at these extracts from the recordings. Why does the third speaker use the phrase *I suppose* so frequently?

a I suppose the, most of the contact I have with computers is at work.

b I suppose these are, are the main uses.

c I suppose the most it's used for at home is – is games …

2 **2.2** *I suppose* is often used like this at the beginning of sentences. How is it pronounced?

Listen, check, and practise.

3 Answer these questions. Start your answers with *I suppose*.

a What do you mostly use a computer for?

b How many e-mails do you send a day?

c What aspects of computers do you like?

React and discuss

1 Are people becoming too dependent on computers? Talk about people you know.

2 'Playing computer games is a waste of time'. Do you agree?

Vocabulary: *make* and *do*

The verbs *make* and *do* are sometimes confused. In general:

* *do* is connected with activity or work: *do the shopping*.
* *make* often means produce or create something new or different: *make money*.

a Complete these extracts from the recording using the correct form of *make* or *do*.

1 *I can't believe the progress I personally have* .... *in my use of it in the last, well, two years …*

2 *(I would like one …) just as an information source, rather than having to* .... *phone calls …*

3 *… they are vital for the kind of work I* .... *…*

4 *… I couldn't* .... *my job without one really …*

b Make lists of expressions you know with *make* and *do*. Compare with a partner, and then compile a class list.

Language focus: emphasis

When we are speaking, we can emphasize ideas by stressing particular words or phrases, but we can also use grammar and vocabulary for emphasis.

1 **2.3** Listen to a recording of extracts **a–f** below. Which of these four ways are used for emphasis in each extract?

- extra auxiliary verbs
- adverbs
- word order
- emphatic words or phrases

a *Computers really equal work in my mind, erm. That's not to say I don't like them. I do.*

b *They really frustrate me, computers do.*

c *Computers – incredibly important for work erm – if one went wrong, I wouldn't know what to do with it at all erm, …*

d *E-mail clearly is a very important part of what you can do with a computer at the moment and I must say that I think it's a wonderful invention, but …*

e *He hasn't got a clue about what to do if his computer crashes, Paul hasn't.*

f *You always accuse me of not answering your e-mails. I do reply to them – eventually.*

2 Work in pairs. Decide which words to stress in these sentences.

a That's not to say I don't enjoy driving. I do.

b It really amazes me, the Internet does.

c I must say I think they're brilliant, the latest computer games.

d That's not fair – I do work hard.

e I expect you think I haven't been listening. Well I have.

f You're always accusing me of not listening to what you say. I do listen.

3 **2.4** Listen, check, and practise.

Exploitation

1 Work in pairs. Think of a response to make conversations. Include an auxiliary verb.

Example

a Can't you work a bit more quickly?
I am working quickly.

b I wish you'd put petrol in the car occasionally.

c You don't like my parents, do you?

d I asked you to remind me to video the football match on TV last night.

e There's no point in getting a new TV – you'd never watch it.

f We only finished lunch ten minutes ago. You can't be hungry already.

2 How many ways can you think of to make the ideas in these sentences more emphatic?

a You're joking.

b It's true.

c Computers are brilliant.

d I understand.

e I think it was difficult, and I know you agree with me.

Speaking

You are going to discuss this statement.

 We should ban computers for one day a week.

Work in groups of four to six. Half the students in each group should agree and the other half should disagree with the statement.

1 Prepare a short persuasive speech saying why you agree or disagree with the statement.

- If you are **for**, think of the new opportunities the ban would provide.
- If you are **against**, think of the potentially disastrous results of the ban.

2 Agree on a time limit for each speaker, then take turns to present your ideas to the rest of the group. Each short speech can be followed by a few minutes of general discussion. Use some of the expressions in the box below.

3 When everyone has spoken, vote on whether you agree or disagree with the statement.

Arguments for

- I (would) agree with this idea because …
- I (would) approve of a ban because …
- Just think of the benefits / advantages of …

Arguments against

- I don't / can't accept this idea because …
- I would be against a ban because …
- Just think of the consequences / disadvantages of …

General expressions

- (I think) it would be in all our interests to …
- I honestly believe that …
- It's my personal view that …
- You have to accept that …
- You can't really believe that …

Exploring words

Computers and computing

1 Complete these sentences with appropriate verbs and nouns from lists **A** and **B**.

| A | back up join log on send sit surf visit |

| B | chat room e-mail files Internet terminal Web websites |

a If you want to contact someone instantly you can .... them an ....

b If they need particular information, many people now .... the ...., instead of using reference books in libraries.

c Many companies, organizations, and individuals have .... which people can ....

d Cybercafés are places where anyone can .... at a .... and .... to the ....

e If you want to make new friends or talk to people about a special subject you can .... a ....

f To avoid losing your work on a computer, you should always .... your ....

2 Work in pairs. Discuss these questions.

a Have you ever contacted people through a *chat room*?

b Have you ever lost work because you forgot to *back up*?

c Have you ever used a *cybercafé*? What for?

d Do you use *e-mail* more or less than traditional letters or the telephone?

e How easy is it to find what you want on the *Internet*?

f What are your favourite *websites*? Have you got or thought about getting your own website?

SPEEDY, private, informal – isn't e-mail wonderful?

It is now considered the simplest way to communicate with people outside your company, and it lets you talk shop with colleagues, too. But perhaps we're getting a little too comfortable with our in-boxes and browsers. A British company certainly must think so – it had to pay £450,000 in damages to a rival company after one of its employees circulated derogatory remarks about the rival's trading performance in an internal e-mail. And who can forget poor Lois Franxhi, who was dismissed from her job after logging on to travel websites 150 times?

3 a Do you think there should be controls on employees' use of e-mail and the Internet when they are at work?

b Read the extract above. What problems did employers and employees face?

4 Match these adjectives (some are from the extract) with their near-synonym and their antonym.

adjective	near-synonym	antonym
a derogatory	insulting	formal
b private	official	fitting
c informal	complex	inoffensive
d speedy	improper	unlawful
e inappropriate	rapid	simple
f scandalous	casual	public
g complicated	confidential	complimentary
h legitimate	outrageous	slow

5 Work in groups.

a How do you think the Internet will affect everyday life in the next 20–30 years? Think about people's home lives, their jobs, and how they spend their leisure time.

b Should there be controls on the kind of material that can be found on the Internet? If so, how could this be done and who should decide what is controlled?

Language commentary

1 The conditional

a Zero conditional – uses

Something that is always true or that happens regularly in certain situations.

If you heat ice, **it melts.**
If I go on a long journey, **I read** or **listen** to music.

b First conditional – uses

- Something possible or likely in the future.
  If it's sunny, we'll go for a picnic.
- Warnings, threats, or promises.
  If you don't work a bit harder, **they won't renew** your contract.
- Instructions.
  If you need any help, **give** me a ring.

▶ Note In conversation the word *if* can be left out.
You want to get into the club – **you'll have to** queue up like everyone else.

- Sometimes the sentence starts with an imperative form of the verb and the two clauses are linked with *and*. This is often used for warnings and threats.
  Do that again **and you'll** be in trouble.

c Second conditional – uses

- Something possible but improbable in the future.
  You wouldn't enjoy the film if you **saw** it.
- Something hypothetical, unreal, or impossible.
  If you didn't live so far away, **I'd come** and see you more often.
  If I were ten years younger, **I'd marry** you.

▶ Note In second conditional sentences, we can use *was* or *were*. *Were* is rather more formal.
  If he were / was here, I'm sure he'd know what to do.

- Advice.
  If I were you, **I'd say** nothing about it to anyone.

d Third conditional – uses

Something imaginary in the past.

If I hadn't gone to that meeting, **we wouldn't have met.**
You'd have enjoyed the play **if you hadn't fallen** asleep.

▶ Note Inversion is an alternative to the *if* clause in third conditionals.
Had I known you weren't coming, I wouldn't have bought so much food. (= if I had known)

e Mixed conditionals

Mixed conditionals relate a past event to something in the present or future, and can mix second and third conditional structures.

If I'd bought a better computer, **I would be able** to work more quickly.
I'd be going on holiday next week, **if I hadn't had** that accident.
If we were still living in the city, **we wouldn't have seen** all this.

First and third conditional structures can also be mixed.

If you're so clever, you **wouldn't have locked** your keys in the car.

f Other conjunctions used in conditional sentences

Other conjunctions can be used instead of *if*.

as long as = on condition that
I'll be quite happy **as long as you don't spend** too much money.
You can borrow the car **as long as you fill** it up with petrol regularly.

provided / providing (that) = on condition that
She can come with us **provided (that) she doesn't mind** sleeping in a tent.
You can stay in our flat while we're away **providing (that) you keep** it clean.

Suppose / Supposing = if / what if
Supposing / Suppose we get held up, what **will** we do?
Suppose / Supposing we got held up, what **would** we do?

unless = except if / if not
Unless we're quick, **we'll miss** the train.
I wouldn't set out in the snow, **unless I was sure** I wouldn't get stuck.

▶ Note *But for* = if something hadn't happened:
We'd have got here on time **but for** the heavy traffic. **But for the fact that the road was flooded**, we'd have been here two hours ago.

2 Emphasis

We can use stress and intonation for emphasis when we speak, but we can also use linguistic devices to emphasize information or opinions.

a Adding the auxiliary verbs *do / did* to statements

He **does** expect everyone to be at the meeting on time.
(He expects everyone to be at the meeting on time.)
I **did** enjoy that new programme on TV last night.
(I enjoyed that new programme on TV last night.)

b Adding adverbs

Adverbs can be used before or after auxiliary verbs.
I **really** am tired. / I'm **really** tired.
She **clearly** was feeling ill. / She was **clearly** feeling ill.
I **definitely** have got flu. / I've **definitely** got flu.

▶ Note The auxiliary verb cannot be shortened if the adverb is before it.

c Unusual word order

Attention can be focused by adding a 'tail', with or without an auxiliary.
They really annoy me, **mobile phones do.**
They really annoy me, **mobile phones.**
(Mobile phones really annoy me.)
They're too hot for me, **Spanish summers are.**
(Spanish summers are too hot for me.)
I'm fed up with waiting for you, **I am.**
(I'm fed up with waiting for you.)

d Emphatic words or phrases

Computers are **incredibly** important to me in my work.
I must say, I didn't think I'd ever buy a mobile phone.
Right, let me repeat what I've just said.

3 Open questions

3.1 Caught in the rain

Lead in

1 a Put these adjectives in order from weak to strong.

damp   soaked   wet

b Put these 'moving' verbs in order of speed.

run   stroll   walk

2 It is raining heavily and you haven't got an umbrella. What is the best thing to do – continue walking or start running?

3 **3.1** You are going to hear three people talking about this situation.

a What happened to the woman? What did she do?

b Would she have got wetter if she had walked?

4 Choose the best meaning for the phrases in **bold** in the extracts.

a *Yeah, yeah – but **it occurred to me** actually – cos I was running down the street to …*

it happened to me   I discovered
I suddenly realized

b *… as much rain is falling on you as if you were walking – **mind you** it would have gone totally against the grain …*

but   and also   because

Reading

1 Read the title and first paragraph of the article below.

a Complete the paragraph with these words.

downpour   problem   rain   run   walk   weather

b What are you going to find out by reading this article?

2 Read the rest of the article and check your ideas.

Scientists rule out running from the rain

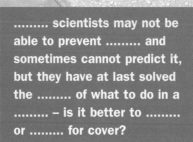

……… scientists may not be able to prevent ……… and sometimes cannot predict it, but they have at last solved the ……… of what to do in a ……… – is it better to ……… or ……… for cover?

5

Uₙ NIVERSITY SCIENTISTS report in the journal *Weather* that it is pointless to run, ending a dispute that has rumbled on for years. A dash means spending less time in the rain, but you will be just as wet at the end of the trip, says Dr Stephen Belcher, a lecturer in meteorology.

To come to this conclusion, Dr Belcher and his colleagues observe that there are two ways in which a person encounters each raindrop: 'Firstly the raindrops can fall directly on to the top surface of the person, and secondly, as the person moves, they will run into those raindrops which are directly in front of them.'

However, the surface area of the front of an individual is much greater than that of the head and shoulders. Using idealized cuboid people to make the calculations easier, the team concludes that wetting from passing through the rain is the dominating factor. Only if we moved very slowly, or were caught in an incredible storm, would it be a good idea to make a dash for it.

3 According to the article, are these statements True or False?

  a If you run in the rain you get less wet than if you walk.

  b Rain always falls on people in the same way.

  c The scientists did their experiments on models, not on real people.

  d It would be sensible to run if you were in a thunderstorm.

  e Scientists now understand exactly why people prefer to run.

4 Work in pairs.

  a Explain in your own words:

    1 why *it is pointless to run in the rain*

    2 why the scientists used *idealized cuboid people*.

  b Then present your explanation to another pair, and together decide whose explanation is clearer and more effective.

The scientists are baffled by why most people prefer to run, says John Holden, another member of the team. He agrees that 'this intriguing problem' should now be passed to the university's psychology department. 'Sometimes I do run,' he admits. 'But I keep trying to tell myself that there's no reason to.'

40

45

The Daily Telegraph

Language focus: *wish*

1 In the conversation, one of the speakers said *I wish I'd brought my umbrella*.

We use the verb *wish* to talk about situations in the past, present, or future, which for some reason are impossible or unlikely to change.

Match these *wish* sentences with their uses.

Sentence	Uses
a *I wish I'd brought my umbrella.*	criticizing another person's actions or showing you are annoyed by them
b *I wish it wasn't raining.*	regretting something that happened or didn't happen in the past
c *I wish I was ten years younger.*	hoping for something in the future
d *I wish you wouldn't smoke in here.*	expressing an impossible fantasy
e *I wish the weather would improve.*	desiring a change in the present situation

2 Rephrase sentences **1a–e** above using as many of the alternative structures from this list as you can.

I really hope …   I'm sorry …   I'd really like …   If only …
Why won't …?   Please …   Unfortunately …
I'd be grateful if …   I regret …   It's a pity …

giving up

Exploitation

1 Rephrase these sentences using *I wish*.

  a I'd really like to stop smoking but I can't.

  b It's a pity you aren't coming with us.

  c I want you to stop telling me what to do.

  d Unfortunately, I didn't bring my camera.

  e I want to be young again.

2 Think about yourself and your life.

  a Note down your thoughts and memories about these subjects.

    • Something you'd like to be able to do but can't

    • A missed opportunity

    • Something you'd like to change about yourself

    • Something a friend does that irritates you

    • Something from your past that you now feel embarrassed about

  b Try to find other students with similar thoughts or memories.

3.2 Time travel

Lead in

Exchange ideas in pairs or groups.

Do you think time travel will ever be possible? Why? Why not?

Listening

1 **3.2** You are going to hear five speakers talking about where they would choose to go if time travel were possible.

a Which times do the speakers mention?

b Listen again and note any reasons the speakers give for their choices.

2 You are going to hear a conversation about time travel. Before you listen, match these words and phrases from the conversation with their meanings.

a *lay down*   1 a secret observer
b *ground rule*   2 communicate / get on
c *make bets*   3 establish / agree on
d *a fly on the wall*   4 animal waste / manure
e *dung*   5 gamble / risk money
f *interact*   6 principle which future action is based on

3 **3.3** Listen to the conversation and answer these questions.

a Before you start thinking about time travel, especially travelling back into the past, what basic rule do you have to decide on?
b What would be the main difference between New York in the past and New York now?
c What is the difference between travelling back to the past and reading about it?
d What would one of the speakers like to find out about her parents?
e Why would one of the speakers prefer to travel into the future rather than the past?

React and discuss

If you were given the chance to travel in time, what would you most look forward to about the experience and what would you be most worried about? Where would you go?

Exploring natural speech

1 How are the phrases in **bold** in these sentences pronounced in everyday speech? Discuss your ideas.

a I **don't know**, I think the Renaissance would just be absolutely amazing …

b I **want to** go back and look at strangers at a time before anybody I know existed.

c A There's a new film at the cinema about time travel – I've just **got to** see it.

  B Have you decided when you're **going to** go?

  A No, but if you can **give me** a lift we could go together.

2 **3.4** Listen, check, and practise.

Language focus: speculating and imagining

1 *Would*, *might*, and *could* are used when we are speculating or describing what we are imagining. Which verbs did the speakers use in the recordings? Try to remember what they said, then check on p.141.

  a *I .... go back to the time of Jesus I think – first century Palestine …*

  b *I think the Renaissance .... just be absolutely amazing …*

  c *I think it .... be more fun to project a thousand years into the future.*

  d **M1** *Well, if I had no choice – .... I want to come back? I don't know till I go into the future.*

     M2 *Yeah, it .... be great there.*

     W *Or, you know what – it .... not exist.*

2 What is the difference in meaning, if any, between these pairs of sentences?

  a *Y*ou **would** *discover your family secrets if you travelled back into the past.*
    *You **might** discover your family secrets if you travelled back into the past.*

  b *In the future, time travel **could** be a reality.*
    *In the future, time travel **might** be a reality.*

3 Here are some more expressions we use to speculate or imagine something unreal in the present or future. Notice the verb tenses used with them.

  ***Imagine** you **were** a famous actor.*
  ***Suppose / Supposing** we **were** millionaires.*
  ***Let's pretend** (that) **we'd never met** before.*
  ***What if** we **didn't return** from the future?*

Exploitation

Complete the speech bubbles.

  a Imagine time travel were possible. Which time .... you visit?

  b Supposing you .... not return to the present, ... you still want to time travel?

  c If you .... spend an evening with any famous person who .... ever lived, who .... you choose?

  d What if you .... the prime minister or president of your country? What changes .... you make?

  e What .... you do if you .... (hear) that an asteroid .... hit the world in two weeks?

Speaking

Work in pairs.

Student A Turn to p.157.
Student B Follow these instructions.

1 You are a journalist for a popular newspaper. You have arranged to interview someone who claims to have travelled to the future. You do not believe in time travel, but you think this could be a sensational story.

2 Prepare for the interview.

Make a list of questions to ask the time traveller. Think about what your readers might be interested to know. Here are some possible subjects.

  a Where?

  b When? (How many years in the future?)

  c The appearance and character of future people

  d Proof / evidence of the visit

3 Do the interview.

Writing

The newspaper story based on the interview with the time traveller has been published. The words of the time traveller have been changed to make the story more sensational.

You are the time traveller and are going to write a letter to the editor of the newspaper to complain about the treatment of your story and ask for an apology. Here are four examples of 'mistakes' from the newspaper and your notes.

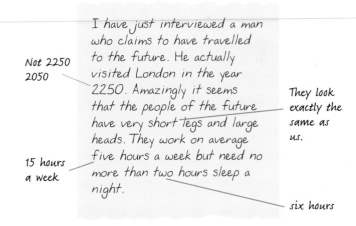

Not 2250
2050

I have just interviewed a man who claims to have travelled to the future. He actually visited London in the year 2250. Amazingly it seems that the people of the future have very short legs and large heads. They work on average five hours a week but need no more than two hours sleep a night.

They look exactly the same as us.

15 hours a week

six hours

1 Plan your letter paragraph by paragraph.

2 How formal should the style of your letter be? You consider this is a serious matter.

3 Write your letter, using formal letter layout. Write **150–200** words.

▶ **Writing guidelines p.152**

3.3 Saving a language

Vocabulary

Finish the words to complete these sentences.

1 Another name for your first language is your m........ t.........

2 A l........ is someone who studies languages.

3 A language spoken by a small proportion of the people in a country is a m........ language.

4 If you have spoken a particular language since you were a baby, you are a n........ speaker of that language.

5 If you can speak a language quickly and easily, you are a f........ speaker.

6 A form of a language spoken in one part of a country, with some different words and grammar is a d.........

7 Ancient Latin and Greek are c........ or d........ languages.

8 English, French, and Russian are m........ or l........ languages.

9 These days many children start learning a f........ language at primary school.

10 In many countries of the world, English is used as a s........ language.

11 If you speak with an a........., you have a non-standard way of pronouncing words.

Reading

1 As you read this article about language, choose which paragraphs A–E answer these questions.

  a Are attempts to save dying languages succeeding?
  b Are there any examples of languages being saved?
  c How bad is the situation?
  d What can be done?
  e Why is this happening?

2 Does this article take a positive or negative view of the future of world languages?

Close up

1.6 What does *some* mean in this context?

1.15 *Genocide* means killing people because they belong to a particular race or group. What other words do you know with the suffix *-cide* meaning killing?

1.17 A *habitat* is the environment in which animals or plants, etc. live. What other words with related meanings contain the root *habit*?

1.18 What is the difference between *famine* and *drought*? Why do they often occur together?

1.43 What are normally found in *nests*? What are the key features of a *nest*?

1.50 What does *very* mean in the phrase the *very brink of extinction*?

The death of

A A LANGUAGE dies only when the last person who speaks it dies. Or more likely it dies when the second-last person who speaks it dies. For then there is no one left to talk
5 to. There is nothing unusual about a single language dying. But what is happening today is extraordinary. According to the best estimates, there are some 6,000 languages in the world. Of these, about half are going to die out in the course of the next century. In the course of the past two or three decades, linguists all over the world have been gathering comparative data. If they
10 find a language with just a few speakers left, and nobody is bothering to pass the language on to the children, they conclude that language is bound to die out soon.

B The reasons so many languages are dying range from natural disasters, through different forms of cultural
15 assimilation, to genocide. Earthquakes, hurricanes, floods and other cataclysms can easily wipe out small communities in isolated areas. A habitat may become unsurvivable through unfavourable climatic and economic conditions – famine and drought especially. Communities can die through imported
20 disease. Cultural assimilation is an even bigger threat. Much of the present crisis stems from the major cultural movements which began 500 years ago, as colonialism spread a small number of dominant languages around the world.

C It's too late to do anything to help many languages,
25 where the speakers are too few or too old, and where the community is too busy just trying to survive to care about their language. But many languages are not in such a serious position. Once a community realizes that its language is in danger, it can get its act together, and introduce measures which can
30 genuinely revitalize the language. The community itself must want to save its language. The culture of which it is a part must need to have a respect for minority languages. There needs to be funding, to support courses, materials, and teachers. And there need to be linguists, to get on with the basic task of
35 putting the language down on paper. That's the bottom line: getting the language documented – recorded, analysed, written down. People must be able to read and write if they and their language are to have a future in an increasingly computer-literate civilization. But can we save a few thousand languages,
40 just like that? Yes, if the will and funding were available.

D There are some famous cases which illustrate what can be done: Maori in New Zealand has been maintained by a system of so-called 'language nests', organizations which provide children under five with a domestic setting in which they are
45 intensively exposed to the language. The staff are all Maori speakers from the local community. The hope is that the children will keep their Maori skills alive after leaving the nests, and that as they grow older they will in turn become role models to new

a language

generations of young children. A language can be brought back
50 from the very brink of extinction. The Ainu language of Japan,
after many years of neglect and repression, had reached a stage
where there were only eight fluent speakers left, all elderly.
However, new government policies brought fresh attitudes and
a positive interest in survival. Several 'semi-speakers' – people
55 who had become unwilling to speak Ainu because of the
negative attitudes by Japanese speakers – were prompted to
become active speakers again. Several seriously endangered
Aboriginal languages of Australia have been maintained and
revived, thanks to community efforts, work by Australian
60 linguists, and the help of local linguistic and cultural
organizations.

E It is too soon to predict the future of these revived
languages, but in some parts of the world they
are attracting precisely the range of positive attitudes
65 and grass roots support which are the preconditions for
language survival.

David Crystal, *High Life*

3 Read the article again and answer these questions. There is
a question for each paragraph.

a What are the signs that a language is in danger of
dying? (para. A)

b How do natural disasters affect languages? (para. B)

c What does the writer suggest can be done to save dying
languages? (para. C)

d What has been done to help save the Maori and the
Ainu languages? (para. D)

e What reasons are there for optimism? (para. E)

React and discuss

It is clear from the article that it will be a very difficult task
to save the world's dying languages. Do you think it is
worth the time, effort, and money that will be needed?

Vocabulary: adjectives and nouns

The adjectives and nouns in these lists are from the article.

1 Note down the combinations that you can remember from
the article – there are 12 altogether.

Examples
active speakers   isolated areas

Adjectives	active	cultural	dominant	fluent	isolated
	local	natural	negative	positive	

Nouns	areas	assimilation	attitudes	community
	disasters	languages	movements	organizations
	speakers			

2 What other combinations of adjectives and nouns from
the lists above are possible?

Role play

Work in groups of four.

The island you live on has a limited amount of money to
spend on protecting the natural and cultural environments.
Three different projects have been proposed but there is
only enough to money to pay for two. Your task is to
discuss and decide which two projects to support.

1 Find out about the projects.

Student A Turn to p.157.
Student B Turn to p.157.
Student C Turn to p.158.
Student D Turn to p.159.

2 Describe and discuss the three projects.

3 Decide which two projects should be supported. Compare
your ideas with other groups.

Exploring words

A question of punishment

1 Discuss these questions in pairs.

  a What is the worst crime you have heard of?

  b How should someone who commits this crime be punished?

2 Read this list of crimes and offences.

  a Which are crimes against the person and which are crimes against property? Some are both. (Write **Pe**, **Pr**, or **B**.)

abduction	arson	assault ....
assisting suicide	bank robbery	bigamy ....
blackmail	bribery	burglary ....
drink-driving	drug-dealing	forgery ....
fraud	hijacking	kidnap ....
manslaughter	mercy-killing	mugging ....
murder	possession of drugs	rape ....
shoplifting	smuggling	speeding ....
stalking	treason	

  b What are the words for the criminals who commit these crimes? In most cases they have one of these endings: *-ar* / *-er* / *-ist*. In a few cases the words are quite different from the words in the list. In some cases there is no special word for this kind of criminal.

  c What are the verbs related to the crimes? In some cases there is a directly related verb, for example, *to murder*. In some cases you will need to use a phrase including the verb *to commit*.

3 Work in pairs.

  a Group the crimes listed above into three categories.

    • Major crimes

    • Petty crimes

    • Minor offences

  b Compare lists with another pair.

    1 Do you have the same crimes in each list? What are the main differences?

    2 Try to agree on the three crimes you consider most serious and the three most minor offences.

4 Here are some of the commonest forms of punishment.

  a Add any other punishments you know to this list.

a fine	a prison sentence	community service
electronic tagging	naming and shaming	

  b What would be appropriate punishments for the three most serious crimes and the three most minor offences? Discuss ideas.

5 Work in groups.

You are going to discuss a case that took place in Britain in 1999.

  a Read the facts of the case. What is your first reaction to this story?

The facts of the case

TWO YOUTHS went to an isolated farm in the early hours of the morning with the deliberate intention of burgling the property. The two were shot by the farmer while they were prowling around in the house. One was wounded in the arm and the other, who was shot in the back, was found dead the following day.

  b Now read more information about the case on p.157. Does this change your ideas?

  c Do you think the farmer should be punished? If so, what should his punishment be?

  d Turn to p.158 to find out what actually happened to the farmer.

Language commentary

1 *wish*

a *wish* –meanings

Wish expresses several related ideas. Notice the verb forms which follow *wish*.

- A regret for something in the past that is too late to change.

  I wish I'd taken her advice.

  I wish I hadn't promised to go with them.

- Dissatisfaction with your current situation, which cannot possibly change.

  I'm tired of behaving in an adult way – **I wish I were** a teenager again.

- Frustration with your current situation, which could change.

  I wish I could pass my driving test. I've tried several times and I keep failing.

- Impatience with someone else's behaviour – *would* suggests that the other person is unwilling rather than unable to change.

  I wish you would be quiet when you come in late. You woke me up last night.

▸ **Note** It isn't possible to say *I wish I would …*

b *If only*

If only is used to express regrets or strong wishes. *If only* clauses can stand on their own, leaving the consequence implied.

If only you didn't have to go so soon …

(Implied continuation   … we could spend more time together.)

If only I could speak English fluently …

(Implied continuation   … I'd be able to get a good job.)

c Alternatives

What a pity / shame you can't come to our party. We'll miss you.

It's a pity / shame you won't be there.

Unfortunately there's nothing I can do to help.

I really hope everything goes well at the weekend.

I regret insulting / having insulted him now.

I'm sorry I made such a fuss.

Why won't / don't you stop complaining?

I'd be grateful if you didn't smoke in the house.

I'd really like you to stay for the weekend.

Please phone me as soon as you can.

2 Speculating and imagining

a *would, might, could* – speculating and imagining the future

- *Would* is used in conditional sentences, or when a condition is implied.

  I would go back in time to the fifteenth century (if I had the opportunity).

- *Might* is used to refer to something you think of as being quite likely.

  We might move next year (if we can afford to / if we can find a place we like).

- *Could* is used to speculate about real possibilities.

  It could be sunny at the weekend. Who knows?

- *Could* (*not*) is also used to mean *would* (*not*) *be able* or *would* (*not*) *be possible*.

  I could never leave you.

b Imaginary ideas

In these alternatives, notice past tense verbs are used to show that this is an unreal situation.

(Just) suppose you weren't married to Laura.

Suppose / Supposing we missed our flight.

(Let's) imagine we were on a desert island.

Let's pretend you'd never seen me before, what would you think?

What if someone stole our car and **crashed** it?

c Conditionals

Conditional sentence patterns are also used to speculate or express imaginary ideas. Notice these two alternative constructions. The second example (inversion) is more formal.

If I'd known you weren't interested, **I wouldn't have kept phoning** you.

Had I known you weren't interested, **I wouldn't have kept phoning** you.

4 Danger

4.1 A near miss

Lead in

Work in pairs or groups.

1 What dangers could be associated with the situations shown in the photos?

2 Which of these newspaper headlines could be associated with the photos?

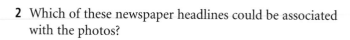

Twenty arrested in midnight drugs raid

Striker hit by flying bottle

Domestic accidents on the increase

Passenger cut free after six-hour ordeal

I WOKE UP NEXT TO A SNAKE

Helicopter rescues four in off-shore drama

Listening

1 You are going to hear someone describing a motorway situation when they felt in danger. What do the words in **bold** mean in this extract from the recording?

… we were approaching a **junction** and I thought well this car's coming up very close behind me obviously he's going to go off up the **slip road** to the junction but he didn't – he came right up behind me and at the last minute **swerved** out to **overtake** me, hit the back of my car but not enough to, to, to send either of us off course, and **sped off** up the motorway, so I thought well you know I'm not having this, so I chased him and **flashed** him and he **pulled over** on to the side of the road …

2 **4.1** Listen to the first part of the recording.

Why did the speaker feel afraid? What did he imagine might happen?

3 **4.2** What happened? Listen to the second part of the recording and answer these questions.

a Where was the speaker?
b How did he feel as the two men approached him?
c What did the two men do or say to the speaker?
d What did the two men give the speaker to reassure him?

4 Make up a suitable newspaper headline for this story.

React and discuss

1 How would you have reacted in the same situation as the speaker?

2 Have you ever been involved in or witnessed a situation similar to this?

Exploring natural speech

Speakers use 'vague language' when they cannot or do not want to be precise for some reason.

1 Underline any examples of this kind of language in the two extracts from the recordings.

a … I was driving home from London to Oxford, erm about, I don't know, about 11 o'clock at night something like that on a Saturday night and the motorway was quite deserted …

b No baseball cap. No baseball bat – anything like that. And they sort of approached me one from either side of the car erm and there were a couple of minutes when I thought mm yeah this was a bad idea …

2 Work in pairs.

Take turns to tell each other something you did yesterday. Try to include some commonly used 'vague language' words and phrases from the box.

Vague language

- *about* (= approximately)   *nearly   just before   just after*
- the suffix *-ish* – (*I went to bed early-ish*)
- *quite* (= not very)   *fairly   rather*
- *stuff   thing(s)   something like that   anything like that*
- *perhaps   maybe   probably*
- *a couple   a few   several   a lot   loads   two or three*

Vocabulary: *danger*

Complete these sentences with *danger* phrases from the list, then discuss possible answers to the questions which follow the sentences.

out of danger   on the danger list
a danger to himself   hidden dangers
danger money

a When he drinks too much Paul's .... and other people.
   What might Paul do in this situation?

b Sue was badly injured in the accident and was .... for nearly a week.
   Where would Sue probably be in this condition?

c Firefighters should get .... for the work they do.
   Can you think of other jobs in this category?

d My mother has been critically ill but she's .... now.
   If everything goes well, what will happen next in this mother's story?

e To a careless person foreign travel can be full of ....
   Give some examples of these in your country.

Speaking

1 Work out the stories behind one of these newspaper headlines. Make notes of the main points.

BOMB SQUAD INVESTIGATES ABANDONED CAR

Thick fog brings motorway chaos

Streets deserted as gunman takes hostages

7-year-old thief a danger to himself

2 Tell the story to a partner as if you were a TV or radio news presenter.

4.2 Anonymous threats

Listening

1 You are going to hear two people talking about dangerous situations they have been in.

a Look at the photos. Guess what the dangers were.

b Predict which of these words or phrases are used in each story. Write 1 or 2 next to each word or phrase.

- *absolutely furious* ....
- *angry gesture* ....
- *clump of trees* ....
- *dark patch* ....
- *eight stops* ....
- *on my own* ....
- *road rage* ....
- *shouted abuse* ....
- *sunroof* ....
- *taxi rank* ....

2 **4.3** Listen to the first story. As you listen, check your answers to **1b**.

3 Are these statements True or False? Listen again and check.

a When the speaker got on the train there were already two passengers in her carriage.

b During the journey the train stopped eight times.

c After the other passenger got off the train the lights went off.

d There was no one at the station when the speaker got off the train.

e The taxi area at the station was well lit.

4 **4.4** Listen to the second story. As you listen, put these events in the correct order.

a The driver threatened the cyclist. ....

b The cyclist indicated that he was angry. ....

c The driver opened his window. ....

d The cyclist apologized. ....

e The driver put his head through the sunroof of his car. ....

f The driver insulted the cyclist. ....

React and discuss

Would you have been frightened in either of the situations you have heard about? Why / Why not?

Exploring natural speech

1 Why do the speakers use *sort of* in these extracts from the recording? What does this phrase add to the meaning? What does it tell you about the speaker?

a I grabbed this person and said 'Where's the taxi rank?' and they pointed over to this **sort of** clump of trees in the middle of this **sort of** like very dark patch …

b I was **sort of** cycling along as I thought I was in the right …

2 Add *sort of* to this story wherever you can, then read your version of the story to a partner.

> He glanced at me with a strange expression in his eyes and told me to follow him. I smiled and did what he said. He took me into a large room. It was a dining room with an enormous table in the middle. I sat down but I felt uncomfortable. I didn't know what to expect. He went out of the room, leaving me alone.

Language focus: narrative tenses

1 Read this extract from the cyclist's story. Which verb tense is most commonly used? Why is this tense appropriate to story-telling?

… I made an angry gesture as they call it in the newspapers erm and he actually followed me and pulled alongside and stuck his head out of the sunroof while driving along, stuck his head out of the sunroof and he basically said you know 'if you do that again I'm going to knock your head off'…

2 Why do we sometimes use the Past continuous?

I was thinking to myself, well this is all right because when I get to the end …

I was sort of cycling along, … and he opened his window …

3 Why is the Past perfect used?

I went to this station … and the friend that I'd met there took me to the station …

What is the difference in meaning between these two sentences?

When I got to the station, everybody had gone home.
When I got to the station, everybody went home.

4 How would you expect these different story beginnings to continue? Make up the next part of the story.

I was cycling home last night …
I cycled home last night …
I'd cycled home last night …

Exploitation

1 Complete this story with the correct past form of the verbs in brackets. You may need to use the passive.

A detective .... (walk)[1] along the corridor of a large hotel. Suddenly, he .... (hear)[2] a woman's voice. 'No! Don't shoot me, John!' Then there .... (be)[3] a shot. The detective .... (run)[4] to the room where the shot .... (come)[5] from and .... (burst)[6] in. In one corner .... (lie)[7] a dead woman and in the middle of the room .... (be)[8] the gun that .... (use)[9] to shoot her. On the other side of the room .... (stand)[10] a postman, a lawyer, and an accountant. The detective .... (look)[11] at them for a moment, then .... (go)[12] up to the postman ....[13] (grab) him and .... say[14], 'I am arresting you for murder.'

The detective .... (never see)[15] any of the people in the room before. How .... (know)[16] that it was the postman who .... (murder)[17] the woman?

How did the detective know that the postman was the murderer?

2 Think about the story behind one of these photographs.

a Discuss your ideas in pairs. Then decide whether to make your story dramatic or humorous.

b Tell your story to another pair who chose the other story. If you are the listening pair, interrupt your partners' story from time to time with comments or questions. Use expressions from the box.

Interrupting

Comments
- I'm not sure I understand.
- What a strange thing to do / say.
- I'm sorry, I didn't catch that.
- That's not very likely.

Questions
- Why did they do that?
- How did they do that?
- What happened next?
- Where / When did this happen?

Writing

You are going to enter a story-writing competition. The winning story will be published in a magazine for young people.

1 Choose one of the stories you have just told or heard in **Exploitation 2**.

2 Plan your story, paragraph by paragraph. Write **150–180** words in 3–5 paragraphs.

3 Write your story in an informal style suitable for the magazine readers.

▶ Writing guidelines p.151

4.3 Cyber danger

Reading

1 You turn on your computer to check your e-mail and find this message.

> If you receive an e-mail with the subject of 'Anything goes' DO NOT OPEN IT – delete it immediately. Warn all in your address book about this virus.

  a What are your first thoughts?
  b Would you pass on the warning to everyone in your address book? Why / why not?
  c Why is *virus* an appropriate word to use for things like *Melissa* which damage computers?

2 Work in pairs, **A** and **B**.

  a What kind of person do you think writes computer viruses? Compare your ideas.
  b **Student A** Read the article on this page.
    Student B Turn to p.157.
    Does the person you read about fit your idea of a virus writer?

3 Work in the same pairs.

  a Tell your partner three interesting facts from the article you have read.
  b Do the two virus writers, David Smith and Johnny, have anything in common?
  c What were their reasons for writing viruses?
  d Work through the **Close up** tasks which follow your partner's article.

React and discuss

1 Have you, or has anyone you know, ever been the victim of a computer virus?

2 Do you think virus writers should be punished? How?

Close up

1.17 Smith is described as *soft-spoken*. How would you describe someone who was the opposite of *soft-spoken*?

1.20 What would be the opposite of **profound** consequences?

1.22 What is a *victimless crime*? Can you think of any crimes which are *victimless*?

Melissa Creator Pleads Guilty

The New Jersey man who disrupted e-mail systems around the world in March by spreading a computer virus he named 'Melissa', pleaded guilty in a plea bargain
5 **with prosecutors on Thursday.**

Computer programmer David Smith, 31, one of the first people believed to be prosecuted for spreading a computer virus, admitted in court entering user groups and electronic mail groups
10 on America Online without authorization.

He faces a maximum of 10 years in prison and a possible $150,000 fine on the New Jersey state charge.

Smith acknowledged that he had deliberately
15 broken into the systems and had known what he was doing.

But the soft-spoken Smith, reading a statement, said in court, 'I did not expect or anticipate the amount of damage that took place ... I had no
20 idea there would be such profound consequences to others.'

'These crimes are not victimless crimes,' New Jersey Attorney General John Farmer said at a news conference. 'This is not a joke.'

25 Farmer pointed out that the virus had paralysed tens of thousands of computer systems and cost companies and other parties tens of millions of dollars in losses.

Reuters Limited

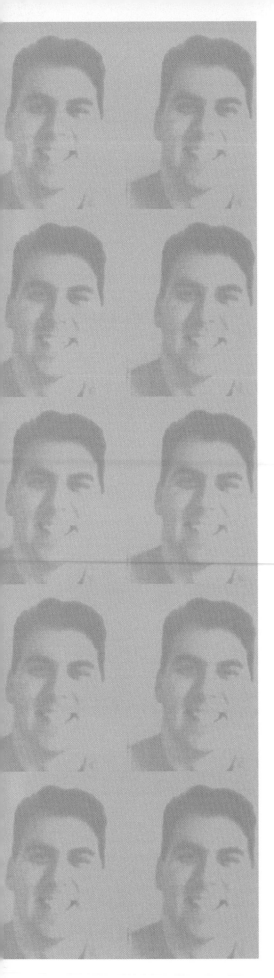

Language focus: reported speech and reporting verbs

1 Here are some examples of reported or indirect speech. What were the actual words (direct speech) in each case?

    a *AOL states that this is a very dangerous virus.*

    b *Computer programmer David Smith admitted … entering user groups … without authorization.*

    c *Smith acknowledged that he had deliberately broken into the systems and had known what he was doing.*

    d *Farmer pointed out that the virus had paralysed tens of thousands of computer systems …*

    e *Johnny explains why he is a virus writer.*

2 What do examples **1a** and **c–e** tell us about reported speech?

3 We sometimes use reporting verbs when we report someone's words. Reporting verbs give us extra information about the way something was said or about the purpose for which it was said.

    a Which reporting verbs are used in sentences **1a–e** above?

    b Match the following near synonyms with the reporting verbs in **1a–e**.

concede	confess	declare	spell out	observe

    c How is the verb *suggest* used as a reporting verb? Which of these sentences are correct?

        1 He suggested reinstalling the software.

        2 She suggested to restart the computer.

        3 I suggested that we saved our work on disk.

        4 They suggested that we change our Internet Service Provider.

        5 He suggested we install virus protection software.

Exploitation

1 Report this conversation without using direct speech. Use appropriate reporting verbs from this list. (There are more verbs than you need.)

accuse (someone of doing something)	admit	apologize (for doing something)	ask
claim confess congratulate (someone on doing something) deny explain insist		
maintain promise suggest tell		

    a **Sue**   You've been using my computer, haven't you, Nick?

    b **Nick** No, I haven't. Why don't you ask Pete?

    c **Sue**   Have you been playing games on my computer, Pete?

    d **Pete** I'm afraid I can't even use a computer, Sue.

    e **Sue**   Sorry. I didn't mean to accuse you.

    f **Pete** I suspect it was probably Jon.

    g **Sue**   How do you know that?

    h **Pete** I saw him sitting at your desk yesterday afternoon.

    i **Sue**   Is that true, Jon? Was it you who used my computer?

    j **Jon**   Yes, it was. Sorry.

    k **Sue**   Don't be sorry. You've got the highest game score ever! Well done!

2 Work in pairs, **A** and **B**.

    a **Student A** Turn to p.158 and read the e-mail.

          Student B Turn to p.159 and read the e-mail.

    b Tell each other about the e-mail you have just read.

Exploring words

Collocation (1)

1 a Choose the best definition of the word *collocation*.

   1 a verb and noun that are usually used together

   2 a combination of words that are frequently used together

   3 a common combination of an adjective and a noun

   4 two or three words that are always used together

b Why are collocations important in language learning?

2 In one of the recordings in the unit a speaker described a *motorway* as being *deserted*. Look at this list of adjectives with similar meanings to *deserted*.

a Which of them can describe the nouns in the list below?

Adjectives	abandoned	bare	busy	crowded	deserted
	empty	full	lonely		

Nouns	beach	bottle	car	feet	house	person
	room	station	street	village		

b Compare your lists in pairs, then think of other nouns which can collocate with each of the adjectives.

c Complete these sentences with appropriate adjective–noun combinations.

   1 At the side of the road we saw many ...., left by their drivers when the petrol finally ran out.

   2 At the end of my holiday, no one came to meet me and I returned to a(n) .... My parents were at work and my brother was at school.

   3 Too many people want to sunbathe and swim. That's why the .... are so .... at the weekends.

   4 I walked through the .... of the town. 'Where is everybody?' I wondered.

d What is the difference in meaning between these pairs of phrases?

   1 *a deserted house / an abandoned house*

   2 *a busy station / a crowded station*

   3 *an empty room / a bare room*

3 We *win a war* but we *conquer a disease*.

a Which of these verbs can describe the nouns in the list below?

Verbs	beat	combat	come to terms with	confront
	defeat	face	fight	meet	overcome	run	solve

Nouns	a challenge	(a) crime	(a) danger	(a) difficulty
	(a) disadvantage	(a) disease	(a) fear	an enemy
	the future	a handicap	a (losing) battle	
	a problem	a risk	a war	

b Complete these sentences with appropriate verb–noun combinations.

   1 People visit phobia clinics to help them .... their irrational ....

   2 Scientists and doctors are always trying to find new ways of .... like cancer.

   3 Society seems unable to .... the .... of drug addiction. Some people think the police are .... a .... against international drug dealers.

c Think of other nouns that can collocate with three of the verbs in the list above.

4 Read the short article below and underline the collocations. Look for these combinations.

- adjective–noun   *an abandoned car*
- verb–noun   *to solve a problem*

5 Discuss these questions in pairs.

a What household chores do you regularly carry out?

b Are there any situations in which you deliberately expose yourself to danger?

c Have you ever seen or been involved in a driving accident?

d How would you assess these risks on Dr Duckworth's 0–8 scale?

Washing-up as risky as driving

Statistician Dr Frank Duckworth's 'Riskometer' is a scale to help people assess the risks in their daily lives. He has given everyday
5 situations a risk rating from zero to eight. Zero represents just existing on the planet for a year, while eight represents committing suicide.

10 One of Dr Frank Duckworth's more surprising findings was that a person who smokes 40 cigarettes a day is exposing himself to nearly as much danger as playing a game of Russian Roulette.

And the chances of dying while doing a routine activity like
15 hoovering, washing-up or walking down the street come into the same category as suffering an accidental fall or being involved in a driving accident.

Dr Duckworth has said, 'I would guess that over a person's lifetime, the risk of death by carrying out household chores lies
20 between five and six on the Riskometer scale.

Metro

Language commentary

1 Narrative tenses

a Past simple – uses

- To refer to a sequence of completed events.
  I **went** across and **stood** under this sort of tree.
- To refer to habitual or repeated past actions.
  I **cycled** to work every day last week.
- To refer to unreal events in the present or future.
  It's high time we **had** something to eat.
  I'd rather you **didn't criticize** me.

b Past continuous – uses

- To refer to a background situation.
  I **was settling** in well and **getting on** with my new colleagues, …
- To refer to a past action in progress when something specific happened.
  As I **was walking** home, I tripped and fell over.

c Past perfect – uses

- To clarify a sequence of events in the past.
  I arrived at the station, went to the waiting room, and started to read the book **I'd bought** that morning.
- To explain a past action.
  I'd left my keys at work so I couldn't get into the house.
  I was exhausted because **I'd been running** for two hours.
- In reported speech.
  He said **he'd tried** to phone me the day before. ('I tried to phone you yesterday.')
- As part of conditional structures.
  If **I hadn't missed** my train, I wouldn't have felt so worried. (Third conditional)

2 Reported speech

a Basic rules

- If the reporting verb is in the past, the direct speech verb often moves back in time.

'I **love** you.'	She **said** she **loved** me.
'I'll **help** you tidy the house.'	He said **he'd** (he would) **help** me tidy the house.

- If the reporting verb is in the present, the direct speech does not have to change when it is reported. You can choose whether to change the tense or not.

'I still **love** you.'	She **says** she still **loves** me.

- The original verb tense does not change if we want to emphasize that what was said by the speaker is still true or relevant.

'I still **love** you.'	She said she still **loves** me.
'**We're going** on holiday tomorrow.'	They said **they're going** on holiday tomorrow.

- The word order in reported questions is the same as for statements. The subject and verb are not inverted.

'How much **do you love** me?'	I asked her how much **she loved me.**
'**Are you going** on holiday tomorrow?'	I asked them if **they were going** on holiday tomorrow.

- Commands are reported with verb + object + *to* + infinitive.

'**Stop!**'	She **told / ordered him to stop.**
'**Slow down!**'	They **told him to slow down.**

- Most modal verbs change in reported speech.

'We **may** go to Spain in the summer.'	She said they **might** go to Spain in the summer.
'**Can** I help you get the picnic ready.?'	She asked if she **could** help me get the picnic ready.
'I **must** go and see the dentist.'	He said he **had to** go and see the dentist.
'I **should** go now or I'll be late.'	She said she **should / ought to** go or she'd be late.

b Other changes

- Pronouns may change.

'**You** can go.'	She said **I** could go.

- Time references may change.

'I wasn't paid **last month.**'	He said he hadn't been paid **the previous month.**

- Place references may change.

'You can't park **here.**'	They said I couldn't park **there.**

- Determiners change.

'Have you heard **this** fantastic news?'	She asked if I'd heard **the / that** fantastic news.

c *say, tell*

Say and *tell* are different; *tell* needs a direct object.

She said she loved me.	She told **me** she loved me.

These verbs also need a direct object, and are usually followed by *to* + infinitive.

---
advise   ask   beg   command   forbid   instruct   persuade   request   urge   warn

---

d Other reporting verbs

There are many reporting verbs which can be used instead of *say, tell,* or *ask.* They are useful because they provide an interpretation of the speaker's intention.

'Yes, I can come.'	He **confirmed** (that) he could come.
'I think it'll rain this evening.'	He **predicted** (that) it would rain that evening.

---
agree   announce   argue   believe   claim   complain   decided   deny   doubt   emphasize   hope   imagine   imply   inquire   insist   reply   report   think   wonder

---

When we report negative words or thoughts, we can make the reporting verb negative.

'I'm sure you **won't enjoy** the film.'	She **didn't think** I'd enjoy the film.

e *suggest*

As a reporting verb *suggest* can be used in different ways.
He suggested **finding** a hotel.
He suggested (that) we **found** a hotel.
He suggested (that) we **should find** a hotel.
He suggested (that) we **find** a hotel.

▶ **Note** It is not correct to say: He suggested **to find** a hotel.

5 Dilemmas

5.1 In the workplace

Lead in

Read about these dilemmas people can find themselves in at work. What is your immediate reaction? Choose one alternative for each problem.

What should I do?

1 One of my colleagues is dishonest. She's stealing office equipment.

a Tell the boss ☐
b Warn my colleague ☐
c Do nothing ☐

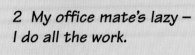

2 My office mate's lazy – I do all the work.

a Complain to the boss ☐
b Ask my colleague to stop being lazy ☐
c Do nothing ☐

3 I have to work from 9.00 a.m. till 4.00 p.m. without a break.

a Demand a break ☐
b Look for a new job ☐
c Put up with the situation ☐

Listening

1 You are going to hear a radio programme offering advice to people in dilemmas at work.

Before you listen, answer these questions to check your understanding of the phrases in *italics* from the programme.

a Who does *public property* belong to? What kinds of things are regarded as *public property*? What is the opposite of *public property*?
b Do you ever *pass on gossip* you have overheard? If so, do you feel guilty about it?
c If you *sink to someone's level*, do you behave well or badly?
d In what circumstances might you tell someone to *mind their own business*?
e If you *jump to conclusions*, do you form an opinion quickly or slowly?

2 **5.1** Listen to the discussion of the first situation.

a What is the e-mail writer's dilemma?
b What suggestions are given by the advisers? What do they agree and disagree about?

3 **5.2** Listen to the second part of the discussion.

a What is the situation?
b What does the e-mail writer want to do?

React and discuss

How would you have responded to the first dilemma you heard about? What advice would you have given?

Exploring natural speech

1 Read this extract from the recording.

I don't think she has the right, I'm afraid, I just don't think she has the right …

2 These sentences introduce bad news or express disagreement or criticism. Add *I'm afraid* to each of them.

a Your work is not good enough. You'll have to do a lot better.

b The business is doing very badly. We can't afford to keep you.

c Your behaviour at work is completely unacceptable.

d The office was broken into last night.

3 **5.3** Listen, check, and practise.

Vocabulary: three-part phrasal verbs

1 Read these extracts from the recording. How are the three-part phrasal verbs in **a–c** different from the two-part verbs in **d** and **e**? Think about the word order.

a *I just don't think she has the right – she has to **put up with** it.*

b *She's got to concentrate on what she's doing and let him **get on with** it.*

c *Well, let's **move on to** our next e-mail from someone in London.*

d *It's an interesting suggestion. I promise I'll **think** it **over**.*

e *I had a real problem with one of my colleagues, but I think I've **sorted** it **out** now.*

2 Answer questions **a–f** using a pronoun object and a phrasal verb from this list.

get away with   go back on   look down on   look forward to
run out of   send off for

a How does he feel about starting his new job?

b Did he lose his job for stealing office equipment?

c Have we got any more photocopying paper?

d How did bosses use to treat employees?

e Did she keep her promise about doing more work?

f I've just seen a job advertisement in the newspaper. How can I get an application form?

Language focus: opinions and suggestions

1 How do the speakers in the recording express their opinions or make suggestions about what other people should do? Complete these extracts from the recording.

a *I .... disagree. I think that if he is going to be so rude …*

b *… there's .... that he can expect her to not take what he's been saying …*

c *I agree, but .... rise above it? .... sink to their level?*

d *........ try and talk to him about it, but to start gossiping …*

e *Yeah, you're .... That's probably the first thing that she should do …*

f *........ .... that she should .... confront it …*

2 **5.4** Listen to the recording and check your answers.

3 Here are some more expressions we can use to give opinions or make suggestions about what someone should do. Can you add any others?

- *She ought to / should / could (always) / might / must / has got to …*
- *Why can't he / doesn't he …?*
- *It might be an idea to (ask) … / It might be an idea if he (asked) …*
- *I (would) suggest she …*
- *I'd advise him / her to …*

Exploitation

Work in groups of three.

1 Discuss the second dilemma you heard about in the recording. Here's a reminder.

> My boss has asked me to book him a double room at a hotel for a conference. The thing is he's not taking his wife with him. I feel like protesting – but I know that if I do he'll just tell me to mind my own business.

Presenter You have no strong feelings on the subject.

Adviser 1 Express your opinions and make suggestions.

Adviser 2 Express your opinions and make suggestions. You sometimes disagree with **Adviser 1**.

2 Choose one of the three dilemmas from the **Lead in** section. Discuss it as a group, then present your ideas to the rest of the class.

5.2 A quiet Sunday bus ride

Reading

1 Look at these verbs and nouns from the article you are going to read.

abuse (*n*) brains children grown-up fight fist kids knuckles lip	
opponent punch-up scrap smack spit swear victim yob a youth	

a Group the words under these headings.

People	Bad language	Violent behaviour	Parts of the body

b Which two words in the *People* group mean the same?

c Which two words in the *People* group have opposite meanings?

d Which three words in the *Violent behaviour* group have similar meanings?

e Which body words are connected with the *hand* and which are connected with the *head*?

2 Now read about one man's dilemma.

a Why did the writer speak to the yobs?

b What was their first reaction?

React and discuss

1 What would you have done in the writer's situation?

2 Have you ever been involved in or witnessed a situation like this?

3 Work in pairs.

Student A You were a passenger on the bus in the story you have just read. You are going to give an interview to a journalist, describing what happened. Read the article again and decide how you felt at each stage of the story. Be ready to invent answers to some questions.

Student B You are a journalist collecting information about the bus incident. You know the basic facts but need more details for your story, so you are going to interview one of the passengers. Read the article again and decide which were the key stages of the story. For each stage, prepare questions to find out how the passenger felt and other details. Interview the passenger.

Close up

1.6 What idea does *stream* suggest in the phrase *a stream of abuse*?

1.39 Is a *close shave* more or less serious than *real trouble*? What does *let alone* mean?

1.47 What is a *gagging order*? (A *gag* is something put in or across a person's mouth to stop them talking.)

1.70 What does the suffix *-ify* mean in *trendify*? (Other verbs: *simplify / intensify / purify*)

1.71 *bus rage* is similar to *road rage*. What do these phrases mean?

1.78 How is *making eye contact* with someone different from *looking at* them?

An everyday dilemma in modern Britain

IT WAS just a quiet Sunday bus ride, until the two youths at the back started messing with the emergency door. Kids like a laugh but this wasn't high spirits.
5 When the driver stopped the bus to tell them off, he just got a stream of abuse.

We have two choices. We either sit and look out of the window and pretend it's not happening, or we speak our minds.
10 Since I had my two young sons, aged six and eight, with me, I asked the yobs, politely, to watch their language.

Stunned silence. I could hear their brains whirring inside their bony heads.
15 Yobs have got so used to our timidity they're surprised to be challenged. Surprised and delighted.

'What the **** has it got to do with you?'
20 'Plenty,' I said. 'I wouldn't swear in front of your kids, so please don't swear in front of mine.'

'Come on then, you ****.'

Faced with a bony fist with HATE
25 tattooed on the knuckles, it's no use suggesting a cosy chat about community values. But why should I fight? My children were already frightened by this grown-up who'd suddenly turned crazy.
30 Outside life carried on as normal. Swans drifted down the river, men fished quietly, some children were flying a kite.

This wasn't happening in some inner city alleyway. It was the middle of a small town, on a Sunday afternoon. Things like this aren't supposed to happen here. [35]

Never, in 12 years of London life, walking about at all times of day and night, did I have a close shave, let alone face any real trouble. [40]

No, the real front line is here, in small towns like this. Our future is one of cameras on high poles, soulless shopping malls, children with idle hands and empty heads and enough dole money for booze. [45]

But it's not the fear of the fist, or the knife I hate. It's the gagging order. Express an opinion, call for some manners and you risk a smack in the mouth. Or worse.

There we stood, the yob and I, eye-to-eye on that little bus. In the end deprived [50] of his punch-up, he spat in my face and then in the driver's.

Despite my anger, I knew it was best to leave it at that. What sickened me was the [55] spitefulness and stupidity of it all.

There's always been fighting. But in the past it was a peer group thing consisting of pals falling out and rival groups of children defending their territory and their [60] infant honour. All in the family so to speak.

Now, it's the family who is the victim. Today the yobs' opponent is anyone: me and you, dads and grandads, even our mums [65] and grandmas.

In my case, there was no big fight. People might say: 'So what? You didn't even get your lip split. It wasn't even an argument.' Nor could we trendify it by [70] calling it 'bus rage', a brief dust-up between irritable passengers. It wasn't even worth reporting to the police.

Some people said I should have decked the leader of the yobs, or at least tried to. [75] Some said I was crazy to risk a scrap, especially when I had my children with me. 'Don't even make eye contact with them,' my wife says. Others said I was lucky: it might easily have been a knife [80] instead of a mouthful of spit.

FOOTNOTE A week afterwards, I was travelling on the train. Two yobs lit up in a no-smoking carriage. People sniffed disapprovingly, but no one said anything. Neither did I. [85]

Nicholas Whittaker, *Daily Mail*

Language focus: inversion

1 What do you notice about the word order in these sentences? What is similar about the first word or phrase?
   a *Never, in 12 years of London life, did I have a close shave, …*
   b *Nor could we trendify it by calling it 'bus rage', …*
   c *Not only did the boys swear at the driver, they also spat at him.*
   d *At no time did any of the other passengers support me.*
   e *Hardly had the bus moved off when the yobs started messing about.*

2 What is the effect of starting sentences like this? Compare these pairs of sentences.
   a *Never have I heard such a dreadful speech.*
      I've never heard such a dreadful speech.
   b *I saw what he did and I heard every word he said.*
      Not only did I see him, I also heard every word he said.

3 Here are some more words and expressions which are used in the same way.

(In) no way   No sooner … than   Not a thing   Never before
Not once   Not a single person   Not until   On no account   Hardly ever
Seldom   Under no circumstances

   Rewrite these sentences starting with one of the words or phrases from the list. As well as changing the word order, you may need to change verb forms.
   a I found out the names of the youths three weeks later.
   b I didn't think once of getting off the bus.
   c I've hardly ever felt as frightened as I did on that journey.
   d Immediately I got on the bus, the driver drove off.
   e I'm quite sure I won't take my children on that bus journey again.
   f Bus drivers are not allowed to interfere if passengers start arguing or fighting.
   g He didn't hear anything from the police after the incident.
   h I've never been involved in a road rage incident before.

Exploitation

Work in groups.

1 Read through these instructions.
   a You are going to make up a story which involves:
      • a narrator (you)   • two other people.
   b The story should describe a 'rage' situation: in the street, at work, on a plane.

2 Brainstorm what happened.

3 Now write the story, which should include these five sentence beginnings.
   • Never before had I seen such a …
   • Under no circumstances could I …
   • Only when he'd / she'd left …
   • Not only did I / he / she …
   • At no time did I / he / she / anyone …

   Use the beginnings in any order. Add your own endings and other ideas.

4 Tell or read your story to the rest of your group.

5.3 How far should we go?

Listening

1 You are going to hear a group of people discussing genetic engineering. Before you listen, discuss these questions in groups.

   a For what practical purposes is genetic engineering being developed?

   b What makes it a controversial subject?

   c Do you have strong feelings about it? Are you for or against?

2 **5.5** Now listen and answer these questions.

   a Do the speakers mention any of the purposes you talked about?

   b What is their general feeling about genetic engineering? Are they for or against, or do they have mixed feelings?

3 Listen again and complete these sentences to make true statements.

   a The speakers agree that it would be good to use genetic engineering to …

   b Knowing the function of every gene means that humans will be able to …

   c Being able to eradicate natural diseases means that humans will live …

   d If humans live to a much older age, this will have economic …

   e The speakers are against using genetic engineering to enable couples to …

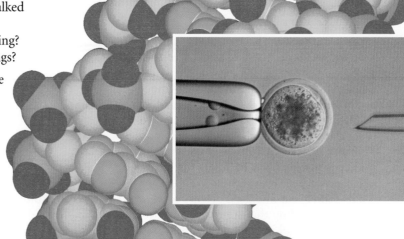

genetic engineering
Changing the structure of the genes of a living thing in order to make it healthier or stronger or more useful to humans.

Vocabulary: adjective-noun collocations

1 Which of the adjectives can be used with each health noun?

Adjectives	drastic effective gradual infectious instant old-fashioned painful serious successful
Nouns	cure disease operation recovery treatment

2 Complete these sentences with adjective–noun combinations. Use ten different words.

a Flu is a(n) .... which can spread quickly from person to person.

b Having a heart transplant is a(n) .... which is used only as a last resort.

c Keith was so ill he had to spend a month in hospital. Now thank goodness he's made a(n) ....

d As yet there is no .... for the common cold.

e Holding your breath is a(n) .... for hiccups.

Speaking

1 Work in pairs or groups.

Choose two or three of these statements about genetic engineering, then discuss them.

- Genetic engineering is an unnatural interference in human life and should be banned.
- We cannot trust scientists to work in the best interests of ordinary people.
- The large companies involved in genetic engineering are more interested in their own profits than in human welfare.
- Genetic engineering applied to crops and animals can ensure a cheap and plentiful supply of food for the whole world's population. For this reason it must be encouraged.
- People should have the right to choose the sex, appearance, and intelligence of their children.
- Genetic engineering should only be used to help us eradicate terrible illnesses like cancer.

2 Make your own list of the pros and cons of continuing with genetic engineering. Include the moral, practical, and economic issues involved.

Example

Pros: It can help us to eradicate diseases.
Cons: We don't know the long-term effects.

Writing

Continue working in the same pairs or groups for parts 1 and 2 of this writing task.

You are going to write a magazine article about genetic engineering, based on the discussions you have just had. (Assume that the magazine is read by people of your age.)

1 Plan the article.
- Decide how many paragraphs you will need.
- What will the topic of each paragraph be?
- Think about your readers. How technical can your writing be?

2 Write a title and a first sentence.
- Why is it a good idea for the title to be eye-catching and the first sentence to be attention-grabbing?

3 Write the rest of the article. Write **160–200** words altogether. The style should be informal, light, and personal. Your own ideas should be clear.

▶ **Writing guidelines p.154**

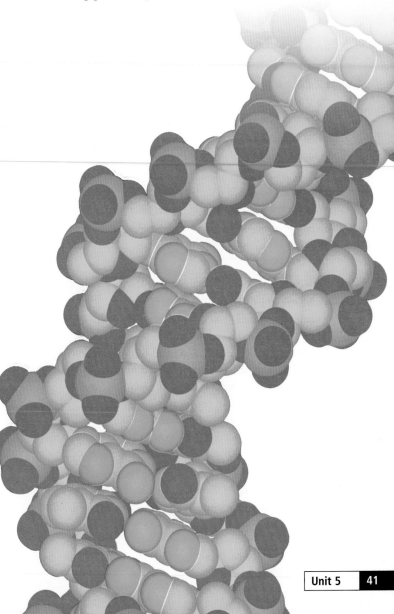

Exploring words

Rights, responsibilities, truth, and lies

1 a What do you consider to be your most important rights as an individual? For example, do you think you have the right to work?

What are your main responsibilities in your personal and professional life?

Compare ideas with a partner.

b Complete these expressions with the correct prepositions.

1. be responsible .... your own actions
2. discuss the rights and wrongs .... an issue
3. .... the public interest
4. blow the whistle .... someone
5. the lesser .... two evils
6. sit .... the fence
7. be .... two minds .... something
8. lay yourself open .... criticism

c Now complete this story of a personal dilemma with appropriate expressions from **b**.

> **ONE OF** my friends is involved in drug-dealing and I'm ....[1] telling the police. I just can't decide. I know that what he's doing is a crime and that it would be ....[2] to inform the police. The trouble is, I hate the thought of ....[3] one of my friends. But the problem's getting worse and I know I can't ....[4] for ever. If I keep my secret much longer I'll ....[5] public criticism. It will be difficult whatever I do, so I suppose going to the police would be the ....[6]. I've ....[7] the situation with my best friend, and she thinks I ought to go to the police straight away. So if my drug-dealing friend gets into trouble, he's only got himself to blame. In the end everyone's got to be ....[8].

d What would you do in this situation? Discuss ideas in pairs or groups.

2 a Which of these people would you trust or believe?

1. Mike's completely *above board*.
2. Jo is *two-faced*.
3. Dave's *as good as his word*.
4. In the end Sue *came clean* and told me everything.
5. The President has been involved in a *cover-up*.
6. Apparently Helen *made up* the whole story.
7. Liz always *sticks to the facts*.
8. Matt's pretty *straightforward*.
9. Jeff's well known for *telling tall stories*.
10. Kate's one of those people who *tells it like it is*.

b Work in pairs. Who would you use these words and phrases to describe? Think of people you know personally as well as public figures.

3 Read this fictional account of a dilemma that a newspaper reporter found herself in.

a What was the writer's dilemma?

Would you be a whistle-blower?

I WAS doing a story for the local newspaper on a young man, let's call him Tim, who had just been named 'Employee of the Year' in our town. Tim had everything. He was good-looking, popular, and successful. In an interview he told me, among other things, that he had a first-class degree from Cambridge and had published a respected book on business management. Subsequently, I made the usual checks only to discover that Cambridge University had no record of him being a student there, and his publisher had never heard of him.

When I confronted Tim with my discoveries, he acknowledged that his stories were fabrications and begged me not to publish the truth.

My editor and I discussed the rights and wrongs of publishing. Would it be in the public interest? Weren't Tim's lies simply a private matter? After all he hadn't hurt anyone. On the other hand, he had misled his boss and colleagues. In the end we felt that the public had a right to know that their hero was a fake and we told Tim that we were going to publish the story.

Tim's mother then contacted us and said that, if we published, Tim would probably commit suicide.

b Discuss these questions.

1. What are the main issues faced by the journalist and the editor?
2. What action do you think they should take?

c Now find out what happened by reading the end of the story on p.158.

d In what circumstances would you be a whistle-blower?

Language commentary

1 Opinions and suggestions

a Making suggestions and giving advice

We often express our opinions about what people should or shouldn't do indirectly. This is because we want to sound polite and not appear aggressive.

The words and phrases in **bold** in the examples below are used to make suggestions or advice less direct.

I (don't) think you ought to / should go on your own.
Why not simply / just talk to him about it?
Why don't you forget all about it?
(Possibly / Maybe / Perhaps) try and talk to him.
It might be an idea to phone before you go.
I / I'd suggest you make a proper appointment.
I / I'd advise you to check with the embassy first.
Don't you think it might be more sensible to take traveller's cheques?
You could (always) hire a car when you get there.
Have you thought about buying a mobile phone?

b Agreeing with someone else's opinion

I couldn't agree more.   You're probably right.
I wholeheartedly agree.   Absolutely!

c Disagreeing with someone else's opinion

I completely / absolutely / fundamentally / totally disagree.
I can't / couldn't (possibly) go along with that.
I know what you mean, but …

d Stating a general opinion

In my opinion / view, there are too many cars on the road.
It's my considered opinion that people spend too much money on food.
If you want my honest opinion, I think smoking should be banned in all public places.

2 Inversion

a After expressions with a negative meaning

After a range of negative expressions, there is inversion of the subject and the auxiliary verb.

No sooner had the game begun **than** it started to rain.
Never, in my whole life, **have I** been so frightened.
At no time did I lose hope.
In no way was he to blame for the accident.
No way am I going to apologize to him. (Very informal.)
On no account must you tell anyone what you've just heard.
Under no circumstances must you take more than four tablets a day.
I didn't see a single person, **nor did I** hear anything.
Not once did anyone thank her for all the work she'd done.
Not only was she physically ill, she was also deeply depressed.
Not since I left university **have I** had such a good time.

b After expressions with a restrictive meaning

Hardly / Barely / Scarcely had the game begun **when** it started to rain.
Only by practising every day **do you** stand a chance of winning the race.
Seldom have I come across such a talented child.

c Use

Inversion is often used to make what we say sound more serious, important, or dramatic. It is a type of 'fronting' which gives the negative idea more importance. In both pairs of examples below, the first sentence is more emphatic.

1 **Never**, in my whole life, **have I** been so frightened.
   I've never been so frightened in my whole life.
2 **Hardly had the game** begun when it started to rain.
   The game had hardly begun when it started to rain.

d Other examples of inversion

- In some formal conditional expressions.
   Should you arrive early, let yourself in. (= If you arrive early … **Should** is inverted to replace a first conditional **if** clause.)
   Were you to change your mind, I'd be most grateful. (= If you changed your mind, … . **Were** is inverted to replace a second conditional **if** clause.)
   Had I realized you were waiting for me, I'd have come straight away. (= If I had realized you were waiting for me, … . **Had** is inverted to replace a third conditional **if** clause.)

- In direct questions (not indirect / reported questions).
   Have you ever seen a ghost?   (I asked her **if she had** ever seen a ghost.)

- It is possible to use inversion after a place expression at the beginning of a sentence, with verbs of movement, for example *be, come, go, sit, stand*.
   On the wall **was an old photograph**.
   In the middle of the square **stands a statue** of the president.

e Inversion of subject and noun (not pronoun)

- It is common in speech to start a sentence with the adverb particle of phrasal verbs. In these cases subject and verb are only inverted when the subject of the verb is a noun.
   Along came the bus and **on we got**.
   The taxi arrived on time, so **in we got** and **off we went**.

- It is optional to invert nouns which are the subject of reporting verbs after direct speech.
   'And how are you today?' **asked the doctor**. (or … **the doctor asked**.)
   'I'm fed up with doing as I'm told,' **screamed the boy**. (or … **the boy screamed**.)

- With *here* and *there*.
   Sh! **Here comes my mum**. (but Sh! **Here she comes**.)
   There goes my last hundred pounds. (but **There it goes**.)

6 Natural assets

6.1 Personal gifts

Lead in

Look at this list of expressions used to describe people's natural talents or gifts.

be + a born (teacher)
a natural (athlete)
a talented (singer)
good at (talking)

have + an aptitude for (languages)
a gift for (making people laugh)
a (musical) talent

1 Can you think of people you know who these expressions could apply to?

2 Can you think of any more natural talents to add to the list?

Listening

1 **6.1** You are going to hear four people talking about their talents. How would you describe each speaker's attitude?

big-headed   modest   matter-of-fact   embarrassed   amused   grateful   mystified

2 Complete this table with what you remember about each speaker. Then listen again, check your answers, and add any more information you can.

	Speaker 1	Speaker 2	Speaker 3	Speaker 4
a Speaker's talent				
b Example given by speaker				
c Other people's reactions				

3 What about you? Do you have a particular talent? Tell a partner what it is and how people react to it.

4 Where do talents or gifts come from? Are they inherited? Are they gifts from God? The people in the next conversation say what they think.

a Predict, from these phrases, some of the things they might say.

an affinity for something   depending on the environment   musical inclination
parents   physical attributes

b **6.2** Listen to the conversation and check your ideas.

c Summarize the main ideas expressed in the conversation.

React and discuss

Do you think everyone has natural gifts? How can they best be developed?

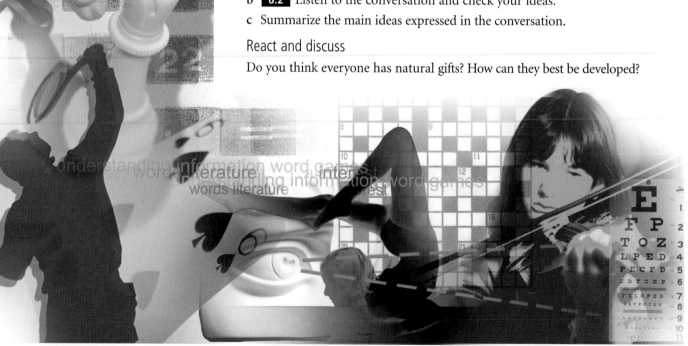

Exploring natural speech

Notice how the two speakers interact. Listen again and follow the transcript. Decide how they connect with each other at the numbered points. Choose from these types of connection.

A adds to an idea
B shows agreement
C finishes an idea
D replies to a question
E shows slight disagreement

A   Oh gosh there are all kind of gifts that people can be born with – you know mental gifts, intelligence, physical attributes – beauty – strength …

B **1** Definitely, yeah. Talent …

A **2** Talent absolutely, musical inclination.

B   And I definitely believe that people are born with certain talents – I think that they can also, you know they can grow depending on the environment that they're in, but …

A **3** Yeah, but I think you either have an affinity for something or you don't …

B **4** Definitely.

A   Like two children take piano lessons – one's going to be amazing and the other …

B **5** … the other is just OK, I agree and I …

A   Do you think it comes from the parents?

B **6** I think, you know, maybe partly, like I said, I think that it can influence a talent, but I think I think some people are born with certain talents and some people aren't …

B **7** And the people that are born with it, is it because their parents, like were their parents musically gifted so they have an inclination?

B **8** I think so, yeah. …

Language focus: *should, ought to, must, have to, need to*

1 Complete these extracts with the appropriate form of *should, ought to, must, have to,* or *need to.* You may have to use negative or past forms of these verbs. Sometimes more than one answer is possible.

  a My children tell me I .... go on the telly.
  b It's a quiz game where you .... think of the word or the phrase.
  c I don't .... carry people's phone numbers around with me. I've got them in my head.
  d I think as a parent, you .... encourage your children to develop their talents.
  e You .... entered for that general knowledge quiz. I'm sure you'd have won.
  f As long as your eyesight is good, you .... take another driving test.
  g You .... worry. You're by the far the most talented person in the room.
  h I really .... go in for that competition this week – I forgot last week.

2 What ideas do the modal verbs in sentences **1a–h** express? Choose an appropriate label for each sentence.

  advice   talking about a duty   command   necessity   order   recommendation
  talking about a responsibility   rule or law

3 Rephrase these sentences using expressions from this list.

  had better (not) + verb   to be (not) supposed to + verb   to be (not) meant to + verb

Example
It would be a good idea to ask them if you want to use the phone.
You'd better ask them if you want to use the phone.

  a You can't park here without a permit.
  b It's against the law to travel without a ticket.
  c Don't tell him you've seen me.

4 What is the difference in meaning between these sets of sentences?

  a 1 *Unfortunately I **have to work** late tonight.*
       2 *I **must work** tonight. I've got an exam tomorrow.*
  b 1 *You **don't have to tell** me what happened.*
       2 *You **mustn't tell** me what happened.*
  c 1 *I **needn't have worn** a suit. It was just a casual party.*
       2 *I **didn't need to wear** a suit. It was just a casual party.*

Exploitation

1 What could you say in these situations?

  a Someone has borrowed your car without asking.
  b You feel embarrassed because someone bought you a present for helping them.
  c Tomorrow's a public holiday – so you've got a day off work.
  d Explain why you didn't go to a meeting. It was cancelled.

2 Work in pairs.

Choose two of the subjects below and talk about each of them for 1–2 minutes. Think about obligations, responsibilities, and needs.

  a The difference between being a child and being an adult
  b How being married is different from being single
  c The changes to your life when you become a parent for the first time
  d How being in prison would be different from living a 'normal' life

6.2 Survivors

Lead in

Work in groups.

What do you know about crocodiles? Note down your ideas under these headings.

- Facts you know are true
- Ideas that you are not so sure about

Reading

1 Read the article and check your ideas.

What, according to Dr Ross, are the main reasons for the survival of crocodiles?

2 Answer these questions.

a What does the writer mean when he says people are *the most fearsome predators ever to stalk the Earth*?

b How do we know that crocodiles have changed little through history?

c How does Dr Ross explain the fact that crocodiles have managed to survive *even in the last few hundred years*?

d Why do you think Dr Ross prefers to describe crocodiles' survival as due to *rapid learning* rather than *intelligence*?

Outlasting the Dinosaurs

An Interview with Dr. James Perran Ross

Crocodiles are the ultimate survivors. Having appeared some 200 million years ago, they have outlived the dinosaurs by some 65 million years.
5 **Even people, the most fearsome predators ever to stalk the Earth, have failed to force into extinction any of the 23 species of crocodilians. What makes them such consummate**
10 **survivors? *NOVA* asked Dr. James Perran Ross, a croc researcher at the Florida Museum of Natural History.**

NOVA Why did crocodilians survive when the dinosaurs went extinct?

15 **ROSS** The short answer is we don't know. But we can look at what crocodiles do now and how they work and speculate on some things that may be involved. Crocodile design has
20 lasted an awfully long time. A great many of the fossils of crocodiles are virtually identical to the crocodiles we see today. They seem to have successfully adapted to their
25 environment and have undergone few changes. I think we have to look at their basic design and concede that it's a good way of being an amphibious predator. It really works. I think one of
30 the aspects that may play to their survival is that they are extremely tough and robust. We're learning now that the immune systems of crocodiles, for instance, are just incredible. They
35 can sustain the most frightful injuries.

NOVA Such as?

ROSS In territorial fights they commonly tear each other's legs off. They go away and sulk for a while and seem to heal
40 up. You often find animals in the wild with missing limbs, missing tails – what must have been very serious injuries. So I think their inherent toughness is one aspect. They are also long-lived. They routinely live for decades. The
45 adaptability of their behavior is also something that may play into their survival. It certainly has in modern times. We haven't lost a species of crocodile to extinction since humans
50 have been dominant on the planet, even in the last few hundred years when our impact has been appalling. The reason appears to be in large part because crocodiles learn quickly and
55 adapt to changes in their situation. They particularly learn to avoid dangerous situations very quickly.

NOVA Would you call that intelligence?

ROSS Well, it's certainly rapid learning.
60 There are some people who keep crocodiles who claim that they are truly intelligent.
I know some people whose opinions I respect who very sincerely believe
65 that crocodiles know individual people and that they learn simple routines very readily, such as when the man with the bucket has food and when he doesn't. They also become tame quite
70 readily. There are a couple of well-documented stories of truly tame crocodiles. The famous crocodile biologist Frederico Medem described a doctor who lived in Villavicencio,
75 Colombia, who had a large *Crocodylus intermedius*, the Orinoco crocodile. He had raised it from a hatchling. It was a female about 10 feet long, and it lived in his house. It played with his children,
80 it played with the family dog.

NOVA

Language focus: determiners

1 *some*

some has a number of different meanings:

- a proportion (not all) of
- a quantity of
- approximately.

Which of these meanings apply to these examples?

a *… they have outlived the dinosaurs by* **some** *65 million years.*

b *Although they don't all agree,* **some** *experts think crocodiles are truly intelligent.*

c *Look! The zoo keeper is giving the crocodile* **some** *food.*

2 *some, any, every*

What is the difference in meaning between these pairs of sentences?

a *I enjoy* **some** *wildlife* **programmes** *on TV.*
I enjoy **any** *wildlife* **programme** *on TV.*

b *Have you got* **some** *money you could lend me?*
Have you got **any** *money you could lend me?*

c **Every** *18-year-old can go to university.*
Any *18-year-old can go to university.*

3 *no, not a, not any*

a Which sentence in each pair sounds more emphatic or more negative?

1 *There's* **no** *food for the crocodiles.*
There isn't **any** *food for the crocodiles.*

2 *He* **hasn't** *got* **any** *friends.*
He's got **no** *friends.*

3 **No** *passport is needed.*
You **don't** *need* **a** *passport.*

b What types of noun can be used with *no*?

4 *few, a few, little, a little*

Which sentence in each pair sounds more positive or optimistic?

a ***A few*** *people are coming to my party.*
Few *people are coming to my party.*

b *We've got* **little** *time left – we'd better hurry.*
We got **a little** *time left – we don't need to hurry.*

Exploitation

1 Complete these sentences with *any*, *some*, or *no*.

a I'll show you a card trick. Take a card, ... card you like, it doesn't matter which one.

b There was a dreadful noise, but in fact there was .... damage to either vehicle.

c The Desert Tarantula can grow to .... seven centimetres long.

d I'll answer .... questions you have at the end of my talk.

e .... qualified doctor would have made a simple error of judgement like that.

f .... people are lucky – they never seem to feel the cold.

2 Complete these sentences in unexpected ways.

1 I know very few people who …
(**Example** … *are more modest than I am.*)

2 Any three-year-old child …

3 Every member of my family …

4 A few students in the class …

5 If you had just a little intelligence, …

6 I've got no money left so …

Speaking: interview

Work in pairs and then in groups of four.

1 Prepare your part in an interview.

Student A You are a well-known media pundit (you have opinions about everything). You have been asked to explain why you think *human beings* have survived for so long despite threats to their existence such as wars, disease, etc. Think of one or two theories and examples.

Student B You are a radio or TV journalist. You are making a programme about the ability of humans to survive in the modern world. Note down some key questions.

2 Do the interview with another pair of students as your 'audience'.

Close up

1.28 What other *amphibious* animals do you know?

1.32 Which of these words rhyme with *tough*?
though / through / thorough / enough / cough

1.40 What is the opposite of *in the wild*?

1.78 A *hatchling* is a young crocodile. What does the verb *hatch* mean? What other creatures *hatch*?

Exploring words

Words and their roots

1 The ending of a word often tells us what class the word is.

a Work with a partner. List the words below under these headings: Adjective, Adverb, Noun, Verb. Some words could belong to more than one class.

> ability   amazement   arisen   astonished   beautiful
> biologist   dangerous   extinction   fearsome   impressive
> inclination   modesty   musical   natural   prehistoric
> researcher   scratching   successfully   survivor   toughness

b Which endings do you associate with each class of word? Do you know other typical endings for this word class?

c The ending of a word can sometimes be misleading. Which word in each set is different?

1 *researcher, smaller, speaker, teacher*
2 *beautiful, grateful, roomful, wonderful*
3 *critic, historic, optimistic, realistic*
4 *capable, regrettable, table, unable*
5 *impressive, negative, outlive, positive*

2 The root of a word is the basic form or part of a word without prefixes and suffixes.

a Add prefixes and/or suffixes to the word roots in this table to make words of other classes. Make as many words as you can, including opposites or negatives.

Noun	Verb	Adjective
a	adapt	
b	agree	
c	amuse	
d art	x	
e base		
f danger		
g	describe	
h	injure	
i	rely	
j	x	true

b Think of nouns which collocate with the adjectives in the list above, for example *a true story / a true identity* but not ~~a true person.~~

3 Complete the article below with appropriate words related to these roots.

> accompany   different   distinct   entertain   fault   perfect
> possible   predict   serious   symmetry

4 Work in pairs or groups.

The article describes why beautiful people are likely to succeed in Hollywood. What kind of qualities would be needed to succeed in the following careers?

a Business
b Social work
c Teaching
d The police force

EVERY SPRING the magazine *Vanity Fair* reports on the young actors it expects to become the future gods and goddesses of Hollywood. It is not always right, but because it was right about Leonardo DiCaprio and Nicole Kidman, the industry takes its thoughts very ....[1].

But when it published its ....[2] for next year there was something very odd about the nine new faces in the ....[3] photo. Six of them are female and three of them are male. Five have dark hair and four are blond.

And there you have it, the sum total of ....[4] features. All nine faces are ....[5] and oval in shape, all nine pairs of eyes large and moist. The lips are full, the bodies are ....[6]. It's almost ....[7] to tell the ....[8] between them. You could even imagine them exchanging roles in a film without anyone noticing. But according to many people in the ....[9] industries, their identical good looks are just not a problem. Nothing sells better than a ....[10] proportioned 17-year-old blank slate.

Language commentary

1 Modal verbs: *should, ought to, must, have to, need to*

These verbs all express different types of obligation.

a *should* – uses

- Suggestions and advice.
  You look really tired – you **should** get more sleep.
- Obligation and duty.
  Society really **should** do more to look after old people.
- Rules and regulations.
  Food **should not** be eaten in classrooms.

b *ought to* – uses

- Advice.
  You **ought to** stop smoking – it's very bad for your health.
- Obligation and duty.
  I **ought to** stop smoking, but it's so difficult.
  We **ought to** report the break-in to the police.

▶ Note *Should* often expresses the personal view of the speaker; *ought to* usually expresses a more external obligation which the speaker cannot influence.

c *must* – uses

Strong advice, obligation, or duty.
You **must** see that film – it's fantastic.
I **must** finish writing this letter tonight.

d *have to* – uses

Obligation, duty, rules, and regulations.
I **have to** attend a meeting every Monday morning at 9.30.
We **have to** pay our fees by next Monday – otherwise we won't be allowed on the course.

▶ Note *Must* and *have to* are sometimes interchangeable but there is a basic difference: *must* expresses the speaker's personal view; *have to* expresses external obligation the speaker can not influence.

▶ Note *mustn't and don't have to* have completely different meanings:
You **mustn't** go out tonight. = This is not permitted.
You **don't have to** go out tonight. = It isn't necessary to go out – it's your choice.

e *need to* – uses

Necessity.
Everyone **needs to** take regular exercise.

f *need to* – forms

There are two negative forms of *need*. They have the same meaning.
You **don't need to** come.   You **needn't** come.

In the past *need* has two forms with different meanings.
I **didn't need to** come.   (I didn't come because it wasn't necessary.)
I **needn't have** come.   (I came despite the fact that it wasn't necessary.)

g Other expressions of obligation

We use *had better* (*not*) + infinitive to give advice or say an action would be a good idea. Unlike *should* and *ought to*, *had better* can only refer to the future.
You'd better check the flight times before you set off.
I'd better not get to work late again this week.

To be (*not*) *supposed to* + infinitive is used to talk about a duty to do something, or a rule or law.
I'm supposed to be at work today, but I'm not feeling well.
You're not supposed to drive more than 90 kph on this road.

To be (*not*) *meant to* + infinitive means to be expected (not) to do something.
You know what the doctor said. **You're meant to stay** in bed.
Haven't you seen the notice? **You're not meant to smoke** here.

2 Determiners

a *some* – meanings

- An indefinite number or quantity of.
  There are **some people** standing in the road.
- A proportion of (not all).
  Some of my friends are a lot older than me.
- Approximately.
  Some 200,000 protestors marched through the city centre.

▶ Note This use of *some* only applies to large / approximate numbers.

b *any* – meanings

- An indefinite number or quantity of.
  There aren't **any** potatoes – I'll have to buy some more.
- It doesn't matter which one / ones.
  I'd be grateful for **any** help you can give me.
  He doesn't eat meat, but he likes **any** vegetables.

c *every*

Every student is expected to pass the exam.

▶ Note *every / any*
Every competitor will win a prize.
(All the runners will get a prize – wherever they finish.)
Any runner could win the race – they're all good athletes.
(All the runners have an equal chance – but only one can come first.)

▶ Note *every / all*
Every child is an individual. (singular)
All children are individuals. (plural)

d *no*

He's got **no** friends.
The postman has just been but there's **no** post for you.
No visa is required.

▶ Note *No* is more emphatic and more formal than negative verb + *any / a*.

e *few / a few, little / a little* – differences in meaning

Few and *little* have a negative meaning, and mean *not many* or *not much*.
He's just moved to London but he knows (very) **few** people there.
We get on well but we've got **little** in common.

A few and *a little* have a positive meaning, and mean *some*.
He's moved to London and he knows **a few** people already.
We've only just met and already we've found that we've got **a little** in common.

7 Senses

7.1 Gut feelings

Lead in

Work in pairs.

1 Complete the table with the answers to these questions.

  a *Hearing* is one of the *five senses*. What are the other four?
  b What parts of the human body are involved in the five senses?
  c What are these parts sensitive to?
  d Which adjectives are related to these senses?

a Senses	b Parts of body	c Sensitive to	d Adjectives
hearing	ears	noises / sounds	audible

2 Some people believe in 'other senses', for example, a sixth sense, gut feelings, intuition, déjà-vu. What do you understand by these?

Can you think of any more 'other senses'?

Listening

1 **7.1** You are going to hear a conversation in which three people are discussing other senses.

  a What other senses do they mention?
  b In general, do they believe in the existence of these other senses or not?

2 Listen again and answer these questions.

  a What does the first speaker mean when he says the five senses are *tangible*?
  b How are *instinct* and *intuition* different from this?
  c Why does one of the speakers mention *cat's fur*?
  d What does the man want the woman to do when he says '*Convince me*'?
  e Why is the woman *biased*?

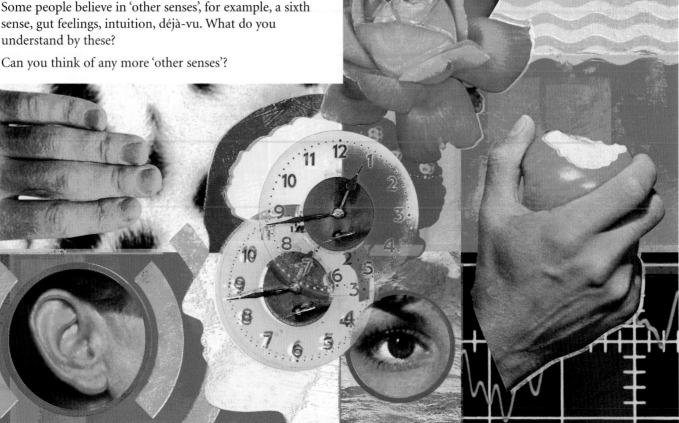

Exploring natural speech

7.2 There are points in the conversation where the speakers do not finish what they were going to say. Read these extracts from the recording, then listen again and decide what the speaker was going to say next at the points marked (**?**).

M1 … whereas if I say 'Do you think this feels like cat's fur or whatever, then there's a point that we can agree on – we can use our tangible senses, but I don't think instinct and intuition is something that's (**?**) – I think some people have more intuition than (**?**) …

M1 Well if I do, I could only take that, I could only accept it as a female point of view, so, yeah, we could debate that all night. I mean, yes, I'm prepared (**?**) Convince me.

Language focus: degrees of agreement

1 a In this extract from the recording, what is the meaning of *Well exactly*? How much do the speakers agree with each other?

    M2 *… when you go into the situation where you think 'I've been here before, I know I've been and I know what's going to happen next.' How can you explain that?*

    M1 *Well exactly* – *it's a vague area. …*

  b Which of these words or phrases have a similar meaning to *Well exactly*?

Absolutely	I don't know	I'm not so sure	Indeed
Nonsense	Of course	Quite	Sure	You're right

  c Rank the nine words and phrases in the list in order from **Strong agreement** to **Strong disagreement**.

  d What other words and phrases of agreement and disagreement do you know?

2 Respond to these statements according to how you feel. Use appropriate words or phrases from the list above.

  a We've all had the feeling of having been somewhere before.

  b The subconscious mind is fascinating.

  c Women are more instinctive than men.

  d Men are more rational than women.

  e People should take notice of their intuition.

Speaking

Work in pairs or small groups.

1 You are going to conduct a survey into how widely various beliefs are held. First, discuss each of these ideas for two or three minutes.

Female intuition — Some people find the idea of women's intuition amusing – in my opinion it explains why women are superior to men.

The significance of dreams — Dreams represent our subconscious thoughts and we should take them much more seriously than we do.

The special relationship between twins — There is an invisible psychological bond between twins which makes them much closer than ordinary brothers and sisters.

Déjà-vu — Everyone's had that feeling of having done something or been somewhere before. Some people think it's proof that we have all had a previous life.

2 Choose two of the ideas and write questions you could ask other students in the class.

Examples
Do you take your dreams seriously?
Do you consider yourself to be superstitious?

3 Conduct the survey. Ask as many other students as you can and make a brief note of their answers.

4 Still in groups, discuss the results of your survey. What conclusions can you draw? Present your findings to the class.

Writing

You are going to write a report summarizing the results of your survey. The report is going to be published in a magazine read mainly by people of your age.

1 Plan the report.
- How many sections will there be? Don't forget an Introduction and Conclusion.
- What would be appropriate headings for the sections?
- What information from your surveys would your readers be most interested in?

2 Think about an appropriate style. Remember, reports are factual. You may want to use numbers, proportions, or statistics to record the results of your survey.

3 Write the report in 160–200 words.

▶ **Writing guidelines p.155**

7.2 Don't stare – it's rude!

Vocabulary

a What have these verbs got in common?

gaze at glance at glare (at)
look at stare (at) watch

b What are the main differences in meaning between *watch* and *look at*? Which verb most commonly goes with the nouns in this list?

a TV programme a football match
a clock a book newspaper headlines
someone's every movement

c How would you feel if you knew someone was *staring* at you?

d What is the difference between *gaze at* and *stare at*? Which of these would you be more likely to *gaze at*?

someone you love the stars the sky
someone you dislike a road accident

e Why might someone *glare at* you if you were driving badly?

f If you didn't have enough time to read a newspaper thoroughly, would you *look*, *glance*, or *stare* at the headlines?

Close up

1.2 What is the purpose of the adjective *so-called* to describe the *staring effect*?

1.25 How could you rephrase *be just as likely to* using the phrase *equal chance*?

1.35 Can you rephrase *so high a success rate*, using *such*?

1.47 What other words or phrases could replace *broadly*?

1.61 A *sceptic* is a person. What is the related adjective?

Reading

1 Read the article below and find the answers to these questions.

   a What is Dr Sheldrake trying to prove in his experiments?
   b Why does Dr Blackmore doubt the results of these experiments?

2 Answer these questions.

   a How might the evidence of fighter pilots be different from the evidence Dr Sheldrake obtained from his experiments?
   b What was the purpose of Dr Sheldrake's second set of experiments?
   c Why were the blindfolded children separated from the others by windows?
   d What is Dr Blackmore implying when she says '*People underestimate the ingenuity of children …*' ?

React and discuss

Have you ever felt that someone was watching you – even though you couldn't see them?

What are you looking at ?

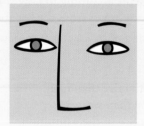

Stories about the existence of the so-called 'staring effect' have circulated for years, with soldiers and surveillance experts claiming
5 that many people somehow know when they are being watched, even through video cameras. Some wartime fighter pilots have even claimed that their lives were saved by being able to
10 sense when they were being tailed by enemy aircraft.

Now Dr Rupert Sheldrake, a controversial biologist, has completed the largest-ever
15 study of the staring effect, involving children in Britain, America and Germany. In the experiments, children sat with blindfolds on, and with their backs to
20 others who either stared at them or looked away. Each time, the blindfolded children simply had to say whether they were being stared at or not.

By guessing alone, the children would
25 be just as likely to be wrong as right. But time and again, they seemed to be able to tell when they were being stared at. In a total of more than 18,000 trials, the children correctly sensed when they were being watched almost 60 per cent of the 30 time. When they were not being watched, the hit-rate fell back to 50 per cent – the level expected if they were guessing.

According to Dr Sheldrake, the odds of getting so high a success 35 rate over so many trials by fluke alone are trillions to one against. 'I've been doing research for many years, and I've never seen 40 any effect as strong as this,' he said. 'Something seems to be going on, because it seems to be repeatable.' These experiments were carried out by 45 different people in different countries, and yet they all found broadly the same results. To counter accusations of fraud, Dr Sheldrake organized a second set of experiments, this time with the added 50 precaution of having the blindfolded children outside and separated by

Language focus: Present perfect

1 Which verb forms were used in the article? Without looking again, choose one of the forms. Then check.

a *Stories about the existence of the 'staring effect'* **circulated / have circulated** *for years …* (l.1)

b *Now Dr Rupert Sheldrake* **completed / has completed** *the largest-ever study of the staring effect …* (l.12)

c *In the experiments, children* **sat / have sat** *with blindfolds on …* (l.17)

d *'I* **never saw / I've never seen** *any effect as strong as this.'* (l.40)

e *To counter accusations of fraud, Dr Sheldrake* **organized / has organized** *a second set of experiments …* (l.48)

2 From **1a–e**, what can you say about when we use the Present perfect? What is the main difference between the Present perfect and the Past simple?

3 Can these time expressions be used with the Present perfect, the Past simple, or both?

yesterday   since 1997   in 1999   for 22 years   when I was 15   recently   just   already   several times   It's the first time …

4 What are the differences in meaning between these sets of sentences?

a *I've done three experiments this morning.*
I've been doing experiments this morning.

b *I've been carrying out experiments like this for many years.*
He's been staring at me for over half an hour.

5 The Present perfect is often used to refer to a past action which has an effect on the present. What could the present effects of these past actions be?

a *I've listened to all the evidence about the staring effect.*

b *I've never worn a blindfold.*

c *I've been training to be a psychiatrist for the past two and a half years.*

Exploitation

Complete these newspaper stories with the correct form of the verbs in brackets – Past simple, Present perfect simple or continuous. You may need to change the word order.

> **1**
> A 25-YEAR-OLD MAN ………¹ (win) this week's lottery jackpot of nearly £13m. Winston Kent from North London ………² (do) the lottery for the first time two weeks ago and cannot believe his luck. 'I know people who ………³ (do) the lottery for years – they ………⁴ (spend) hundreds of pounds and ………⁵ (win) nothing.'
>
> **2**
> ONE OF BRITAIN'S top athletes ………⁶ (drop) out of next month's European Games because of a back injury. Kate Partridge ………⁷ (fall) awkwardly twisting her lower back during a training session last weekend. She ………⁸ (tell) reporters 'This is the first injury I ………⁹ (ever, have). I'm absolutely heart-broken. I ………¹⁰ (look forward) to the European Games since I ………¹¹ (join) the British team two years ago.'
>
> **3**
> WHEN 14-YEAR-OLD Max Greer ………¹² (leave) home on Friday morning, his mother assumed he was going to school, but when a teacher ………¹³ (ring) to ask where Max was, she began to worry. Two days ………¹⁴ (now, pass) since Mrs Greer last ………¹⁵ (see) her son and she is seriously concerned for his safety. 'I ………¹⁶ (telephone) people all weekend – in fact I ………¹⁷ (contact) almost everyone who knows Max. No one ………¹⁸ (see) or ………¹⁹ (hear) anything. He ………²⁰ (just, disappear) into thin air.'

windows from their staring counterparts. 'This eliminated the possibility of sounds being transmitted knowingly or otherwise ₅₅ between the children,' he said. The results, though less impressive, were essentially the same.

Dr Susan Blackmore, a psychologist at the University of the West of England, and ₆₀ a sceptic of paranormal claims, said such experiments were fraught with dangers. One was that people who do the experiments do not send in results unless they are positive. Also cheating could ₆₅ never be ruled out. 'People underestimate the ingenuity of children – what's a blindfold to a savvy kid?'

Dr Sheldrake, however, says that all the issues raised by Dr Blackmore have been ₇₀ fully taken into account. He believes that the results are impressive enough to merit studies of precisely how the staring effect works. His own theory involves some kind of 'electromagnetic morphic field' that ₇₅ surrounds the human body and is disturbed when the person is being stared at, even from behind.

'If you look at somebody, light comes in and you project an image of that person ₈₀ out to coincide with where they are, so in some sense your mind reaches out to touch them,' says Sheldrake.

Robert Matthews, *The Sunday Telegraph*

7.3 Common sense

Lead in

1 How is having *common sense* different from being *well-educated* or *intelligent*?

> A person's natural ability to make good natural judgements and to behave in a practical, sensible way. *Don't worry about the instructions – use your common sense.*

2 Think of common sense solutions to these problems.
- You have a strict monthly budget month but, with two weeks still to go before the end of the month, you have nearly run out of money.
- There are not enough parking spaces at work (or college) for all the people who want to travel by car.

Reading

Work in pairs.

1 Before you read about common sense in business management, discuss these questions which contain key phrases (in *italics*) from the article.

a What is your idea of a *challenging job*?
b What are your personal *goals* as a student or an employee?
c What factors can affect the *morale* of a group of employees?
d What kind of *negotiations* take place in most business organizations?
e How can an employee's *performance* be measured?
f Which groups of people are commonly *reprimanded*? Who *reprimands* them?

2 Read the 10 points taken from a test of common sense in business management.

a As you read, use your common sense to decide whether they are True or False.
b **7.3** Compare answers with a partner, then listen to the recording to check your answers.

React and discuss

1 Do any of the answers or explanations you have heard surprise you? Have you had any experiences which contradict the 'official' answers?

2 Add any of your own common sense ideas for work.

Will your common sense

		T	F
1	If you pay someone for doing something they enjoy, they will come to like this task even more.		
2	Most people prefer challenging jobs with a great deal of freedom and autonomy.		
3	Most people are more concerned with the size of their own salary than with the salary of others.		
4	In bargaining with others it is usually best to start with a moderate offer – near to the one you desire.		
5	In most cases leaders should stick to their decisions once they have made them, even if it appears they are wrong.		

help you as a manager?

		T	F
6	When people work together in groups and know their individual contributions cannot be observed, they tend to put in less effort than when they work on the same task alone.	☐	☐
7	As morale or satisfaction among employees increases in any organization, overall performance almost always improves.	☐	☐
8	Providing employees with specific goals often interferes with their performance: they resist being told what to do.	☐	☐
9	In general, groups make more accurate and less extreme decisions.	☐	☐
10	If you have to reprimand a worker for a misdeed, it is better to do so immediately after the mistake occurs.	☐	☐

Vocabulary

1 Which verbs can go with which nouns?

Verbs	express	give	make	put in	stick to	take

Nouns	a decision	(an) effort	feedback	an idea

2 Complete the sentences, then answer the questions.

a Are you good at .... decisions that affect your personal life?

b What kind of feedback does your teacher .... you on your progress in English?

c How easy do you find it to .... your ideas in public?

d Once you have .... a decision, do you find it difficult to .... it?

Language focus: making generalizations

1 Re-read points **1–10** in the common sense questionnaire and highlight all the language used to generalize.

Example
Most people prefer challenging jobs …

2 Which verb tense is most frequently used for making generalizations?

Exploitation

Work in pairs. Make generalizations about some of the subjects below, using expressions you highlighted in the common sense questionnaire and from this list.

Generalizing expressions
as a rule   broadly speaking   by and large   for the most part
generally speaking   on the whole

a very wealthy people

b politicians

c young parents

d people with mobile phones

e people who live in large cities

f only children

Speaking

Work in groups.

1 Make a list of your own common sense ideas about effective ways of learning English. Use generalizing language where appropriate. Think about these aspects of learning English.

- Learning new words and phrases
- Remembering the spelling of difficult words
- Reading more quickly
- Writing more accurately
- Improving pronunciation
- Getting more speaking practice

2 Share your ideas with the rest of your group, then together, make a list of 'Top 10' common sense tips.

3 Present your tips to the rest of the class.

Exploring words

Colloquial words and expressions

1 Match these colloquial words for everyday objects with the photos. What are the more formal words for these things? Notice how many of the words end in -*y* or -*ie*.

cardy   ciggie   hanky   pickie   sarny   specs   telly   wellies
woolly   zapper

2 A speaker in one of the recordings said: *There's **a heck of a lot** we don't know about the human mind* … This is a very informal expression meaning 'a great deal'. Do the expressions in *italics* in these sentences mean 'a lot' or 'a little'?

a   I buy lottery tickets every week and *a fat lot of* good it does me.

b   I sold my car for a *mingy* £200.

c   *Loads of* people turned up for my party.

d   My brother's got *no end of* ideas for making money.

e   Her uncle left her *oodles of* money in his will.

f   My team has scored *a measly* two goals so far this season.

g   I seem to have *masses of* homework to do this week.

3 a Match the two parts of these conversations.

A	B
1 It's *boiling* in here.	a Have an early night, then.
2 I'm *parched*.	b Hardly surprising – he's been drinking all night.
3 I'm feeling a bit *peckish*.	c Take your coat off, then.
4 It's been a hard day – I'm *shattered*.	d Do you want some of my Coke?
5 I failed the exam and I'm *gutted*.	e We'll be having lunch soon.
6 He can't walk. He's completely *sozzled*.	f Don't worry. You can take it again.

b   **7.4** Listen, check, and practise saying the expressions in **A**.

c   Answer these questions in pairs.

1   What would you choose if you were *parched* or *peckish*?

2   What makes you *shattered*?

3   Have you ever felt *gutted*?

4 a Which of the words in *italics* in these sentences refer to people and which refer to things? Which words could we use to replace them?

1   Where's *what's-his-name*?

2   Pass me that *thingummyjig*, please.

3   There's a blue and red *whatchamacallit* in my case (– can you bring it with you?)

4   There's this *bloke* in our street … (always angry.)

5   I can't find that little *doodah* (we use for keeping the door open.)

6   I saw *thingy* the other day (– I told her I'd give her a ring some time.)

b   Work in pairs. How are the words in *italics* pronounced?

c   **7.5** Listen, check, and practise.

d   Work in groups.

Take turns to describe a person or a thing, using words from **4a**. The rest of the group has to guess who or what is being described.

Language commentary

1 Present perfect

In general the Present perfect links the present with the past in some way.

a Experience

It can refer to our experience of the past up to the present time. The time words in **bold** emphasize this link.

I've **never** flown in a helicopter.

Scientists have **recently / just** discovered a new species of spider.

Have you **ever** been to Australia?

I **still** haven't seen the new James Bond film.

She hasn't phoned me **yet**.

b Explanation

It can provide background information about or explain a current situation. The final clauses in **bold** make this link obvious.

I've spent all weekend preparing for this meeting – **so the meeting is bound to be a success.**

They've worked non-stop for 24 hours – **that's why they look so tired.**

c With time expressions

The Present perfect can be used with certain specific time expressions which relate the present to the past.

We've lived here **for three years**. (and we still live here)

They've worked in London **since 1998 / (ever) since they came back from Zimbabwe**. (and they still work there)

d Continuous

The continuous form of the Present perfect emphasizes the duration of an activity or the fact that it was a repeated activity.

We've been running flat out for nearly two and a half hours now.

I've been practising for the marathon **regularly** – in fact **every week** for the last six months.

This provides a useful contrast with the simple form. Compare these two examples.

I've done three experiments this morning.

I've been doing experiments this morning.

In the first example, the focus is on completion – in this case a quantifiable result. In the second example, the focus is on the continuousness of the activity.

2 Making generalizations

We can make generalizations in two main ways: by using particular expressions, or by choosing particular structures.

a Using generalization expressions

In general / Generally speaking spring is colder than autumn.

By and large / On the whole / Broadly speaking I agree with what you're saying.

As a rule I play tennis at the weekend.

b Using quantity words and expressions

Most people watch several hours of television a day.

Few people I know like football.

A / The majority of my friends hate football.

Everyone likes hamburgers and chips.

Other words like this are *no one / anyone*.

c Choosing appropriate structures

- *Will* can be used to refer to typical actions.

  If I get home from work in good time, **I'll often go** for a 10-km run.

- The Present simple is also used to refer to habitual actions, and frequency adverbs also help us to generalize.

  I **always / usually get** home at 5.30, change, and **go** for a run.

- *Tend to* is used to describe likely or typical behaviour.

  Politicians **tend to** talk too much.

- Plural nouns with no articles refer to those categories in general.

  Children love **animals**.

8 Control

8.1 Family pressures

Lead in

How far do you think parents should push their children to succeed at school, at sport, or in show business? Talk about your own and your friends' experience and any well-known cases you have heard about.

Even before they were born, Richard Williams was determined that his daughters, Venus and Serena, should be tennis champions.

Reading

1 You are going to read an article about Sufiah Yusof, who disappeared from her Oxford college at the age of 15. What can you work out about her story from these words and phrases from the article? Discuss your ideas in pairs.

---

family hothouse   young prodigies   accelerated learning
missing from home   emotional abuse   brainwashing
insular family

---

2 Read the article and check your ideas.

What are the two explanations for Sufiah's disappearance?

Escape from the

FAROOQ YUSOF has five children, all of whom he has taught himself, and all of whom have become mathematics prodigies. His youngest daughter, Zuleika, is preparing, at six, to sit her maths GCSE. Sufiah, 15, who is studying for
5 a masters degree at Oxford University, began her degree at 13. Her brother Iskander passed his 'A' level maths at grade A aged 13; her sister Aisha did the same at 14. The eldest brother, Isaac, 19, is deciding between becoming a professional tennis player and taking up a place at Warwick
10 University.

All this, says Mr Yusof, has been done with the intention of proving that the learning process in children can be nurtured and accelerated.

But in the case of Sufiah, things have gone wrong. Missing
15 from home for a couple of weeks, she has now contacted her parents by e-mail. 'I see you've taken the liberty of running to the national newspapers with the story of how your "naive and innocent daughter" has run off from a "happy home" with some nasty socialists and boyfriends. Has it ever crossed
20 your mind that the reason I left home was because I've finally had enough of 15 years of physical and emotional abuse ...?

'You ruined my brother's life because you wanted him to make lots of money for you winning tennis tournaments. Me, I was lucky. Oxford has been marginally better because I'm
25 away from you most of the time.'

Close up

1.17   How is the adjective *naive* pronounced? What is the noun related to *naive*?

1.19   Can you rephrase *crossed your mind* using the verb *occur*?

1.29, 31   What are the words *brainwashing* and *debriefing* normally associated with?

1.46   What single-word verbs could replace *plump for*?

1.46   Can you think of another way of saying *If you want to hothouse your children ...*?

3 Answer these questions.

   a What did Mr Yusof want to prove by the way he educated his children?

   b Who says these things and what are they talking about?

      1 *… you've taken the liberty of running to the national newspapers …*

      2 *I've finally had enough …*

      3 *Oxford has been marginally better …*

      4 *We have no hope deep inside.*

   c What is the article writer's attitude to Sufiah and her father?

4 Which of these descriptions do you think fit(s) Sufiah?

   a naive and innocent daughter / a brainwashed young woman / a resentful parent-bashing teenager / pretty normal

React and discuss

1 Who is more at fault in the case you have read about – the father for pushing his children, or the university for accepting a child of 13?

2 How do / did you feel about academic success? Is / Was it more or less important to you than having fun with your friends? Do / Did you ever feel under too much pressure?

family hothouse

Her poor parents insist that those cannot be the words of their daughter. Mr Yusof insists that she must be in the hands of some mysterious third party. 'They have got into her mind. "Brainwashing", I think, is the correct term.'

'Even if we get her back, it won't be the same Sufiah. If she is found, she will need debriefing. I have said there will be no charges. But we have no hope, deep inside. From our perspective, this is the end of the story for Sufiah.'

But from other perspectives, it's the beginning of the story for Sufiah. Her e-mail, far from being the work of a brainwashed young woman, reads exactly like the e-mail of a resentful and parent-bashing teenager. Despite her strange life and her accelerated education, Sufiah seems pretty normal.

It seems clear that Sufiah was too young, at 13, to go to university, and her disappearance has sparked calls for further research into the sort of damage accelerated learning can do.

Among the tales of young prodigies, the same themes arise again and again. First, it appears most often to be the father who desires to push his children hard in a particular direction. Second, it appears that tennis, maths and chess are the subjects to plump for if you want to hothouse your children. Third, there appears to be no room for the rest of the world in the lives of the children involved. The Yusof family is an insular one, centred entirely around family life.

Extracted from an article by Deborah Orr,
first published in *The Independent* 7 July 2000

Language focus: reference words (1)

1 When we speak or write, we use certain words and phrases to refer back to something we have already mentioned. What do the *reference* words in **bold** in these extracts from the article refer to?

   a *… her sister Aisha did **the same** at 14.*

   b ***All this**, says Mr Yusof, has been done with the intention of proving …*

   c ***They** in turn have released the e-mail to the press.*

   d *Her poor parents insist that **those** cannot be the words of their daughter.*

2 Complete this extract with appropriate reference words from this list.

all this	him	one	that	The man	them	then	they

Richard Williams was watching women's tennis on television in the 1970s and was struck by the vast prize money. The problem was that his three daughters were already too old for ………[1] to turn ………[2] into tennis stars. Venus arrived in 1980 and Serena in 1982. From ………[3] on, Williams consulted psychologists about how to create a tennis star and coaching videos about how to train ………[4].

However much truth there is in ………[5], one thing is clear. ………[6] wanted to make his daughters into tennis champions even before ………[7] were born, and ………[8] is exactly what he did.

Deborah Orr, *The Independent*

Vocabulary

1 *Take up* has many meanings. Match examples **a–f** with meanings from this list.

accept	adopt	continue	move into	occupy	start

   a Isaac may *take up* a place at Warwick University.

   b I think I'm too old to *take up* squash.

   c They're going to *take up* my idea for improving the car park.

   d I'm not sure what happened next. Perhaps you could *take up* the story now.

   e I'm afraid you'll have to move that piano – it's *taking up* too much space there.

   f Police officers *took up* their positions outside the front and back doors.

2 Discuss these questions.

   a What sports or hobbies would you like to *take up*? (When will you take them up?)

   b Have you ever had any of your ideas *taken up*? (What were the ideas? Who took them up?)

   c What *takes up* a lot of space in your house or apartment?

8.2 Gun control

Lead in

1 Is gun control an important question in your country?

   a Who is allowed to carry guns? The police? Ordinary citizens?

   b Do people need a licence to own a gun? How easy is it to get one?

2 Read the Second Amendment to the Constitution of the USA.

> A well regulated Militia, being necessary to the security of a free State, the right of the people to keep and bear Arms, shall not be infringed.

   a What does this amendment allow American citizens to do?

   b Why do you think some Americans want this amendment to be abolished?

Listening

1 You are going to hear a report on gun control in the USA. Before you listen, guess the answer to these questions.

   a How many gun-related crimes are committed in the USA each year?
     A 250,000   **B** 500,000   **C** 1,000,000

   b How many gun-related murders are committed each year?
     A 9,000   **B** 11,000   **C** 13,000

   c How many guns are there in circulation in the USA?
     A 50 million   **B** 150 million   **C** 250 million

2 **8.1** Listen to the first part of the report and check your guesses.

3 **8.2** Work in pairs. Listen to the complete report.

   a **Student A** Listen and take notes about the National Rifle Association* and New Yorkers against Gun Violence.
     Student B Listen and take notes about the Million Mothers' March and the gun lobby.

   b Tell your partner what you found out about your two groups.

   c Now discuss your personal views on the subject.

     • Should ordinary people be allowed to carry guns?
     • What would be the main effects of banning guns?
     • How practical would it be for the US government to ban guns?

*NRA/National Rifle Association: an organization that lobbies for the right to bear arms.

Exploring natural speech

Notice how, in natural speech, some words run into each other. Often a consonant sound at the end of one word merges with the consonant sound at the beginning of the next word.

1 In this extract from the recording, mark the consonant sounds which merge.

Gun control is a subject which concerns most people in the United States – whether they want to defend their right to own and use weapons – or whether they see them as the curse of modern America. And it's easy to see why it's such an emotive issue when you study the statistics. Each year half a million gun-related crimes are committed in the US – including thirteen thousand murders. And with nearly two hundred and fifty million firearms in circulation it's clearly not an easy task to keep track of who has a gun and why they want to keep it.

2 **8.3** Listen, check, and practise.

Language focus: *what* and *it* clauses

1 These two sentences are similar to sentences in the recording you have just heard. Can you remember how the speaker used *what* to add emphasis? Check on p.143.

  a *They're arguing that the gun manufacturers have not taken care.*

  b *It is certain that the process is being watched closely by campaigners …*

2 The *what* clause focuses attention and prepares the reader or listener for something important. It could be an explanation, a strong opinion, or a new subject.

Add *what* clauses to these sentences.

Example
Gun control concerns most people in the United States.
What *concerns most people in the United States* **is** *gun control.*

  a The gun lobby argues that people have the right to carry guns.

  b Their opponents say that so many guns on the streets lead to serious crime.

3 Sometimes we have to add the auxiliary verb *do*.

  a What I felt like **doing** was walking out. (I felt like walking out.)

  b What I'd love **to do** is go skiing. (I'd love to go skiing.)

4 We can also use an *it* clause (*it* + *be* + information + *who* / *that*) to emphasize particular information.

It was *an illegally-owned gun* **that** *was used in the crime.*

In this sentence *illegally-owned gun* is important. To make this obvious you could add other information:

It was an illegally-owned gun, **not a legally-owned gun**, *that caused the accident.*

5 What is the important information in these sentences? What could you add to make this obvious?

  a It was her father who persuaded her to have her own gun.

  b It's the increase in crimes of violence that worries me.

  c It was the Columbine High School killings that made me realize the destructive power of guns.

  d It was going on the Million Mothers' March that made me change my mind.

Exploitation

1 Complete these sentences.

  a What I like best about summer is …

  b What I dislike most about my job is …

  c What I think the government should do is …

2 Make *what* sentences about these subjects, then compare ideas in pairs.

  a My way of keeping fit *What I do to keep fit is …*

  b My greatest worry

  c The best thing about my family

3 Correct the factual errors in these statements by using *it* clauses. (The correct answers are in brackets.)

  a John Lennon was shot in 1990. (1980)

  b His sister was with him when he was shot. (his wife)

  c A group of three gunmen killed Lennon. (a single gunman)

  d John Chapman shot John Lennon. (Mark Chapman)

Speaking

1 In groups, discuss what can be done to reduce violent crime and especially the use of guns either in your country or in the United States. Include these aspects of the subject.

- The extent of the problem
- The causes of violence
- The role of the police, the legal system, and the government
- The role of parents, schools, and the general public
- The role of the media

Draw up a five-point action plan.

2 Present your plan to the rest of the class.

8.3 Waste control!

Lead in

1 Think about the rubbish your family regularly has to get rid of. Answer these questions.

- What does your household rubbish consist of?
- Do you sort the rubbish into different types?
- Do you put it into plastic bags? (How many a week?)
- Who takes your rubbish away?
- Where does it go? What happens to it there?

2 Compare answers. How many families use plastic bags?

3 **8.4** You are going to hear two British people talking about this subject. How do they answer the questions?

Reading

1 Before you read the article, use the words below to find the correct answers to questions a–e.

| biodegrade | disposable | fossil fuel |
| landfill site | recycle | |

a What is the name for the place where rubbish is taken and then buried?

b What is another word for *decompose*?

c Which verb means *to use something again instead of throwing it away*?

d What are coal and oil two types of?

e Which adjective means *intended to be thrown away after use, instead of being used several times*?

2 Read the article. What damage can plastic waste do to

a the sea and coastal areas?

b wild animals?

Ecological Nightmare

A Plastic is a fraud. It cheats the laws of nature. It is born, but does not ever really die. Plastic is designed to be impervious to natural decay, which is 5 why it's so useful for wrapping sweaty sandwiches in. Because it doesn't erode, this makes it an ecological nightmare. Twelve billion plastic bags are handed out to shoppers in Britain 10 every year.

B Most plastic ends up in a landfill site. It will never biodegrade, but thanks to the biological conditions which exist in landfills, neither will 15 organic waste such as onion skins and nail clippings or hamburgers, which can remain intact for decades, 27m tonnes of it accumulating year by year. If someone in the future excavates 20 these sites, they almost certainly will be living on a planet empty of blue whales, elephants and tigers. What they will have, however, are billions and billions of bags with the word *Asda* 25 or *Miss Selfridge* stamped on the side.

C Government targets may mean that plastic bags in the future will be recycled, but this will be tricky. One problem is that a variety of plastics 30 exist which cannot be recycled together. Contamination or mixing of plastics may render the material unusable, and even when successful, plastics can only be recycled a few times. Of the 15 million plastic bottles 35 used in the UK every day, less than 3% get recycled.

D The seabed is becoming increasingly 'plasticized'. Half a kilometre down, plastic bags 40 float on the bottom of the Mediterranean in densities of up to 80 items per hectare; and 550 plastic bottles per kilometre were recovered in a recent survey of Bristol Channel 45 coast. In Indonesia, plastic bags have been reported clogging up the pumps at water refineries. Turtles in the Bay of Biscay commonly die of ingestion of plastic bags. Seabirds too, have plastic 50 fragments in their stomachs, and plastic molecules in their muscles.

E The irony of plastic waste as a serious environmental problem is that, unlike fossil fuel 55 consumption or rainforest destruction, it is easily solvable. Plastic is an immensely useful material. We use it, however, as though it has no downside at all. We must reduce our use of 60 plastic. As shoppers we should use non-disposable bags to carry shopping, or simply refuse a bag when we buy something. We have a national obsession with wrapping everything in 65 plastic; it is unnecessary and, environmentally, deadly.

Sasha Norris, *The Guardian*

3 Which paragraph, A–E

a describes some of the effects waste plastic has on the natural world?

b suggests a change in people's behaviour as the solution to the problem?

c establishes the difference between plastic and other forms of waste?

d describes why recycling plastic is not a simple process?

e describes problems related to burying plastic and other types of rubbish?

React and discuss

Will what you have read in this article change your shopping habits? Why? / Why not? What would change your behaviour – the cost of plastic bags? New laws?

Language focus: the future

1 What are the different forms of the *will* future used in the article? Look at these examples.

a *Most plastic ends up in a landfill site. It **will never biodegrade** …*

b *If someone in the future excavates these sites, they almost certainly **will be living** on a planet empty of blue whales.*

c *Government targets may mean that plastic bags in the future **will be recycled**.*

2 The *will* future has three main uses. Which uses do the extracts above illustrate?
- to make predictions or describe expectations
- to make promises or threats
- to refer to future facts or certainties.

3 *Going to* can be used to make predictions. What is the main difference in meaning between these two sentences?

a *That seabird is **going to die** – it has just eaten part of a plastic bag.*

b *I expect more seabirds **will die** as a result of waste polluting the sea.*

4 What is the difference in meaning between these sentences?

a *By the year 2020 **we will have stopped** using plastic bags.*

b *In the year 2020 **we will stop** using plastic bags.*

5 Match the examples of the future **a–e** below with one of these uses.
- a future trend   • a scheduled event   • an arrangement
- an intention   • an offer

a ***I'm going to use** paper bags. I'm determined to stop using plastic bags.*

b ***I'll go** to the supermarket this week if you like.*

c ***I'm meeting** the environment officer at 10.30 next Thursday morning. Come if you like.*

d *In a hundred years' time people **will be retiring** earlier.*

e *You'd better hurry – the supermarket **closes** in ten minutes.*

Exploitation

1 Only one of these examples uses the correct form of the future. Which one? Correct the others.

a I've just booked a last-minute holiday in Greece. Our flight will leave at midnight. I'm sending you a postcard – I promise.

b I give up smoking by the end of the year. I'm absolutely determined this time.

c In the future we'll all be eating more vegetables and less meat.

d My sister will be having a baby. I can't wait to be an uncle.

e Let's go to the cinema this evening. I pay.

f I'll have lunch with my father today – we've arranged to meet in town.

2 Work in groups of three. Each choose one of these attitudes.

A Optimist   B Pessimist   C Realist

Discuss one of these subjects.
- Your country in the year 2020
- World problems in the next 100 years

Writing

Write a short magazine article on the subject you have been discussing. Present your personal point of view. You want to keep people's attention, and not put them off by being too serious. What do you think is a suitable tone? Write your article in **160–200 words**.

▶ Writing guidelines p.154

Close up

1.32 Which common verb could be used instead of *render*?

1.49 What is the difference in meaning between *ingestion* and *digestion*?

1.59 Does *downside* have a positive or a negative meaning?

1.63 What kind of word is *refuse* here? How is it pronounced? What other meaning and pronunciation can it have?

Exploring words

Countable and uncountable nouns

Many nouns have different meanings depending on whether they are countable or uncountable. It is important to be able to distinguish between these meanings.

1 Work in pairs.

a Read the article about noise control. How many nouns can you find that can be countable or uncountable?

b What is the difference in meaning between the countable and uncountable versions of the nouns you have found? Choose three nouns and make sentences to illustrate the different meanings.

c Exchange sentences with another pair. Have you and your partner made up similar examples?

Noise Control

PIPEDOWN is an organization which fights one of the irritations of modern life: piped music, also called muzak or lift music. Piped music is made possible by sophisticated systems which supply sound to all
5 parts of buildings.

It is the misuse of muzak in public areas which Pipedown is against. The organization helps the millions of people who hate this form of noise pollution but can't do anything about it.
10 The problem is that many people dislike silence – in shops, restaurants, railway stations or other public places. Cows are supposed to produce more milk if piped music
15 is played to them.

The same idea is used to encourage people to spend money. Piped music also spoils conversation as
20 well as real music.

2 Underline all the nouns in sentences a–e below, then list them under these headings.

• always countable	*bus*
• always uncountable	*information*
• can be countable or uncountable	*hair*
• singular words ending in -s	*species*
• plural words which do not end in -s	*children*

a Crime in general and crimes of violence in particular are increasing.

b There must be a better means of controlling traffic here. In other places they have banned cars altogether.

c Our rubbish is mostly food, paper, and packaging. We recycle newspapers, card, and bottles, but there are no facilities for recycling metal or plastic.

d Many people think there ought to be control over the information on the Internet.

e She said she left her parents because she'd had enough emotional abuse.

f Piped music is a form of noise pollution.

3 Work in groups.

Choose two or three of these subjects and talk about them for about two minutes each.

• Violent crime
• The pros and cons of private cars
• The best way of disposing of rubbish
• The Internet as a source of useful information
• Ideal parents
• Music in public places

Language commentary

1 *What* and *it* clauses

Starting sentences with *what* or *it* clauses allows us to put special emphasis on particular information. We focus a listener's or reader's attention by preparing them for what we are going to say next.

a *what* + verb *be*

What I like best when I'm really hungry is freshly-cooked doughnuts. (When I'm really hungry, I like freshly-cooked doughnuts best.)

What you must remember is that you haven't been doing this job very long. (You must remember that you haven't been doing this job very long.)

What they needed was a good long rest. (They needed a good long rest.)

- Sometimes we need to add an auxiliary verb.
  What the school is doing is raising money for a new swimming pool. (The school is raising money for a new swimming pool.)

- We can also repeat the subject of the sentence.
  What I did was I phoned him and explained everything. (I phoned him and explained everything.)
  What you should do is you should tell him to mind his own business. (You should tell him to mind his own business.)

b Similar constructions

All (I) did was …	One thing (that) …
Something (that) …	The (only) thing that …

All I did was ask him for a lift. (I asked him for a lift – that was all.)

The (only) thing that surprised me was the height of the tower. (The height of the tower surprised me.)

One thing I forgot to do was to renew my passport. (I forgot to renew my passport.)

Something I've never done is drive(n) to work – I've always walked or cycled. (I've never driven to work – I've always walked or cycled.)

c *It* + *be* + information + relative clause

- These examples emphasize the subject of the verb.
  It was my brother who told him to phone you. (My brother told him to phone you.)
  It's my arm that's broken, not my leg. (My arm's broken, not my leg.)

- In these examples the object of the verb is emphasized.
  It was my sister (that) you saw, not me. (You saw my sister not me.)
  It's a Volvo (that) he wants, not a Saab. (He wants a Volvo, not a Saab.)

- The *it* clause can be used to focus on other information.
  It won't be until this afternoon that we find out the result. (We won't find out the result until this afternoon.)
  It was on the TV news that I first heard about the earthquake.
  (I first heard about the earthquake on the TV news.)

2 The future

a *will* – uses

- Predictions.
  Scientists are predicting that an asteroid **will hit** the Earth in the year 2050. Hundreds of people **will be killed**.

- Expectations.
  We'll arrive about 7.30 in the evening. **We'll see** you there.

- Future facts and certainties.
  High tide this evening **will be** at 7.46.   **I'll be** 32 next week.

- Promises, offers, warnings, and threats.
  If I damage your car, **I'll pay** for the repairs.
  If you park there, **they'll take** your car away.

- Decisions at the moment of speaking.
  Stop rushing around – **I'll pick** the children up from school.

b Present tenses – uses

- Scheduled events: Present simple.
  We haven't got much time – our plane **leaves** in half an hour.

- Arrangements: Present continuous.
  I can't see you on Thursday – **I'm having** dinner with my boss.

c *going to* – uses

- Plans, intentions, resolutions.
  The government **is going to give** more money to pensioners.
  If we make a profit this year, **we're going to invest** more money in the business.
  I'm going to get fit by eating less and taking regular exercise.

- Predictions based on present evidence.
  Can you hold my cup for me? **I'm going to sneeze.**
  It's going to snow this evening – it's turned very cold.

d Future continuous – uses

- Future trends.
  In the future more people **will be working** from home.

- An action that is expected to be happening at a point in time.
  In half an hour, **we'll be watching** the film.

- An action that is expected to fill a period of time.
  I'll be revising for my final exams all weekend.

- An action that is the result of a routine or an arrangement.
  I'll be finishing work at about 5.30 – I'll see you then.

- Asking polite or tentative questions.
  Will you be using the phone again this evening?

▶ Note Sometimes *will be* + *-ing* is used to refer to 'predictable' present activities:
Don't phone him now – **he'll be having** his evening meal.
This is like the use of *will* for predictable or typical behaviour.

e Future perfect simple and continuous – uses

Looking back from the future at actions that will be completed.
By this time next year I hope **I'll have found** a new job.
On November 17th **we'll have been living** here for five years.

▶ Note This form can also be used to speculate about actions which are complete at the time of speaking.
There is no point contacting him now; **he'll have left** for work.

9 Music matters

9.1 My music

Lead in

9.1 You are going to hear snippets of different styles of music. How many can you identify? Match the snippets with the appropriate words from this list.

Ballroom dance   Celtic   Choral   Classical   Country   Disco
Folk   Heavy Metal   Latin   Modern jazz   Opera   Pop
Reggae   Rock 'n roll   Soul   Traditional jazz   World music

Listening

9.2 You are going to hear four people talking about their musical preferences. As you listen, answer these questions. (There may be more than one answer to each question.)

1 Which speakers like these types of music?
   • classical   • pop   • jazz   • dance   • film

2 Who likes these people's music?
   • Mozart   • Ella Fitzgerald   • Michael Jackson   • Bach

3 Who likes music that makes them feel calm and relaxed?

4 Who likes singing in the car?

Exploring natural speech

9.3 The second speaker uses four adjectives to describe his musical tastes.

I've always loved Michael Jackson music and sort of really .... **1** stuff – everything that's in the charts. I know that it's .... **2** but it's erm, I don't know, fun to dance to and it's .... **3** – you hear it once and I don't know next time you hear it, you sort of know, know the lyrics and you want to sing along. And when you go to night clubs or wherever, it's fun to dance to. Erm, but more serious stuff, I, I really like Ella Fitzgerald and .... **4** stuff but yeah, that's about it.

1 What have the adjectives got in common? Listen and complete the extract.

2 How are the four adjectives formed? Think about the kinds of words they are related to.

3 Which adjective(s) mean(s)
   a similar to something?
   b pleasant and easy to remember?
   c unoriginal, mediocre, banal, common?

4 Rephrase these sentences using adjectives ending in -y.
   a This meat tastes as if it is made of rubber.
   b I hate chewing gum that tastes like fruit.
   c He's worked as a builder all his life – that's why his hands are like leather.
   d I don't like that camera. It looks as if it's made of plastic.

React and discuss

1 What is your favourite kind of music? How does it make you feel?

2 Do you play or have you ever played music yourself?

Language focus: adverbs of degree

1 Adverbs of degree are used to modify adjectives, verbs, or other adverbs.

Underline the adverbs of degree in these sentences (**a–f** are from the recording).

a … *I am quite an intense person.*
b *I really like Ella Fitzgerald.*
c *I have quite specific music tastes.*
d *I particularly like the way someone like Stanley Kubrick uses it …*
e *I think that that's very clever and very moving …*
f *… I sing in the car a lot which is quite embarrassing at traffic lights because it's quite obvious that I'm singing very loudly.*
g *I'd say I've got fairly wide tastes in music.*
h *I have to admit I find opera singers slightly annoying.*
i *I rather like classical music but most of my friends absolutely hate it.*

2 What two meanings can *quite* have? Sentence **1f** shows both meanings.

3 Adverbs of degree are used in different positions in sentences. Which adverbs from **1a–i** can be used

a before an adjective? *I'm .... tired.*
b before an adverb? *She's driving .... fast.*
c before a main verb? *They .... enjoy parties.*
d before an indefinite article + adjective + noun? *He's .... a lazy person.*
e after an indefinite article and before an adjective + noun? *He's a .... clever person.*

4 Group the adverbs from **1a–i** according to meaning. Use the four headings below. When you have included all the adverbs, add any more you know to the table.

Full degree	High degree	Medium degree	Small degree
particularly	really	fairly	slightly

Exploitation

Compare yourself with a partner.

1 What kind of person are you? Include adverbs of degree in your answers.

*How **intense** are you? / How **sociable** are you? / How **intellectual** are you?*
*How **talkative** are you? / How **brave** are you? / How **self-confident** are you?*
*How **creative** are you? / How **optimistic** are you? / How **generous** are you?*
*How **stubborn** are you? / How **impulsive** are you? / How **reliable** are you?*
*How **persuasive** are you? / How **moody** are you? / How **patriotic** are you?*
*How **inquisitive** are you? / How **practical** are you? / How **organized** are you?*

2 How much do you enjoy these occasions and activities?

Work   Holidays   Weekends   Parties   Watching sports   Sport / Shopping
Spending time with friends   Spending time with your family

Speaking

1 **9.4** You are going to hear three people having a conversation about music.

a What are they discussing? Why?
b Do you agree with any of their suggestions?

2 Work in groups of three or four.

You are going on holiday together, travelling by car. Like the people in the recording, you decide to take some music with you for the journey.

a Think of three albums you personally would like to take.
b Tell the rest of your group about your choices. Give your reasons.
c Agree as a group on which six albums to take. Everyone needs to feel their choices have been taken into account, but you also need to have a variety of different kinds of music.

9.2 The player and the listener

Vocabulary

You are going to read an extract from *The Piano*, the novel based on the award-winning film. Here are some of the words and phrases used in the extract.

absorbed	discerning	engrossed	harmony	insatiable
longing	melody	rhythm		

a Decide whether they are used to refer to music or people.
b Which two adjectives from the list mean *very interested* and could complete this sentence? *It's no use trying to talk to him. He's completely .... in his work.*
c Which adjective can describe *appetite / desire / need / curiosity*?
d Which adjective describes a person who has good taste in food, music, wine, clothes, etc.?
e Which three nouns mean the same as *beat*, *tune*, and *combination of different notes*?
f Which noun means *great desire*?

Reading

1 Read Part 1 of the extract from the novel.
   a Why did Ada visit George Baines?
   b How did her daughter occupy her time while Ada was with George?
   c What was her main reason for visiting him now?

2 Read Part 2.
   a How did Ada's playing compare with the kinds of music George had heard before?
   b What effect did her playing have on Baines?

3 Read Part 3.
   a How did Ada feel about George Baines' reaction to her playing?
   b Why do you think Baines closed his eyes?
   c Why do you think Ada glanced *warily* at him?

The Piano

Part 1 Flora and Ada made the walk to George Baines' hut for the next piano lesson through the endless rain.
5 Baines kept a friendly mongrel dog whom he called Flynn, and Flora's pleasure was to torment Flynn with a stick. The dog complied with her games passively, taking refuge
10 under the hut when her enthusiasm grew too great, whereupon Flora tried to force him out into the driving rain by pushing her weapon through a hole in the veranda floor, her excited leaping and shouting keeping tempo with her mother's rhythmic melodies.
15   Inside, George Baines paced the floor of his hut while Ada McGrath played in her insatiable manner, the music at once lyrical and insistent. She had dropped all efforts to teach Baines, and now played for her own pleasure, stealing time for herself from beneath
20 his gaze.

Part 2 Baines had heard singers and players in the drinking houses of many ports; he had sung sailors' tunes himself at sea; he had stamped his feet and
25 danced with women who lifted their skirts and whirled gaily. It was nothing like this. His listening was not refined, nor discerning, and yet Ada McGrath's playing made him hear,
30 made his mind open and fill with emotion. He felt he could listen to her play forever. He observed that she played a steady rhythm with her left hand, and a counter rhythm with her right. One piece seemed to flow into the next
35 without cessation. These were not parlor songs, or jigs, or popular tunes; they were harmonies from somewhere else. Baines was drawn to Ada, to her self-contained silence at the keys. It was as though the music brought this silence strangely alive.
40   Baines kept his head bowed, but as the playing became more confident and she became more absorbed, he raised his eyes to watch. He sat at a far corner of the room, enjoying the whole vision of this woman at her piano.

Part 3 Presently Baines took his chair to a closer position and opposite angle. Ada glanced up as she felt him passing behind her. She thought it odd that he always seemed satisfied to listen, not wanting to play was beyond her imagining. She became engrossed in the music once again while his attention focused on her as she bent farther from or closer to the keys.

45

50

55

Again Baines shifted his chair, carrying it round the back and to the other side of the piano. Ada watched him as he moved, conscious of his scrutiny, the shifting heat of his presence. From this position Baines could see more clearly and thus enjoy her fingers moving fluidly on the keys and the small details of emotion on her face. Her hands were so very supple, her fingers tapered, strong but delicate and fine. Twice he closed his eyes and breathed deeply, suffused with longing. When his eyes were closed, Ada glanced at him warily.

60

65

Jane Campion and Kate Pullinger,
The Piano

Close up

1.12 A *weapon* is a general word for something used for fighting. What was Flora's *weapon*?

1.29 What is the meaning of *nor*? How could you rephrase *not refined, nor discerning*?

1.38 What kind of *keys* are being referred to? What other meanings does *key* have?

1.40 *bowed* is from the verb *bow* meaning to lower your head. What other meanings does *bow* have? How can it be pronounced?

1.55 *Farther* is one of the comparative forms of *far*. What is the other?

1.61 *Thus* is a rather literary word. What alternatives could be used in spoken language?

Language focus: formal and informal style

1 The extract from *The Piano* is written in a formal literary style. Match examples **a–e** from the text with the appropriate features of formal style.

Examples		Feature of formal style	
a	Sentence 3, paragraph 1	1	precise rather than everyday vocabulary
b	her games **passively, taking refuge** under the hut – l.9	2	long sentences with several clauses
c	*whom* – l.6	3	uncontracted verb forms
d	*paced* instead of *walked around* – l.15	4	use of participle clauses to link ideas
e	*he had* sung sailors' tunes himself – l.23	5	formal rather than conversational grammar

2 Find more examples of these formal features in the extract.

Exploitation

1 Rewrite this extract, making it sound less formal and more conversational. Pay particular attention to the words and phrases in **bold**. Think about sentence length.

> Baines kept a friendly mongrel dog **whom** he called Flynn, and **Flora's pleasure was to torment** Flynn with a stick. The dog **complied** with her games passively, **taking refuge** under the hut when her **enthusiasm grew too great, whereupon** Flora tried to force him out into the **driving** rain by pushing her **weapon** through a hole in the veranda floor, her excited **leaping** and shouting **keeping tempo** with her mother's **rhythmic melodies**.

2 Work in pairs.

  a **Student A** Turn to p.158 and complete writing tasks 1 and 2.

    Student B Turn to p.159 and complete writing tasks 1 and 2.

  b Now exchange your writing with your partner. Compare what your partner has written with the original version of the story.

  c Discuss the differences between the versions.

9.3 The good and the bad

Lead in

1 Add words to these lists.

- Music people   *band …*
- Instruments   *drum …*
- Musical features   *tune …*
- Types of music   *progressive rock …*
- Types of recording   *album …*

2 **9.5** You are going to hear three people talking about music.

   a What kind of music is each person talking about?
   b What specific aspects of the music do they mention or describe?

3 Listen again and answer these questions.

   a How do we know that the first speaker really enjoyed the CD she describes?
   b Why was the second speaker surprised that he enjoyed the music so much?
   c Why do you think the third speaker was not surprised by how much she enjoyed the concert she describes?

Reading

1 Discuss these questions.

   a What makes you decide to buy a particular CD or listen to a particular piece of music on TV, radio, or live?
   b Would a good review ever persuade you to buy a CD or go to a concert? Would a bad review put you off?
   c Would a friend's opinion have more or less effect on you than a published review?

2 Read one of the reviews and answer the questions below.

   Student A Read the review of Genesis at Earls Court.

   Student B Read the review of the CD by El Hadj N'Diaye.

   a What does the reviewer like and dislike?
   b How many stars would the reviewer have given? Use this rating system.

***** Unmissable   **** Recommended   *** Enjoyable
** Mediocre   * Terrible

3 Work in pairs.

   a Tell your partner about the review you have read. Say what the reviewer particularly liked and/or disliked.
   b From what you have read, and from your own musical tastes, would you go to the concert or buy the CD?

   4 Add any words from the reviews to the list in **Lead in 1**.

Genesis at Earls Court

THERE AREN'T MANY BANDS of whom it can be said that the drum solo is the best part of the show, but then there's only one Genesis. I'd trailed down to Earls Court wondering if I'd missed something for all these years, and that Genesis had maintained their extraordinary popularity by secretly becoming thrilling and provocative.

Of course they hadn't, but first let me say how impressive the production was, with its strange lighting pods climbing diagonally across the stage, the array of huge screens displaying chunks of animation, computer graphics, film and live video.

What a shame all this technology couldn't make the music even slightly interesting. Although pieces like *No Son Of Mine* at least have a tune, a trip down Genesis's memory lane is like being locked in a musical-aversion chamber, where synthesizers plonk aimlessly, and guitars huff and bluster till they're blue in the face.

Adam Sweeting, *The Guardian*

El Hadj N'Diaye

Voice guitar

Thiaroye

Siggi Musique (48 minutes)

While Senegal's El Hadj N'Diaye has created quite a stir in France and Belgium over the last two years, he has so far remained little known elsewhere. *Thiaroye* is bound to change all that. This album is suffused with deep emotional intensity captured in 12 arrangements of masterful simplicity. The focus of the music is N'Diaye's stirring voice. Besides being a remarkable musician, he is also an outstanding lyricist whose songs, dedicated to various social groups, have gained him the title 'voice of the voiceless'.

The album also contains some of the most convincing love songs ever written.

The heartbreaking *Say Get* really makes you feel the pain of separation, whilst *Weet* describes loneliness with light melodies and intriguing allegories. The gripping blend of haunting melodies, floating guitars and inspired lyrics makes *Thiaroye* an utterly compelling album.

Katharina Lobeck, *Songlines*

Writing

1 You are going to write a review of a musical experience you have had.

   a Decide what you are going to review. It could be a concert you have been to, a TV show you have seen, or a CD. Choose something you have strong opinions about. Decide whether to write a good or a bad review.

   b Tell a partner about the concert, show, or CD you are going to review. Ask each other questions. Does your partner have an opinion about 'your' music?

2 Prepare to write your review by making a brief paragraph plan, for example:

   • a brief description of what you are going to review – concert / CD
   • what you liked and / or disliked
   • a final comment or recommendation to readers.

   Include a rating based on the star system in Reading 2b.

3 Write your review in 120–160 words.

▶ Writing guidelines p.156

Exploring words

Collocation (2)

1 The adjectives in this list can be used to describe *music*.

a What else can they describe? Choose appropriate nouns from the list.

Adjectives	calming catchy cheerful depressing lively loud moving
	relaxing romantic

Nouns	book comments film holiday influence meeting person
	shower slogan smile story swim title tune

b Complete these sentences by choosing the best adjective–noun collocation.

1 I've been to a *relaxing / depressing* meeting at work. The management announced that the company was losing money and would be making half the employees redundant.

2 This week's Number One song has a really *loud / catchy* tune – I can't stop humming it.

3 *The Diary of Anne Frank* is the *cheerful / moving* story of a young girl in the Second World War.

4 After a long tiring day at work, there's nothing I like better than a *relaxing / cheerful* shower.

5 I lose my temper very quickly. My sister's the opposite. She has a very *romantic / calming* influence on me.

c Work in pairs. Talk about the differences between the following pairs. Think of examples to illustrate the differences.

1 a *depressing* film / a *moving* film

2 a *cheerful* person / a *lively* person

3 a *romantic* holiday / a *relaxing* holiday

2 What is the difference in meaning between these pairs of words? Complete the sentences with the appropriate words.

a *classic / classical*

1 I also quite like erm .... music when it's adapted in films …

2 … it's nice music to drive to, and they're just they're .... pieces, they're sort of .... melodies.

b *economic / economical*

1 I used to agree with the government's .... policies, but I'm not so sure now.

2 We'll have to be more .... with petrol if we can – it's getting really expensive now.

c *historic / historical*

1 I love .... novels – anything set in the past.

2 Everybody agreed – the day the two leaders met was a(n) .... occasion.

d *comic / comical*

1 You look really .... in those flared jeans.

2 He's one of the best .... actors around at the moment.

3 Complete this film review by choosing one of the two adjectives in each case.

That was a really *haunting / gripping* [1] film, I was on the edge of my seat from beginning to end. The storyline was absolutely *intriguing / poignant* [2] – you
5 were never sure what was going to happen next and the ending itself was particularly *moving / thrilling* [3] – I was certain he was going to get killed. And then when he eventually told her he
10 loved her – that was an especially *intriguing / poignant* [4] moment.

The way the music came in was *gripping / remarkable* [5]. That *haunting / remarkable* [6] melody has been going
15 through my head since we came out of the cinema. I thought the cast was pretty *impressive / thrilling* [7] – too; Xavier Vitier has always been one of my favourite actors.

4 Work in groups. Take turns to talk about one of these subjects.

- An intriguing storyline in a film, book, or TV programme
- A poignant moment in a film, book, or TV programme
- A TV programme or film with an impressive cast
- A TV programme, book, or film with a thrilling ending

Language commentary

1 Adverbs of degree

a Uses

- Most adverbs of degree can be used with adjectives, adverbs, quantifiers, and verbs.
  I'm feeling **extremely tired**.
  He's speaking **really quickly**.
  You've given me **rather a lot of** food.
  I **rather like** driving on motorways.

- *Rather*, *really*, *absolutely*, and *hardly* can be used in front position.

- Adverbs of degree can be grouped according to their strength of meaning.

b Full degree *absolutely, completely, entirely, totally, quite*

(These are only used with ungradable or extreme adjectives and adverbs.)
I'm **completely convinced** this is the best thing to do.
After the game the whole team were **totally exhausted**.
They've redecorated their flat **absolutely perfectly**.

c High degree *awfully, extremely, really, terribly, very*

I'm **extremely happy** with the result of the election.
Unfortunately I read **very slowly**.

- *Very much*, not *very*, is used with verbs.
  I **very much hoped** you'd be able to come on holiday with us.

d Medium degree *fairly, pretty, quite, rather*

I'm **pretty sure** we've met before.
We're all working **fairly hard** at the moment.

e Small degree *a bit, a little, slightly*

I feel **slightly / a little embarrassed**.   Could you drive **a bit faster**?

f Negative *hardly, scarcely*

She **scarcely knows** what she's saying.   I'm **hardly awake**.

g *quite* – meanings

- *Quite* has two meanings:
  I'm **quite good** at swimming, but I'd like to be better. (= fairly)
  I tried to start my car this morning but it was **quite impossible**. (= completely)

- *Quite* is used before the indefinite article.
  He's **quite a good** swimmer.

h *rather* – meanings

- In a negative or unfavourable comment, *rather* means the same as *quite*.
  I thought it was **rather a disappointing** film.

- In a positive comment, *rather* means *surprisingly*.
  I thought that programme was **rather interesting**.

- *Rather* can be used before or after the indefinite article.
  That was **rather an interesting** programme. / That was **a rather interesting** programme.

i *too* – meanings

Too and *very* have different meanings.
Even though I'm feeling **very ill**, I'm going to work.
I'm **too ill** to go to work. (*too* = so ill that something is impossible)

2 Formal and informal style: general guidelines

Different situations require different degrees of formality, from the most formal written language of a legal letter to the most colloquial everyday conversation you might hear in a bar. There are no strict rules in this area but the guidelines below point out a few generalizations.

Formal	Informal
Uncontracted verb forms **He is** coming – **I am** sure.	Contracted verb forms **He's** coming – **I'm** sure.
Complex sentences The dog complied with her games passively, **taking refuge** under the hut when her enthusiasm grew **too great, whereupon** Flora tried to force him out into **the rain by pushing** her weapon through a hole in the floor.	Shorter sentences The dog put up **with her games. He took** refuge under the hut when she got **too enthusiastic. But then** Flora tried to force him out into **the rain. She pushed** her weapon through a hole in the floor.
Formal structures Was this the man **to whom** you had already spoken? **There are** many things left to do. **Fewer people** read the classics now.	Conversational grammar Was this the man you'd already spoken **to**? **There's** lots of things left to do. **Less people** read the classics now.
Precise vocabulary Baines **paced** the floor of his hut. I have just **received** your letter. I tried to **telephone** you this morning.	Non-specific vocabulary Baines **walked up and down** his hut. I've just **got** your letter. I tried to **call** you this morning.
Single-word verbs He was the first to **raise** his hand when the teacher asked a question. I shall be **returning** to that subject later.	Phrasal verbs He was the first to **put up** his hand when the teacher asked a question. I'll be **coming back** to that subject later.
The Passive **He was prevented** from seeing his children. **I was laughed at** wherever I went.	The Active **They prevented / stopped him** from seeing his children. **People laughed at me** everywhere I went.

10 From place to place

10.1 Travel

Lead in

1 Which of these types of place have you visited in the last few years?

- another continent
- a foreign country
- a capital city
- a tourist area in your country
- a remote area
- an island
- a seaside resort
- a famous building or landmark
- a place associated with someone famous

2 Talk to other students. Find someone who has been to some of the same places as you. Find out why they went. For example, was it for a holiday or on business?

Listening

1 You are going to hear a short documentary report about the increasing popularity of adventure holidays. Before you listen, discuss these questions.

a What types of adventure holiday can you think of?
b What ages and types of people enjoy the kind of holidays you have been talking about?
c Why do you think adventure holidays are becoming more popular?
d Why are beach holidays becoming less popular?

2 **10.1** Listen and check the answers speakers give to questions b–d. What types of adventure holiday are mentioned?

React and discuss

1 If you could choose, what sort of adventure holiday would you go on? Would you want there to be an element of danger or challenge?

2 When you visit somewhere new, do you prefer to go as a traveller or a tourist?

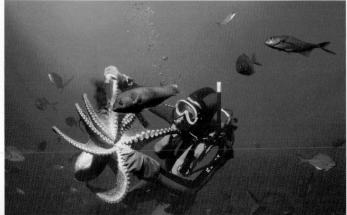

Exploring natural speech

The word *just* means *only* or *simply* and is often used in conversation to make what we say sound less serious or important.

1 How is *just* pronounced in this extract?

I'm **just** really interested in getting to know exactly what's going on in the country and really seeing the place rather than going out and **just** having a relaxing time. I **just** think this gives a more comprehensive look at a country rather than **just** going to relax really.

2 **10.2** Listen, check, and practise.

Vocabulary

1 Underline the vague language expressions referring to people's ages in this extract from the recording.

Michelle Cook, who's worked as a tour leader with an adventure holiday firm for more than ten years, says the interest doesn't just come from students or twenty-somethings. 'We actually take people from fourteen to seventy-nine years old. In the past I've led tours with people in their eighties and they've been the life and soul of the group.'

2 Here are some more ways of referring to people's ages. Which of these are examples of vague language?

Pete is *twenty-five.*
He's in his *mid-twenties.*
He's *twenty-something.*
Jackie is *nearly 17.*
She's *a teenager.*
She's *in her late teens.*
Florence *has just turned 80.*
She's *in her early eighties.*
She's *an octogenarian.*
She must be *at least fifty.*
She's *fifty if she's a day.*

3 Work with a partner. Talk about the ages of members of your family or people you work or study with. If you don't know someone's exact age, use a vague language expression.

Language focus: *as* and *like*

1 *As* and *like* are sometimes confused in English. What is the difference in meaning between these pairs of sentences?

a 1 *Michelle Cook worked **as** a tour leader.*
  2 *Michelle Cook worked **like** a tour leader.*

b 1 ***As** a traveller, I like to see how other nationalities live.*
  2 ***Like** a traveller, I like to see how other nationalities live.*

2 In everyday speech, *like* can sometimes be used instead of *as* or *as if*. In which of these sentences can *like* replace *as* or *as if*?

a *It's not **as** exciting **as** many people want their holidays to be.*

b *So it looks **as if** the quest for challenge and excitement and the desire to be a traveller rather than a tourist, will continue to shape the kind of holiday people decide to take.*

c ***As** the tour leader points out, the trend towards adventure holidays is likely to continue.*

d *It's **as if** people have got tired of relaxing holidays and want something more active.*

e ***As** we're going on holiday tomorrow, I'm not going in to work today.*

Exploitation

Complete this short news story with *as*, *as if*, or *like*. Sometimes both are possible.

GLYNN THOMAS, who works ....[1] a professional artist, recently celebrated his 50th birthday. ....[2] a present, his wife paid for him to go on a trekking holiday to Nepal.

The experience was ....[3] nothing he had ever done before. At times he felt ....[4] he had gone back several centuries in time. ....[5] many in the group he was with, Glynn found the whole experience fascinating.

.........[6] a trek, however, it was not particularly challenging, because it was in the foothills rather than the mountainous part of the Himalayas. And ....[7] porters carried all the backpacks, it was quite a relaxing holiday! Glynn had plenty of time to paint and take photographs.

Speaking

Work in pairs or groups.

1 Plan a two-week adventure holiday for yourselves. Think about these points.
- Type of holiday – is it for travellers or tourists?
- Will there be an element of adventure or even danger?
- Ways to spend your time – devise an outline programme for the two weeks.
- Details – place? time of year? type of accommodation?
- Cost – set your own price limit.

2 Present your holiday plan to the rest of the class. Try to persuade them that your idea is best.

10.2 First impressions

Lead in

Work in pairs or small groups.
Discuss your ideas.

1 What images come to mind when you think of the South Pole or the North Pole?

2 If you were at one of the Poles, how do you think you would feel, physically and mentally?

Reading

1 You are going to read a traveller's account of the last stage of his journey from the North Pole to the South Pole. What could each of these phrases from the account be describing?

---

scudding to a halt   in a dream
brightly-lit   almost paralyzing
numb-faced   short of breath
anoraked figures

---

2 Now read the article quickly.

a How does the writer feel about his arrival at the South Pole?

b How would you describe the style or tone of the article – factual? impressionistic? personal? impersonal?

Close-up

1.26 If stacks of wood and pieces of equipment are the *flotsam and jetsam* of a builder's yard, what do you think *flotsam and jetsam* means?

1.43 What does *proffer* mean? What other verb is it similar to?

1.44 How do you walk if you *trudge*?

1.67 Why does the writer use the word *crunch* to describe his last few steps to the South Pole? What is he walking through?

1.86 What does *It depends which way you look at it* mean?

Welcome to the Pole!

12.30 a.m. Over the noise of the engine Dan, the pilot, shouts that we are 47 minutes from the Pole.
1.00 a.m. Radio communication from 5 air traffic control at the South Pole base.
'There is no designated runway and the US Government cannot authorize you to land. How do you copy?'
10 *Dan:* 'OK.'
'OK. Have a good landing.'
1.10 a.m. We can see the South Pole ahead. It is somewhere in the middle of a complex of buildings dominated 15 by a 1,560-foot dome. Vehicles and buildings are scattered around the site.

We land at the Amundsen-Scott South Pole Station, scudding to a halt on a 20 wide, cleared snow runway. Two well-wrapped figures from the base wait for us to emerge from the plane, and shake our hands in welcome.
It's as we walk towards the dome, 25 past Portakabins and stacks of wood, insulation equipment, all the flotsam and jetsam of a builder's yard, that I become aware of how much effort is required just to keep going. It's as if

I'm in a dream. However hard I try, the 30 dome doesn't seem to get any nearer.
After what seems like a lifetime we descend between walls carved from the ice to a wide underground entrance. 35
Pulling open a door as heavy as that on a butcher's deep-freeze, we enter a warm, brightly-lit canteen. A man in Bermuda shorts is piling a tray with chilli dogs, turkey soup, potato chips 40 and lemon poppyseed cake. One of the chefs rubs cake off on his overalls and proffers a hand. 'Welcome to the Pole!' After coffee we trudge back outside. Scott, Fraser, Nigel and Clem go off to 45 dig up the tent that was left here last year, so that we can eat and sleep. Rudi goes back to the plane. I'm about to join them when I realize that in the midst of all these rules, regulations, 50 coffees and poppyseed handshakes, I have completely forgotten why we are here.
The temperature, with wind chill, is a cutting, almost paralyzing minus 50 55 centigrade, and it's 3.15 in the morning at 10,000 feet when I set out for the final lap of this extraordinary journey. A few hundred yards from the

3 Read the article again and answer these questions.

   a How do you explain the conversation between the air traffic controller and the pilot?

   b Why do you think it requires so much 'effort just to keep going'?

   c Why is the door to the canteen so heavy?

   d Why does the writer say 'I have completely forgotten why I am here'? Why is he there?

   e How is it possible for the writer to walk round the world in eight seconds?

React and discuss

1 Would you like to visit one of the Poles?

2 What other remote places on earth would you like to visit?

---

dome out on the snow is a semi-circle of flags of all the nations working in Antarctica, in the middle of which is a reflecting globe on a plinth. This is the Ceremonial South Pole, at which visiting dignitaries are pictured.   60   65

   Crunching slowly past it, numb-faced and short of breath, I come at last to a small bronze post sticking three feet above the ground. It exactly marks 90 degrees. From this spot all directions point north. At this spot I can walk around the world in 8 seconds. I am on the same longitude as Tokyo, Cairo, New York and Sheffield. I am standing on the South Pole.   70   75

   In the distance I can see a group of anoraked figures pacing the snow, stopping occasionally, forming a circle, pointing then striking at the earth with a shovel. Eventually Clem and Nigel, Fraser and Rudi give up looking for the tent and we all stand together at the bottom of the world. Or the top. It depends which way you look at it.   80   85

            Michael Palin, *Pole to Pole*

Language focus: story-telling

1 Which combination of verb tenses does the writer use to describe his arrival at the South Pole? Underline the main verbs in these extracts.

   a *Two well-wrapped figures from the base wait for us to emerge from the plane, and shake our hands in welcome.*

   b *A man in Bermuda shorts is piling a tray with chilli dogs, turkey soup …*

   c *… I realize that in the midst of all these rules, regulations, coffees and poppyseed handshakes, I have completely forgotten why we are here.*

   d *… it's 3.15 in the morning at 10,000 feet when I set out for the final lap of this extraordinary journey.*

2 What would be the more normal verb tenses to use to describe something that happened to you?

3 Why does the writer choose present tenses? What is the difference in effect of these two sentences?

   • *I **am** standing on the South Pole.*

   • *I **was** standing on the South Pole.*

4 When would you use past forms to tell a story, and when would you use present forms?

Exploitation

1 We use present forms instead of past forms to make a story more conversational, and so more interesting. Retell this story using the Present simple, Present continuous, or Present perfect.

> *It was Tuesday and I was driving to work when my mobile phone rang. The traffic was very busy and by the time I picked up the phone to answer it, it had stopped ringing. It was my girlfriend's number, so I called her back. While I was waiting for her to answer, a police car overtook me and flagged me down. I stopped the car and opened my window. The police officer pointed out that it was an offence to use a mobile phone while driving and fined me £40 on the spot. As soon as I got to work, I rang my girlfriend to find out why she had called. I asked her what she'd phoned for. She said she was missing me and wanted to check I was OK.*

2 We often use present tenses when we tell stories or jokes.

Example
A horse goes into a pub, walks up to the bar, and asks for a pint of beer. The barman looks at the horse, leans over and says in a quiet voice, 'Why the long face?'

Tell your partner a story or a joke.

Writing

1 Write an account of your first visit to a place. It could be somewhere very special, or a town or city.

   • Write in the first person (*I*) and in the personal, impressionistic style of the South Pole article.

   • Describe the place itself and your reactions to what you saw and did.

Write your account in about **100** words.

2 Exchange paragraphs with a partner. Read each other's descriptions and ask more questions about your partner's visit.

▶ **Writing guidelines p.151**

Exploring words

Compound nouns

1 These are some of the ways of forming compound nouns in English.

A noun + noun (this is the most common type)
B noun + verb + -*er*
C noun + verb + -*ing*
D adjective + noun
E verb + particle (these are often related to phrasal verbs)
F particle + verb

a Find compound nouns formed in these ways from the list below. There are two nouns of each type.

---
beach holiday   break-in   bullfighting   bypass   checkout
dishwasher   grandparents   greenhouse   hotel room
housekeeping   input   window cleaner
---

b Work in pairs. Add two or three more examples to each group, then compare your examples with another pair.

c Match the verbs and nouns that go together in these lists and then make the name of an occupation. (Normally the first word of a compound noun referring to a job is singular: a person who *cleans windows* is a **window** *cleaner* not a ~~windows~~ *cleaner*. However, there are a few exceptions to this generalization.)

1 clean	•	antiques
2 commentate on	•	buses
3 deal in	•	clothes
4 decorate	•	fires
5 drive	•	interiors (of houses)
6 fight	•	pianos
7 manufacture	•	portraits
8 paint	•	roads
9 sweep	•	sports
10 tune	•	windows

2 a Where does the stress normally go on compound nouns? Compare ideas in pairs.

1 *I really like horse-riding – I can't stand bullfighting.*
2 *He's a window cleaner not a firefighter.*
3 *Let's go on a beach holiday this year, not an adventure holiday.*
4 *This is a hotel room not a campsite.*
5 *Use the dishwasher, not the washing machine.*
6 *Can I work on the checkout instead of in the storeroom?*

b **10.3** Listen, check, and practise.

3 In these two sets of compound nouns the stress is on the second word. What have the words in each set got in common?

---
1 kitchen table   bathroom window   office door
station platform   garden chair
---
2 cheese sandwich   plastic bag   silver ring   stone steps
tomato omelette
---

4 Read this article describing Asian markets.

a Find and underline the 11 compound nouns.

b Compare answers with a partner and then decide which type of compound each noun is (from **1A–F**).

A market is where growers come to sell their fresh produce. It's always an eye-opener. In Thailand I discovered a herb mixture, which consisted of lemon grass and lime leaves tied together ready to put into a dish and cook.

At a weekend market in Bangkok, there was a man with a big black rubbish bag full of drinking coconuts. The nuts had been roasted and were covered in scorch marks. The man cut off the top of a nut, put a straw in the small hole and handed it to me. I had never tasted coconut juice so sweet.

When I was a child in Sri Lanka, my father would take me with him to the street markets. They were covered by a roof but the sides were open, and there were no flyscreens to keep the flies out.

Places in the Heart

5 Work in pairs.

a Write a short paragraph about an ideal place of some kind. It could be a beach, a country village, a night club.

• Write no more than four sentences – describing what you can see, hear, smell, do, or buy in this place.
• Use at least five compound nouns.

b Read your paragraph out to the rest of the class.

c The class can vote on which place sounds the most attractive.

Language commentary

1 *as* and *like*

a *as* – uses

- To refer to status, function, or occupation.
  As the director, she has a responsibility to the staff.
  My brother is working **as** a nurse in a London hospital.
  It's really a sofa, but you could use it **as** a bed.

- In comparative expressions.
  He's nearly **as** tall **as** me.
  That isn't **as** expensive **as** my last car.

- To mean *because*.
  As I'm not at work today, could you e-mail me any important information?

- To mean *at the same time* or *while*.
  As I opened the door, I realized this was my last chance.

b *like* – uses

- To make comparisons.
  Even though she's been a teacher here for nearly five years, she behaves **like** a student.
  Like most people, my son left home when he was 18.

- To mean *similar to*.
  Everyone says I'm **like** my grandfather, even though I look **like** my grandmother.

▶ Note To refer to differences we can use the opposite, *unlike*.
  Unlike most of the people I know, I dislike football.

c *as (as if)* or *like*

Sometimes it is possible to use *as* or *like*:
I haven't changed my mind. I feel exactly **as / like** I did yesterday. (= the same way as)
You look **as if / like** you need a good sleep. (**like** is informal)

2 The Historic present

a Narrative tenses

The most common verb tenses used for telling a story involving a sequence of events in the past are past tenses.
By the time **we arrived** at the hotel **we were** worn out. **We'd been driving** since five o'clock and **had had** only two short breaks. **We were hoping** for a hot meal, but the chef **had already gone** home, so **we had to make do** with tired sandwiches in the bar.

b Dynamic effect

We can make a sequence of events sound more dynamic by using present tenses: this is the 'historic present'. This story uses the Present simple, the Present perfect simple and continuous and the Present continuous.
By the time **we arrive** at the hotel **we are** worn out. **We've been driving** since five o'clock and **have had** only two short breaks. **We're hoping** for a hot meal, but the chef **has already gone home**, so **we have to make do** with tired sandwiches in the bar.

c Anecdotes

This sequence of tenses is commonly used to tell anecdotes and jokes.
A guy goes to see his grandmother and takes his friend with him. While he's talking to his grandmother, his friend starts eating the peanuts on the table, and finishes them off. As they're leaving, his friend says to the grandmother, 'Thanks for the peanuts.' She says, 'That's OK, since I lost my teeth I can only eat the chocolate off them.'

3 The Present simple: other uses

a Common uses of the Present simple

- To refer to a regular action or habit.
  He **travels** abroad two or three times a year.

- To refer to something that is always true.
  The sun **sets** in the west.

- In sports commentaries.
  Adams **runs** with the ball, **goes** past one defender, and **passes**.

- To refer to a future timetable or schedule.
  We'd better hurry – our plane **leaves** in just under an hour.

b 'Performative' verbs

These verbs are used to make declarations in conversation, and are most commonly used in the simple, not continuous, form.

accept	admit	advise	apologize	congratulate	declare
demand	deny	forbid	forgive	insist	object	predict
promise	propose	protect	recommend	refuse	request
suggest	thank	warn			

I **admit** I was wrong.   I **promise** to write every week.

c Introductory expressions

The simple form is used with introductory expressions which show understanding or knowledge.

believe	gather	hear	presume	see	realize	understand

I **understand** you've been away.
I **believe** Peter wants to see you.

d 'State' verbs

These verbs refer to states or stable situations rather than actions, and are most commonly used in the simple form.
This computer **belongs** to my father.
NOT ~~This computer is belonging to my father.~~
State verbs belong to five different meaning groups.

being	appear seem exist consist of involve look mean resemble weigh
having	own belong contain hold include possess have (it) involves
opinions	consider doubt expect hope imagine know suspect think
feelings	dislike envy fear hate like love mean mind regret respect trust
senses	feel hear see smell taste

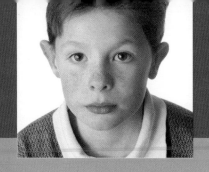

11 Remember

11.1 Memories

Lead in

1 Read this account of an early memory.

    a Why is the occasion so memorable for the writer?
    b What sights, sounds, and smells can he remember?

2 Compare your answers with a partner.

> My first country memory is of an afternoon in high summer and me riding with my cousin Willie Purtill on a donkey and cart along a laneway thick with fuchsia and brambles. I must have been about six years old and we were returning from the creamery at
> 5 Lisselton on the main road between my father's town, Listowel, and the seaside village of Ballybunnion. An empty milk churn sat between us and Willie tapped his fingers methodically on the metal casing. His other hand held the reins and from time to time he clicked his tongue, a reminder to the ancient and slow-moving
> 10 donkey that we were depending on him to get us home. Around us the farmland of North Kerry stretched from Cnoc on Oir (the Mountain of Gold) down to the Atlantic Ocean at Ballybunnion, a wide stretch of land where the pasture is interspersed with snipe grass and the dark loam of the bogs. It was now the first week of
> 15 the harvest and we could smell the aromas of new-mown hay and ripening blackberries mingling with the sea salt that drifted in from the Atlantic.
>
> Fergal Keane, *In the Heart of the Country*

Listening

11.1 You are going to hear two people talking about their earliest memories.

1 How old were the speakers?

2 Where were they or what situation were they in?

3 What other people were involved?

Exploring natural speech

1 **11.2** Read this extract from the conversation you have just heard, then listen again and follow the conversation. What do the words in **bold** refer to?

  G …and erm, basically I was on a family holiday with my mum, my dad and my brother and **we**[1] were staying with my uncle and his wife and **they**[2] erm had some very strange rules of their house that you had to abide by if you stayed with **them**[3] and I was quite sort of fussy as a kid, anyway they had these rules and we had to stick to **them**[4] as we were staying **there**[5] and we sat down to dinner one night and one of **his**[6] rules was that you had to eat everything that was on your plate.

  B No!

  G Yeah, you had to completely finish your food.

  B What if you didn't like **it**[7]?

2 How do you explain what the boy's mother said in this extract from the conversation?

  B Yeah, my head was bleeding and I had to go to hospital and have thirteen stitches …

  G Err!

  B '**Unlucky for some**[8],' my mum said …

React and discuss

1 Do you think that it's true that people tend to remember the bad things rather than the good ones?

2 Sounds, smells, and tastes often bring back memories. Are there any particular sounds, smells, or tastes which bring back memories for you?

Language focus: *must, can, can't (+ have)*: certainty and deduction

1 How certain are the speakers about their age?

  a *I must have been about six years old at the time.*
  b *I was probably about 17 at the time.*
  c *I know I was 22.*
  d *There's no doubt about it – I was 15.*
  e *I might have been 13 or 14, I suppose.*

2 We do not normally use the affirmative form *can have* for expressing deductions. Why do you think it is possible in these examples?

  a *I can only have been about four, maybe slightly older.*
  b *He can hardly have remembered something from when he was only two.*
  c *They can never have been able to spend time alone.*

3 We use *must, can, can't*, etc. *+ have* when we are making a deduction based on evidence.

Example
I must have been about six years old. (Evidence: *I had just started school.*)

What could the evidence be for these statements?

  a Someone phoned while I was out, but it can't have been my brother. He's …
  b It can only have been my sister. She's …
  c It must have rained very hard there. …
  d Somebody must have been having a party here. …

4 What is the difference in meaning between these pairs of sentences?

  a *She couldn't have got there. No trains ran that day.*
     She can't have got there. She said she'd phone as soon as she arrived.

  b *It must be Mario. I'd recognize his voice anywhere.*
     It must have been Mario (who emptied the jar). No one else likes honey.

Exploitation

Work in pairs or groups. Look at these pictures and work out what happened.

Example
The woman jumping might have …

Speaking

Work in groups. Talk about one of your earliest memories. You could mention these aspects of your memory.

* a sequence of events
* a domestic scene
* a place
* a person / some people
* a time of the day or year
* an atmosphere or a feeling (e.g. happiness / fear)

Use appropriate modal forms from the **Language focus** and expressions from this box.

Remembering

* I (can) remember + *ing*
* As far as I can remember, I …
* I can still see (the look on her face).
* I'll never forget (what he said).
* I clearly / distinctly remember …
* I seem to remember …

Writing

You are going to write about an early memory. It could be the one you have just been talking about.

1 Think about these aspects:

  * place   * sequence of events
  * time   * atmosphere and feelings
  * people   * noises or smells.

2 List a few phrases you might use for each aspect.

3 Write your paragraph in about 150 words.

4 Exchange paragraphs with a partner and read about each other's memories. Ask questions to find out more about your partner's memory.

▶ **Writing guidelines p.151**

11.2 Memory

Lead in

1 Match the words with the objects shown in the pictures.

> biscuit lipstick match pill rose zip
> mousetrap pipe rhino boy screw
> shoe sunglasses toy duck train ticket

2 Now close your book and write down as many of the objects as you can remember.

3 Compare lists with other students, then open your book and check.

4 Complete these sentences with the correct form of one of these verbs. (Sometimes more than one verb is possible.)

> remember   remind   recall   recognize
> memorize

a I've seen her before, but I just can't .... her name.

b He .... me of his father. He's got the same smile.

c The car came round the corner. I've tried but I just can't .... what happened next.

d It only took her ten minutes to .... the names of 30 students.

e .... me to phone my brother later. I promised I would.

f I hardly .... you. You look different with short hair.

Reading

1 Read the article.

a How many different kinds of memory are mentioned?

b What are neuroscientists doing research on now?

Close up

1.2–1.3 How many *centuries* are there in a *millennium*? What is the word for a period of 10 years?

1.3 Which words could replace *barely* here?

1.44 Where is the stress on *photographic*? And on these words: *photographer* / *photograph*?

The mystery of memory

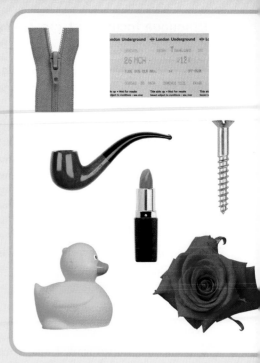

A Fascination with memory and how to improve it goes back millennia; yet the sciences of memory are barely a century old. At first they were the province of psychologists, who taught us to distinguish short-term from long-term memory. Many things are recalled only for a few seconds or minutes – strings of numbers and people's names – before being permanently lost. What isn't lost gets transferred into long-term memory, which seems to last almost for ever.

B Remembering involves recovering things from longer term memory and placing them into 'working memory'. Then there is the difference between procedural memory – remembering 'how' (to ride a bicycle for instance) and declarative memory (remembering that those objects with two large wheels, saddles and handlebars are called bicycles). Procedural memory is more stable than declarative. Alzheimer's sufferers remember how to ride a bike long after they have forgotten what it is called.

C There are other distinctions. Recognition versus recall, for example. Think how hard it is to recall a friend's face, and how easy to recognize the person when you see them. Play the memory game, showing someone a tray of objects for a minute or so, then removing it, and asking them to remember what they have seen. Most people find it hard to remember more than 15 different items. Do the experiment differently though, and show them a series of objects or photos one after the other for a few seconds, then perhaps weeks later offer them a choice between photos they have seen before and new ones, and people can recognize correctly 10,000 or more.

D And finally, so-called 'eidetic', or photographic memory – what most of us have of our early childhood; snapshot-like fragments, associated with smells or tastes or colours. Children below the age of eight seem to remember like this, and most of us lose the ability as we grow older.

D The human brain contains some 100 billion nerve cells, each capable of making up to 100,000 connections with its neighbours. It is the pathways made possible by these myriad interconnections which must contain the answers to how memories are made. The idea is simple: each time a new memory is made, a new pattern of connections is created, which in some way stores the new memory, much as the 'memory' of a scene is stored on the tape of a video recorder.

E Think about trying to remember the name of a person you met yesterday; you might try a variety of strategies. Where did you meet? What were they wearing? What letter did their name begin with or what did it rhyme with? Who did they remind you of? What did you discuss? All these are different access points by which we might attempt to retrieve the missing name. And almost certainly each of these features is stored in a different region of the brain.

F The great mystery with which neuroscientists are currently wrestling is to understand how all these different regions and brain processes are bound together to give us coherent conscious experience.

Adapted from an article by Steven Rose

2 Which paragraph, A–G

a describes a test which shows that people find it easier to recognize things when they see them than to recall them?

b describes an ability that humans grow out of?

c lists methods people use to try to remember what someone is called?

d refers to the first areas scientists defined?

e describes the problem scientists are currently working on in this area?

f points out the difference between remembering names and remembering how to do something practical?

g attempts to explain the way the human brain stores memories?

Language focus: relative clauses

1 a Without looking back at the article, complete these extracts with a relative word or phrase. Then check.

1 *At first they were the province of psychologists, ... taught us to distinguish short-term from long-term memory.* (1.4)

2 *What isn't lost gets transferred into long-term memory, ... seems to last almost for ever.* (1.10)

3 *Play the memory game, showing someone a tray of objects for a minute or so, then removing it, and asking them to remember .... they have seen.* (1.29)

4 *All these are different access points .... we might attempt to retrieve the missing name.* (1.68)

5 *The great mystery .... neuroscientists are currently wrestling is to understand how all these different regions and brain processes are bound together ...* (1.74)

b There are six more relative pronouns which are not used here. What are they?

2 a How are the relative clauses in the first two sentences in **1a** different from those in the other extracts?

b What is the difference in meaning between these sentences?

1 *My daughter who works as a teacher has a photographic memory.*

2 *My daughter, who works as a teacher, has a photographic memory.*

3 a Underline the relative clauses in these extracts. Which relative pronouns could be added?

1 *... offer them a choice between photos they have seen before and new ones, ...*

2 *Think about trying to remember the name of a person you met yesterday ...*

b When is it possible to leave out relative pronouns?

4 What does *which* refer to in these two sentences?

a *I clearly remember going past a big white house **which** was surrounded by trees.*

b *I clearly remember going past a big white house, **which** is amazing because I was asleep for most of the journey.*

Exploitation

1 Add appropriate relative pronouns to these sentences.

a 1998 was the year we moved into the apartment .... we're in now.

b Unfortunately, the person to .... this parcel is addressed doesn't live here now.

c That's the man I was telling you about – the one .... has just come out of prison.

d They're unreasonable people .... opinions I despise.

e She said she's enjoying her job, ... surprised me because she looks so stressed.

f I got held up in the traffic and didn't arrive until midnight, by .... time people had already left.

2 Which of the relative pronouns in sentences **1a–f** could be left out?

3 Make up three definitions for each of these.

an adult	a politician	a village	a newspaper	old age

a a definition which a child could understand.

b a more complete definition.

c an amusing definition.

Speaking

1 Close your book. How many objects can you still remember from the **Lead in**?

2 Compare with a partner. Which things did both of you remember? What do you think made these things memorable?

3 Now open the book and check.

11.3 Help!

Lead in

1 How good are you at remembering the following?

- birthdays and anniversaries
- meetings at work
- promises to other people
- resolutions you make (to yourself!)
- appointments, for example at the dentist

2 Do you have a special way of trying to remember? For example, writing on your hand?

3 **11.3** Listen to some people talking about the same subjects.

   a What kinds of things do they forget?

   b How do they try to remember?

Reading

1 Look at this short text. What is it and where is it from?

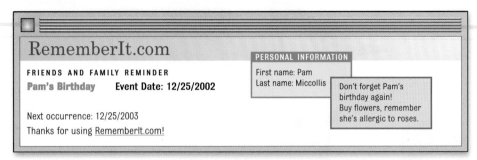

2 Now read about the organization which provides this service.

   a What kinds of reminder can RememberIt.com send you?

   b What other services does it offer?

RememberIt.com

email _____
password _____

REMEMBERING AND FORGETTING

If you can't forget the femme fatale who rocked the White House in 1999, but have forgotten a loved one's birthday year after year, a quick e-mail reminder could be the solution to your dilemma. A new survey conducted by RememberIt.com, an information management and online reminder service, reveals that most people remember public

5 events such as political scandals and severe weather conditions, but forget birthdays of friends and family.

The survey polled 1,000 Americans about the most unforgettable public events of 1999, personal events most likely to be forgotten and the most common reminder techniques used. When asked what public event of 1999 people most remembered, 46.7

10 per cent recalled the Monica Lewinsky scandal, followed by Hurricane Floyd at 27.5 per cent. Birthdays and anniversaries took the lead in personal events that were most often forgotten at 33 per cent, while 24.8 per cent of those surveyed were most likely to forget meetings and appointments. In addition, the survey showed 68 per cent of people polled preferred to receive written reminders, a large portion of the group

15 favoring e-mail reminders.

RememberIt.com offers online tools to help users remember and plan for a variety of events and commitments such as birthdays, vacations, medical appointments and car maintenance. In addition, members can set and track their goals and New Year's resolutions online, to help them lose weight or save for an important purchase. The

20 easy-to-use site helps users manage events online and receive personal e-mail reminders.

rememberit.com/

React and discuss

1 Do you think this service is really necessary? Why? Why not?

2 Has forgetting something important ever had serious results for you?

3 Would you like to be sent reminders like this?

Close up

1.1 What is a *femme fatale*? Can you think of any famous examples?

1.9 How do we say numbers like these: *46.7* and *27.5*?

1.11 What is the difference between a *birthday* and an *anniversary*?

1.20 *easy-to-use* is an adjective in the phrase *the easy-to-use site*. How could this phrase be rewritten using a relative clause?

Language focus: articles

1 Without looking back, choose the correct articles in these extracts. (^ = no article needed). Then check.

a *If you can't forget **a / the** ¹ femme fatale who rocked **the** / ^ ² White House in 1999, but have forgotten **a / the** ³ loved one's birthday year after year, **a / the** ⁴ quick e-mail reminder could be **a / the** ⁵ solution to your dilemma.* (l.1)

b ***A / the** ⁶ new survey conducted by RememberIt.com, **a / the** ⁷ information management and online reminder service, reveals that most people remember public events …* (l.3)

c ***A / the** ⁸ survey polled 1,000 Americans about **the** / ^ ⁹ most unforgettable public events of 1999, …* (l.7)

d *RememberIt.com offers **the** / ^ ¹⁰ online tools to help **the** / ^ ¹¹ users remember and plan for **a / the** ¹² variety of events and commitments such as **the** / ^ ¹³ birthdays, …* (l.16)

2 Complete these statements about the use of articles with *a, an, the,* or ^. Use the extracts to help you. Sometimes an example can illustrate more than one rule.

a When mentioning something for the first time, we use ……… .

b When there is only one of something (it is unique or the context makes it clear), we use ……… .

c With uncountable nouns referring to something general, (not specific) we use ……… .

d With superlative adjectives, including *first, same* we use ……… .

e The article that could be replaced by the word *one* is ……… .

f When referring to something or someone that everyone knows, we use ……… .

g When referring to something that has already been mentioned, we use ……… .

h When referring to something non-specific – it doesn't matter which one, we use ……… .

i When we are classifying a person or thing, e.g. saying what their job or function is, we use ……… .

j With plural countable nouns, referring to something in general, we use ……… .

Exploitation

Choose the best articles to fill the spaces in this text – *a, an, the,* or ^.

It should be ………¹ easiest thing in ………² world to remember to get your mother ………³ birthday present. After all, she's ………⁴ most important person in your life.

While I lived at ………⁵ home, I never forgot ………⁶ single birthday. Someone always reminded me. ………⁷ few days before ………⁸ big day, my father would say. 'Don't forget to get Mum ………⁹ present.'

At ………¹⁰ age of 18, I went to ………¹¹ university. I made ………¹² new friends. For ………¹³ first time there was no one telling me what to do. I wasn't used to ………¹⁴ freedom. I didn't forget my family, but they became less important. I phoned once ………¹⁵ month and went ………¹⁶ home twice ………¹⁷ year.

It was ………¹⁸ Wednesday in ………¹⁹ June. I'd just got out of ………²⁰ bed when ………²¹ phone rang. 'Steven?' It was my Mum. 'Do you know what ………²² date is?'

Speaking

Work in groups.

1 What Internet services have you used? How helpful have you found them? Make a list of sites that other students might find useful. Write a two-line description of each site.

Example

Ticketmaster
Brilliant place to start looking for tickets to live music events in the UK. You can search by area, venue, or artist.

2 What do you think these Internet services do for people? Would you be interested in using any of them?

Blind Date   JobsUnlimited
CDnow   Travelocity
UpMyStreet   The Burgled Helpline

3 Think of a new online service which might be popular.

a Make up a catchy name for your service and write a brief description of what it can offer.

b 'Sell' your idea to the other students in the class.

The web site referred to on these pages is in the public domain and its address is provided by Oxford University Press for information only. Oxford University Press disclaims any responsibility for the content.

Exploring words

Loan words used in English

English has borrowed many words from other languages. Some, for example *bungalow*, *village*, are well established and we no longer think of them as 'foreign'. Others are still obviously 'foreign' because of their un-English pronunciation, for example *femme fatale*.

1 Look at the headlines and notices.

  a How many 'foreign' words can you spot?

  b What do they mean?

  c Which languages do you think they are borrowed from?

Junta cracks down on angry crowds

Ballet star kidnapped

Paparazzi to blame for princess' accident

New Drug Czar appointed

At last housework robot!

Dial-a-**pizza**

Trekkers Paradise
2 weeks in the Himalayas for £500

Black Cat Café
Massive menu

Indian Restaurant and takeaway
Tandoori dishes a speciality

New Lifestyle Club
Members-only Gym and Sauna

2 **a** What do these words borrowed from French mean?

> bouquet bourgeois cache cliché crèche cul-de-sac
> duvet entrepreneur gateau genre

  b How are the words in 2a pronounced?

    1 Compare ideas with a partner.

    2 **11.4** Listen, check, and practise.

  c Can you think of any other French words or phrases used in English with similar pronunciations? Start by thinking of words with these endings: *-é* / *-ée* / *-et* / *-eau* / *-eur*.

3 **a** Read this short story which contains a number of other loan words used in English.

  b Underline the loan words. (Look for combinations of letters that are unusual in English, particularly at the ends of words.)

> I live in an expensive part of the city, well away from the hoi-polloi. It was a quiet summer's afternoon – siesta time, you could call it. I'd just come out of the sauna and planned to spend an hour or two dozing on the patio.
> 5   Then it started! My new neighbour had just bought a new grass cutter and was having a blitz on his neglected lawn. That was bad enough, but then his wife came out with her radio playing loud music. The noise reached a crescendo when the children came out and played their
> 10 noisy games.
>   I looked over the fence and asked my neighbour, as politely as I could, if he could keep the noise down a bit. After all, it was a Sunday afternoon. He turned off the machine and walked towards me in a distinctly macho way.
> 15 He apologized and gave me this spiel about how he was looking after his garden to improve the neighbourhood.

4 Work in pairs or groups.

  a Are English words commonly used in your language? Make a list of the commonest.

  b Are English words used in preference to their equivalents in your own language? Why?

  c How do you feel about this trend?

Language commentary

1 Modals: *must, can, can't + have*

a Near certainty

Must be, can't be, must have been, can't have been are used to express near certainty based on evidence or logic.
You **must be / must have been** really tired.
(The speaker assumes this because he knows what the person has been doing.)
He **can't be / can't have been** serious about living abroad.
(The speaker doesn't believe this is possible.)

b *can*

We do not normally use *can* or *mustn't* to express near certainty, but *can* is sometimes used in questions and with *only, never, hardly*.
Where **can she be**? / Where **can they have been**?
I **can only have been** out of the house for ten minutes.
He **can hardly have done** everything himself.

2 Relative clauses

a Relative pronouns: *who (whom), whose, which, that, when, where, why*

* *Who* refers to a person.
  It was my mother **who** taught me to ride a bicycle.

* *Whom* is formal and is used mainly after prepositions.
  The family **with whom** I'm staying have been most generous.
  The more common form of this sentence is:
  The family **who** I'm staying **with** have been most generous.

* *Whose* is a possessive relative pronoun which refers to a person or a thing. It is always followed by a noun.
  The people **whose** flat we've bought have moved to Canada.

* *Which* refers to a thing.
  The tree **which** fell down in the storm had stood there for nearly 200 years.
  The tree **which** I crashed into fell down.
  Which can also refer to an idea expressed by a clause.
  My car brakes failed as I went round the corner, **which** took me by surprise.

* *That* refers to a person or thing.
  The car **that** crashed into me was going too fast.
  All the people **that** I met in Athens were friendly.

* *When* refers to times.
  New Year is a time **when** people make resolutions.

* *Where* refers to places.
  Do you remember the place **where** we met?

* *Why* refers to a reason and usually follows the word *reason*.
  Lack of money is the main reason **why** I had to turn down his invitation to go on holiday.

b Defining and non-defining relative clauses

* We use defining relative clauses to specify which person or thing we are referring to.
  That's the problem **(that) I was referring to**.
  The postcard **(which) you posted at the beginning of May** took three weeks to get here.

* We use non-defining relative clauses simply to add extra, but non-essential information.
  The journey, **which lasted three hours**, was very dangerous.
  Elzbieta, **who comes from Poland**, is an art student.

▶ Note *That* cannot be used as the subject of a non-defining relative clause.
Marc, **who** comes from Zimbabwe, is a mechanic. (NOT ~~that~~)

c Leaving out relative pronouns

Relative pronouns can be left out when the relative word is the object of the relative clause.
The person **I'm writing to** lives in Ireland. (or the person **to whom** I'm writing...)
2000 was the year **I started work**. (or 2000 was the year **when / that** I started...)
Do you remember the place **we met**? (or Do you remember the place **where / that** we met?)
Is that the real reason **you left early**? (or Is that the real reason **why** you left early?)

3 Articles

a The definite article *the*

the = specific / there's only one / the one we know about.
When is **the** doctor coming? (= Our family doctor.)
He's at **the** university. (= The local university.)
She's **the** best gymnast in her class. (= In her class she's unique.)

b *the* – other uses

* *The ... the ...* comparative constructions.
  The harder I work, **the less** I seem to get done.

* *The* + adjective to refer to groups of people.
  The young often make fun of **the old**.

* Names of seas, oceans, rivers, mountain ranges, islands.
  The Pacific / The Amazon / The Alps / The Philippines

* Names of a few countries.
  The Netherlands / The United Arab Emirates

* Names of cinemas and theatres.
  Shall we go to see the film at **the Odeon**?

c The indefinite article *a / an*

a / an = general / non-specific.
He's **a** doctor. (= That's his job or function.)
There's **a** university in Newcastle. (= One of many.)
She's **a** good gymnast. (= She's just one of many gymnasts.)

d No article

* Uncountable nouns with a general meaning.
  Drinking **water** is good for you.

* Plural countable nouns with a general meaning.
  People love driving **cars**.

* In phrases relating to places, situations, or institutions.
  Do you go to **church**?

be in; go to	class	court	heaven	hospital	prison
be at; go to	sea	school	university	war	work
be at; go	home				

12.1 Crazes

Lead in

Look at the pictures below. What are the things and what do you think they have in common?

Listening

You are going to hear five people talking about their past crazes.

1 **12.1** Which speaker, 1–5, talks about
   a their tastes as a teenager?
   b being a member of a club connected to their hobby?
   c an activity they had in common with all their friends?
   d an obsession which lasted four or five years?
   e a craze which a parent found annoying?

2 Listen again. How do you think the speakers feel now about their past crazes?

> **craze** /kreɪz/ n (**a**) ~ (**for sth**) an enthusiastic but usu brief interest in sth that is shared by many people: *the craze for exercising at all hours of the day and night* ∘ *the current/latest teenage dance craze that is sweeping Europe*. (**b**) an object of such an interest: *Pet pigs are the latest craze.*

Exploring natural speech

1 What is the effect of the repetition of the phrase *I knew* in this extract from the recording?

Every break time every lunchtime at school we would play football in the playground. Erm it had a disastrous effect on my shoes – my mother was having to buy me shoes, I remember, every, every three or four months or so cos I wore them out so quickly erm I used to buy regularly a football magazine which I would read avidly every Saturday morning – I **knew** the names of all the teams in the football league, I **knew** their grounds, I **knew** their colours, I **knew** the names of most of the players in all the teams – it was a complete obsession and the odd thing is that now I have absolutely no interest in football **whatsoever** …

2 The word *whatsoever* at the end of the last sentence means roughly the same as *at all*. Do you think it is stronger than or not as strong as *at all*?

React and discuss

1 What are the current crazes among children and young people in your country? What about a few years ago?

2 Is it only children and teenagers who have crazes?

3 How do crazes start? How and why do they spread?

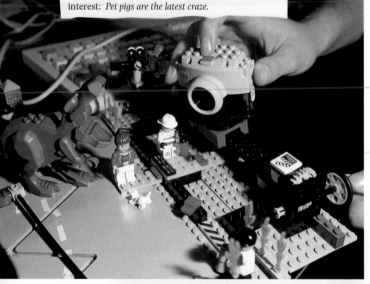

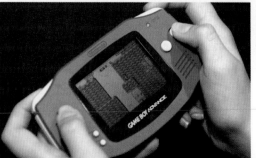

Language focus: *used to* and *would*

How much do you know about *used to* and *would*?

1 We use *used to* and *would* to talk about past habits. **True** or **False**?

2 We can use *used to* and *would* to refer to a single past action. **True** or **False**?

3 *Would* is more common than *used to* in informal English. **True** or **False**?

4 Which sentence suggests that the speaker no longer watches their favourite football team every week? **a** or **b**?
a I used to watch my favourite football team every week.
b I would watch my favourite football team every week.

5 We can always use *would* instead of *used to*. **True** or **False**?

6 Only one of these sentences is correct. Is it **a** or **b**? Can you explain your answer?
a I used to be keen on heavy metal music.
b I would be keen on heavy metal music.

7 Which are the correct question and negative forms of *used to*? **a** or **b**?
a Did you used to play football? / I didn't used to play football.
b Did you use to play football? / I didn't use to play football.

8 What is wrong with this sentence?
I used to collect stuffed animals for 15 years.

9 What could be the difference in meaning between these two sentences?
a I went to Spain for my holidays.
b I used to go to Spain for my holidays.

10 What is the difference in meaning between these two sentences?
a I'm used to travelling abroad.
b I used to travel abroad.

Exploitation

1 Complete this text with *used to / would* or the appropriate form of the verb in brackets. Vary the verbs you use to make sure that the description sounds natural as a whole.

When I .... (be)[1] a kid I .... (collect)[2] everything under the sun – the usual things like stamps and coins, but some strange things like cheese labels and stones. The best thing about collecting these things was that they .... (be)[3] free. The cheese labels are a good example. When I .... (be)[4] about six we .... (move)[5] house and .... (go)[6] to live near a supermarket. My mum .... (go)[7] shopping nearly every day. Of course, she .... (take)[8] me with her and soon I .... (become)[9] fascinated with the different cheeses and the labels on them. I .... (insist)[10] my mum bought a different kind every time she .... (go)[11] shopping. As soon as we got home, I .... (remove)[12] the labels very carefully and stick them in my special album. By the age of nine I .... (have)[13] 1,453 labels in my collection.

2 Think about yourself and your life between the ages of five and 10 or between 10 and 15. Write sentences using *used to* or *would* to describe **a–e**:

Example
your free time
I used to go to the cinema every Saturday morning with my friends. After the film we'd go shopping or have a picnic.

a family life – daily routines, parents, brothers and sisters, your home
b school life – lessons, subjects, teachers, friends
c appearance – clothes, hairstyles, build (height, etc.)
d favourite forms of entertainment – music, TV programmes, sport, games
e likes and dislikes – people, food, holidays

Speaking

1 What things were you interested in between the ages of five and 10? Make a list. Include toys, games, animals, sports, music, hobbies, school activities, TV programmes.

2 How interested were you in each activity? Use these expressions.

quite interested in	enthusiastic about	really keen on
crazy / mad about	absolutely obsessed with	

3 Compare lists with other students. Find people who shared some of your interests.

12.2 Fast food fashions

Lead in

Discuss these questions in groups.

1 Which are the most popular *fast food chains* in your country?

2 What are the most popular types of *fast food*?

3 Do all types and ages of people in your country enjoy *fast food*? What about you?

Reading

1 How much do you know about hamburgers?

   a When were hamburgers first sold in the USA?
   A late 19th century   B early 20th century
   C mid 20th century

   b What did the first McDonald's shops sell?
   A ice cream   B hot dogs   C traditional food

   c How many burgers does the average American eat in a week?
   A one   B two   C three

   d What percentage of Americans get their first job working for McDonald's?
   A fewer than 5%   B 5%   C more than 5%

2 Read the article and check your answers.

3 Answer these questions. You may have to interpret the writer's words.

   a What factors explain the rise in popularity of hamburgers in the USA?

   b Why are hamburgers particularly popular with young people?

   c What point is the writer making when he says his vegetarian son liked Big Macs and McNuggets?

   d What does the writer mean by: *what are euphemistically (and anonymously) called cheap hamburgers*?

   e Why is *the history of the hamburger in your hands* particularly important these days?

React and discuss

How do you think fast food will develop in the future?

--- Close up ---

1.2   *heroic* is an adjective. Which nouns mean 'a person that is *heroic*' and 'the quality of being *heroic*'?

1.1–1.8 Which two words in this paragraph tells us that the Mongols rode horses?

1.26   What is the difference in meaning between *Hamburgers* and *hamburgers*?

1.48   Why does the writer use the phrase *one is told*? Who is *one*?

1.50   Which vegetable is *spud* the slang word for?

1.65   How do you eat something if you *scoff* it?

The rise of

The Big Mac, food historians tell us, has heroic origins. The Mongol hordes, as they galloped over the steppes, would place minced beef under their saddles. After a long day's pillage, they would settle down to their rare (that is, 'raw') burger: boeuf tartare.

The twentieth century history of favourite fast food is as American as cherry pie. The modern hamburger was, historians tell us, pioneered at concessionaire stalls at the 1904 St Louis World Fair.

It was a brilliant innovation: time and motion technique applied to catering. The meat could be kneaded into a pellet, flipped on the hotplate, and clapped in a bun (to keep the customer's fingers grease-free) faster than a nickel could change hands.

The name itself was mysterious. It is true that on the north German coast they relish their patties; they call them *Deutsches Beefsteak mit Brötchen*. Hamburgers, my Hamburg friends tell me, do not eat hamburgers.

The history of the American hamburger is a triumph of 20th century merchandising. No one managed to get a trademark on the word. Any minimum wage menial could cook hamburgers and any street vendor could peddle them. The trick was to market them better than the competition.

In 1936, the Wimpy was brand leader – named after the burger-scoffing character in Popeye. Bob's Big Boy chain is credited with the doubleburger and the drive-thru.

But it was McDonald's, initially a hot-dog franchise, which in the 1950s under Ray Kroc brought the burger into

the burger

the modern age (wisely they decided against Big-Kroc). What McDonald's sold was, famously, less a product than a style of eating: efficient, quick, and one size for the whole family.

The Big Mac, and its rivals, are now to America and its gastronomic colonies what the potato was to 19th-century Ireland. Americans, it is calculated, eat on average three hamburgers a week. Some seven per cent of the American workforce, one is told, had their first job at McDonald's.

What is glossed over in the image is that the hamburger, like the Irish spud, is the staple food of poor people, particularly poor young people. Kids are chronically short of cash, in a hurry, and prone to get hungry at unsocial hours.

At my preferred American drive-thru, In-and-Out, you can get your burger, fries and shake for under three dollars, in three minutes, at three o'clock in the morning. Delicious.

But even at the best outlets, you can never be entirely certain what you're eating. For much of his early childhood, my son proudly proclaimed himself a vegetarian, while scoffing his daily Big Mac or McNuggets, blissfully unaware of their remote origins as meat.

McDonald's and the other big franchises select their meat with scrupulous care. One is less sure about what are euphemistically (and anonymously) called 'cheap hamburgers'.

One of the most sensible and cost effective health measures our government could take would be to instruct young Britons to be intellectually curious about what they are eating. Forget Genghis Khan. It's the history of the hamburger in your hand that you need to know.

John Sutherland, *The Guardian*

Language focus: omitting words

1 a What words have been left out at the points marked ↔ in these sentences?
   b What kinds of words are they?
   1 *At my preferred American drive-thru … you can get your burger, fries and shake for under three dollars, in three minutes, at three o'clock in the morning. ↔ Delicious.*
   2 *Q ↔ Got the time?*
      A ↔ Sorry. ↔
   3 *↔ Traffic's just terrible in the mornings. ↔ Never known anything like it.*
   4 *↔ Thought I might go out for a pizza tonight. ↔ Coming?*

2 We also leave out words and phrases because it is unnecessary to repeat them. Look at these examples.
   I really thought I was going to win the jackpot this week, but (I) didn't (win the jackpot).
   I've often tried to give up smoking but (I've) never succeeded (in giving up smoking).

Exploitation

1 Which (unnecessary) words or phrases make these conversations sound unnatural?

   a A Is there any chance of you giving me a lift?
      B Sure I can give you a lift. Get in.

   b A Have you seen my dad recently?
      B Yes, I have seen your dad recently. I saw him this morning.

2 It is useful to be able to leave out words when space is limited, for example in postcards, e-mails, etc.

   a Cross out any unnecessary words or phrases to enable you to get the text below on to a postcard. Try to reduce it to about 70 words. (Sometimes you may prefer to rephrase rather than simply leaving words out.)

   b Compare shortened versions with a partner. How similar are your versions?

   > Since last Friday I've been from Perth to Adelaide and then I went on to Mount Gambier which is a remote farming town. I climbed a volcano there and I saw koalas, and kangaroos in the wild. On Tuesday I hired a car and Tina and I drove along the Ocean Road past the rocks you can see in the picture. The views were really breath-taking. I have never seen anything like it before. We're planning to visit a rainforest tomorrow.

   c In pairs, take turns to remove one word at a time from one of your shortened texts to make it even shorter. How many words can you remove before it loses its meaning?

12.3 Films

Lead in

1 What different types of film are there? (*action films ...*)

2 Which is your favourite type?

3 Tell each other about your favourite film. Use some of the expressions from the box.

> **Talking about films**
> - It starred .... and co-starred ....
> - The special effects were ....
> - It was filmed on location in ....
> - It had .... subtitles.
> - It was dubbed into ....
> - There was a (fantastic) scene where ....
> - The plot was (really complicated).
> - It's a (real) classic.
> - The dialogue was (brilliant).

Listening

1 You are going to hear someone talking about successful films.

   12.2 Listen to the first part of the recording. Listen for the following:

   a Four types of film
   b The names of two actors.

2 Listen again and complete these sentences with information you hear.

   a The speaker regards *Casablanca* as a ....
   b The speaker compares Western films to ....
   c In Westerns, there are two different types of character, ... and ....
   d Western films always end with ....

3 **12.3** Listen to the second part of the recording. According to the speaker, what makes a good film?

Exploring natural speech

In natural speech people express thoughts as they come into their mind. As a result, ideas are unfinished or repeated and clarifications are added as we think of them. By contrast, before we give a formal talk, we order and plan what we are going to say.

Look at this extract from the recording and rewrite it as it might be spoken as part of a formal talk.

A film … transports you it's the, the whole atmosphere, the music and that especially when you see it at the cinema, and you have to go and make an effort to go see it, erm and you sit there in the dark and this massive movie is, is playing – and you know there's the music and the effects and the sound and the pictures and it's just the whole experience.

React and discuss

1 What do you think makes a good film?

2 What makes a star? Give examples of people you think have 'star quality'.

Vocabulary: phrasal verbs with *off*

1 How does *off* affect the meaning of verbs? What is the difference in meaning between these two sentences?

a *He goes riding in the park.*   b *He goes off riding into the sunset.*

2 *Off* can add a range of different meanings to a verb.

a Put the phrasal verbs in sentences 1–8 into one of these four meaning groups, A–D.

A Leaving	B Stopping or cancelling	C Beginning	D Obstruction or separation

1 The camera crew's strike was *called off* at the last moment.
2 The film was so controversial that it *sparked off* riots outside the cinema.
3 The cheapest seats in the cinema were clearly *divided off* from the more expensive ones.
4 It took us an hour to get to the cinema even though we *set off* very early.
5 The film *kicked off* with a car chase through the streets of New York.
6 The star *broke off* negotiations with the film company because they weren't prepared to pay him his normal fee.
7 All the roads around the cinema were *blocked off* for the film première.
8 It was a real action-packed film. There were some amazing effects as the rocket *blasted off*.

b Which single-word verbs could be used instead of the eight phrasal verbs above?

c Now put these phrasal verbs into groups A–D. Write sentences to illustrate their meanings.

close off	drive off	lead off	put off	ring off	seal off	take off	wave off

Listening and speaking

1 **12.4** Listen to a group of people describing a frightening scene in a film.

a Do you know the films they mention?

b What was frightening about the scenes they describe?

2 Now look at these extracts and answer the questions.

> **A** There's that **bit** in *Psycho* … when I think there's a girl hiding under the staircase, **isn't there**? And whoever it is, **is coming** in, he **runs up** the stairs and you're not quite sure if **he's noticed** her or not and he's sort of looking around the house and **you** know that he's about to come down and find her …

• What does *bit* mean here?
• Why does the speaker use this question tag?
• Why are these verb tenses used?
• Who is *you*?

> **B** I love the bit in I think its *Misery* – is it called *Misery*? – with Kathy Bates **where** where she's **she's gone out** for a drive and he's in the house and he has to try and get out of the room which she's locked him in and, you know, he gets all the way …

• Which word does *where* refer back to? What other word could be used instead?
• Why is the Present perfect used here?

3 Work in groups. Talk about a frightening scene in a film you have seen.

a What elements helped to make a particular scene frightening?

b How did the frightening scene make you feel – physically and mentally?

Exploring words

Fashion

1 Complete these sentences with *fashion* words and phrases from the list.

---
come (back) into fashion   fashion-conscious   a fashion victim
(go) out of fashion   the latest fashion   unfashionable
---

a My mother has never been very .... She can't stand buying new clothes.

b Everyone's wearing bright clothes now. They're ....

c I never throw away any of my clothes – just in case they .... again.

d I feel sorry for kids who spend loads of money on the latest clothes. They're just ....

e No one's wearing shoes like that now. They .... several months ago.

f As soon as anything of mine is ...., I throw it away and replace it.

2 These adjectives can all be used to describe clothes.

a Which have positive, which have negative, and which have neutral connotations? Make three lists.

---
bright   casual   classic   conservative   cool   dressy   dull
elegant   flashy   flattering   formal   naff   neat   neutral
ordinary   posh   presentable   shocking   smart   snazzy
special   sensible   sporty   stylish   tasteful   traditional
trendy   unflattering
---

b Now work in pairs.

Use words from the list above to describe the clothes and shoes in the pictures.

c Which of the things in the pictures would you be happy to wear? Which would you refuse to wear? Why?

3 Work in groups.

a Discuss two questions from **List 1** and two from **List 2**.

List 1

- What are your normal, everyday clothes? How similar are they to your friends' everyday clothes?

  exactly the same / similar / a little different / completely different

- Do you ever dress up? What kind of clothes do you wear?

- Do you ever dress very formally? On what occasions?

List 2

- How important is it in your country for young people to wear fashionable clothes?

- Do you know any fashion victims?

- Have you ever kept anything unfashionable that later came back into fashion?

b Find other students who discussed the same questions as you and exchange opinions.

d **12.5** You are going to hear a group of people talking about which clothes they would wear. Listen for and tick the adjectives they use from the list in **a** above. Add any others they use.

Language commentary

1 *used to* and *would*

a *used to* and *would*

Used to and *would* refer to habitual or repeated past actions. We often choose to use them (instead of the Past simple) when we are looking back nostalgically at the past.

We used to get up at six o'clock, wash in cold water, have a bite to eat, and be out of the house by 6.30.

At 6.30 **we'd leave** the house. We **wouldn't get** back till seven in the evening.

b *used to* – uses

Used to refers to habitual past actions that no longer happen,

I used to walk everywhere. Now I drive like everyone else.

or to actions that didn't happen in the past but do now.

You **didn't use to** smoke, did you?

c *would* – uses

Would can refer to habitual past actions.

Early on Christmas Day the whole family **would get up** early and **go** to church.

We'd open our presents as soon as we got home.

▶ Note

Here *would* is the past form of *will* used to refer to typical or habitual behaviour.

Often if I get home late, **I'll have** a shower, watch TV and go straight to bed.

In the same way *used to* can be thought of as the past form of Present simple to refer to habitual behaviour.

I **used to eat** out twice a week. Now I **eat** at home most of the time.

d Past states

Used to but not *would* can also refer to past states as well as actions.

I **used to** (NOT ~~would~~) have perfect eyesight, now I have to wear glasses for reading.

He used to (NOT ~~would~~) be slim and fit. Just look at him now!

e *be / get used to* + *-ing*

In these two expressions *used to* means accustomed to. It is followed by *-ing*.

At first it was difficult but now **I'm quite used to getting up** early.

I expect **I'll get used to** living so near the town centre, but at the moment it seems very noisy.

2 Omitting words

In natural speech and writing we leave out unnecessary words or phrases, often to avoid repetition. This is called *ellipsis*.

a Words left out

In these examples the words which can be left out are in brackets; in all these cases ellipsis is used to avoid repetition.

My mum can play the piano but (**she**) can't read music. (Repeated subject)

He thinks (**about football**), talks (**about football**), and dreams about football. He's obsessed with it! (Repeated object)

On Sundays she wears her best coat, (**her best**) hat, and (**her best**) shoes. (Repeated pronoun and adjective)

I thought she was coming tonight but apparently she isn't (**coming tonight**). (Repeated verb)

I couldn't find my glasses so I had to borrow Tom's (**glasses**). (Repeated object)

I haven't written to her yet but I will (**write to her**) this evening. (Repeated verb)

b Possible ambiguity

Sometimes it is confusing to leave out words.

I like cheese and ham sandwiches.

This has two different meanings

I like sandwiches with cheese in and I like sandwiches with ham in.

or

I like sandwiches with cheese and ham in.

To make the meaning absolutely clear, we may need to be more precise and include all the words.

I like cheese sandwiches and I like ham sandwiches, but I don't like cheese and ham sandwiches.

c Conversation

In everyday conversation, it is not always necessary to use complete sentences. In the examples below, the following types of words and phrases are left out.

1 auxiliary verbs   2 verbs   3 pronouns
4 object of verb   5 *There's*   6 time / place expressions

• Questions.

Want a lift?	(Do you want …?)
Seen my mobile phone anywhere?	(Have you seen my mobile …?)
You coming?	(Are you coming …?)
Not tired, are you?	(You're not tired …?)

• Statements.

I've always liked black and white films – (**I**) still do (**like black and white films**.)

(**There's**) Nobody there – I'll have to try again later.

Sorry (**I**) can't stop. (**I**) must dash. (**I'll**) phone you at the weekend.

d Answers to questions / Responses to commands

It is usual to use ellipsis in replies to questions and commands; it could be impolite or potentially offensive not to do so.

Q Do you come here often?
A Yes, I do (**come here often**).

Q Ever thought of living abroad for a year or so?
A I'd love to (**live abroad for a year or so**).

Q Do you play tennis?
A I try to (**play tennis**).

C Phone your sister and tell her you're going to be late!
R I have (**phoned my sister**). / I will (**phone my sister**).

13 Conflict

13.1 Personal and professional

Lead in

1 What situations can lead to conflict in people's personal and professional lives?

2 What is your attitude to conflict? Tick any of these statements that are true for you.

   a I avoid conflict whenever possible.
   b I find it easier to deal with conflict at work.
   c I'm prepared to compromise in order to resolve conflict.
   d I don't enjoy conflict, but it doesn't upset me.
   e Conflict in my personal life really upsets me.
   f I try to resolve conflicts as quickly as possible.

Listening

1 **13.1** Listen to seven people talking about their attitude to conflict. Which of the statements in **Lead in 2** are true for each of the speakers? (Sometimes more than one statement is true for a speaker.)

2 Listen again and answer these questions about what the seven speakers say. Use the words in brackets in your answers.

   a What makes it easier for Speaker 1 to deal with conflict at work? (*structure*)
   b How does Speaker 2 manage to prevent herself getting upset about conflict? (*step back*)
   c Does Speaker 3 see his attitude to conflict as a strength or a weakness? (*failing*)
   d Why does Speaker 4 have to deal with conflict immediately? (*rest*)
   e What according to Speaker 5 should people be ready to do in conflict situations? (*compromise*)
   f Why is the fact that Speaker 6 cries and is upset a disadvantage? (*resolve / conflict*)
   g How is Speaker 7 different from her boyfriend? (*laid-back*)

React and discuss

Tell a partner about a real-life situation where you have had to deal with conflict. If you were in the same situation again, would you behave differently?

Exploring natural speech

1 Why do the speakers start their answers with the word *conflict* in these extracts rather than use 'normal' word order?

a **Conflict** – I'm getting better at it – much better than I used to be, but it's not enjoyable, it's never enjoyable having to deal with conflict …

b Well **conflict** – I'd rather not talk about it, that's basically how I deal with …

2 Reply to these questions in a similar way.

a How do you feel about family rows?

b What's your attitude to war?

c Do you find it easy to deal with disappointments?

d Do you ever have problems with your neighbours?

Listening and speaking

1 **13.2** You are going to hear part of a role play in which two people are trying to resolve a conflict. Listen and answer these questions.

a What is the situation? What is the cause of the conflict?

b What is the difference in attitude between the two men?

c Note some of the language the second man uses to try to calm the situation down.

2 Work in groups of three or four.

a Choose one of the conflict situations below and share out the roles.

Situation 1	Busy street during the rush hour
Roles	
Cyclist	You have just hit a pedestrian who was running across the road. You were listening to music on your Walkman, so you may not have been concentrating as much as you should have been.
Pedestrian	You were hurrying to work. You ran across a road and were hit by a cyclist. At the time you were hit, you were talking on your mobile phone. You were not seriously hurt, but your clothes are dirty and you will be late for work.
Other pedestrian/s	You saw exactly what happened.

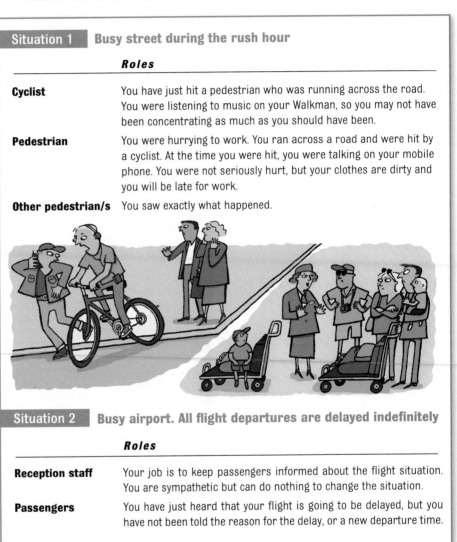

Situation 2	Busy airport. All flight departures are delayed indefinitely
Roles	
Reception staff	Your job is to keep passengers informed about the flight situation. You are sympathetic but can do nothing to change the situation.
Passengers	You have just heard that your flight is going to be delayed, but you have not been told the reason for the delay, or a new departure time.

b Prepare your part in the role play.

Use some of the language in the box and the expressions you noted in **1c**.

- Don't lose your temper. / There's no need to lose your temper.
- I don't want to get into an argument.
- It was just an accident.
- It's nobody's fault. / No one's really to blame.
- Let me (try to) explain.
- Look, calm down. / Take it easy.
- There's nothing I can do about it.
- What's it got to do with you? / It's none of your business.

c Work in groups and try to resolve the situation.

13.2 Only a game

Lead in

Think about your childhood.
Discuss these questions.

1 Did you often visit playgrounds?
Where were they? What were
they like?

2 How well did you get on with other
children?

3 Did you ever get involved in
arguments or fights? How did they
start? How did they end?

Reading

1 You are going to read an article
about a *playground with a difference*.
These six words are used in the
article. What is the difference in
meaning between each pair?

  a *bullying fighting*
  b *hit hurt*
  c *uncoordinated unfit*

2 Now read the article. Find three
reasons why Asbjorn Flemmen
thinks fighting could be good for
children.

3 Answer these questions.

  a According to Asbjorn Flemmen,
  what are the effects of
  overprotective adults on children?

  b In what way do children use
  rules?

  c How do Professor Olweus' ideas
  differ from Flemmen's?

  d Does the Skudeneshavn
  experiment support Flemmen's
  ideas or those of his critics?

React and discuss

Compare ideas in small groups.
Do you feel the same about Asbjorn
Flemmen's views?

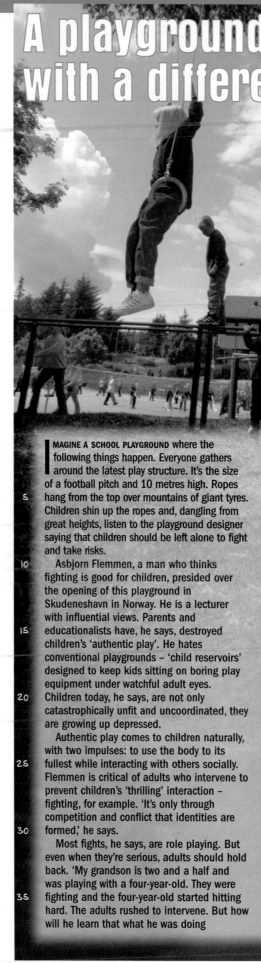

A playground with a difference

IMAGINE A SCHOOL PLAYGROUND where the
following things happen. Everyone gathers
around the latest play structure. It's the size
of a football pitch and 10 metres high. Ropes
hang from the top over mountains of giant tyres. 5
Children shin up the ropes and, dangling from
great heights, listen to the playground designer
saying that children should be left alone to fight
and take risks.

Asbjorn Flemmen, a man who thinks 10
fighting is good for children, presided over
the opening of this playground in
Skudeneshavn in Norway. He is a lecturer
with influential views. Parents and
educationalists have, he says, destroyed 15
children's 'authentic play'. He hates
conventional playgrounds – 'child reservoirs'
designed to keep kids sitting on boring play
equipment under watchful adult eyes.
Children today, he says, are not only 20
catastrophically unfit and uncoordinated, they
are growing up depressed.

Authentic play comes to children naturally,
with two impulses: to use the body to its
fullest while interacting with others socially. 25
Flemmen is critical of adults who intervene to
prevent children's 'thrilling' interaction –
fighting, for example. 'It's only through
competition and conflict that identities are
formed,' he says. 30

Most fights, he says, are role playing. But
even when they're serious, adults should hold
back. 'My grandson is two and a half and
was playing with a four-year-old. They were
fighting and the four-year-old started hitting 35
hard. The adults rushed to intervene. But how
will he learn that what he was doing

will make his friend cry and that he himself
won't like that? You can tell a child that
hurting others is wrong, but they only learn 40
from real feelings.'

In free play, children's conflicts revolve
around how they will play, what they will play
and who they will play with. They constantly
make rules – not to keep things under control, 45
but to make the outcome more unpredictable.
Flemmen describes two children with a
football. One wants to shoot at goal from too
close, so the other refuses to play. The first
child hesitates, then says: 'OK then.' 50

'OK then', repeats Flemmen, 'the two most
important words in the language. They've
agreed on a compromise which allows the
thrill to continue. They are at the edge of
what they can manage; this is what triggers 55
development.'

Of course Flemmen has his critics.
Professor Dan Olweus, an authority on
bullying, insists that while teachers should be
taught to distinguish between play and real 60
fighting, children should not be left alone.
'Research shows there's a direct relation
between the number of adults supervising
and the amount of bullying – more adults
equals fewer bullies.' 65

But the evidence from Skudeneshavn is
impressive. Parents and teachers are stunned
by the improvements in children's levels of
fitness. They are equally thrilled by the social
effects. The school no longer separates the 70
small children from the big ones and the
adults all insist that bullying has
disappeared.

Ros Coward, *The Guardian*

Language focus: -ing forms

1 Here are six of the uses of the -ing form of the verb in English. Which of the uses **a–f** apply to extracts **1–6** below from the article? Some extracts illustrate two uses.

Uses

a part of a continuous or progressive verb tense
b an adjective
c a noun
d after certain verbs
e to introduce a clause (often after a conjunction)
f instead of a relative clause

Extracts

1 … listen to the playground designer **saying** that children should be left alone …
2 … a man who thinks **fighting** is good for children.
3 … keep kids **sitting** on **boring** play equipment under watchful adult eyes.
4 … to use the body to its fullest while **interacting** with others socially.
5 They were **fighting** and the four-year-old started **hitting** hard.
6 … a direct relation between the number of adults **supervising** and the …

2 -ing forms are often used to link ideas.

*He climbed up the tree, **forgetting** he didn't have any shoes on.*

Join these pairs of sentences using an -ing form. You may have to use negatives and passives.

a He ran out of the playground. He slammed the gate behind him.
b They think they may get into trouble. Parents don't let their children play in the street.
c She sent a text message. She didn't realize the teacher was watching her.
d The woman was interviewed several times. This was before she was arrested.

— Close up —

1.6 *shin up* is an informal alternative for a more common verb. Work out which verb from the context.

1.6 What other word in paragraph 1 has a similar meaning to *dangle*?

1.17 What is normally kept in *reservoirs*?

Exploitation

Replace the words and phrases in **bold** in these conflict stories with -ing forms and any words in brackets. You will sometimes need to join sentences.

1 Passengers **who were travelling**[1] on a flight from Miami to Puerto Rico were amazed when a deranged passenger walked to the back of the plane and then started to run up the aisle. **He slapped**[2] passengers' heads along the way. He then kicked a pregnant flight attendant and bit a young boy on the arm. Cabin crew restrained the man (by) **they jumped**[3] on him and **held**[4] him down. He was arrested when the plane landed.

2 On another flight, for some unknown reason, a **drunken passenger** (who)[1] started throwing peanuts at a well-built man **who was** (sit)[2] with his wife. **He was minding**[3] his own business. When the first peanut hit him in the face, he ignored it. **After he was struck**[4] by a second peanut, he looked up to see who had thrown it. He gave the man a dirty look, **and expected**[5] him to stop immediately. When a third peanut hit him in the eye, he'd had enough. 'Do that again' he said, 'and I'll punch your lights out.' But the peanut-thrower couldn't resist. **He threw**[6] one last peanut. **The victim got out of his seat and**[7] punched the man so hard that witnesses heard his jaw break.

Up high in the sky, The Guardian

Writing

The two 'flying stories' above were taken from a collection of conflict stories published on an Internet website. You are going to write a similar single-paragraph conflict story.

1 Decide on a story. Choose one of these alternatives.

a Something that actually happened to you as a child.
b A story with one of these endings.

• *Eventually the captain intervened to separate the struggling passengers.*
• *The smile disappeared from his face as he was rushed to hospital with a suspected broken leg.*

2 Write your story in **100–150** words. Use an informal style appropriate for casual Internet readers.

▶ **Writing guidelines p.151**

13.3 Families at war

Lead in

1 Discuss these ideas in pairs or groups.

   a What kinds of things do you and members of your family argue about?

   b Which members of your family do you have arguments with?

2 **13.3** Now listen to five people talking about the same subjects. How do they answer the questions? (Not all the speakers answer both questions.)

Reading

1 Read the profiles in which people describe one of their parents.

   a Who are the writers describing?

   b What factual details do we find out about the person the writers are describing?

2 What are the similarities and differences between the two descriptions? Think about

Focus
   • Which description focuses on the importance of a significant event?
   • How is the other description different?

Attitude
   • What are the writers' feelings towards their parents?

Style
   • Which description is more conversational?
   • How is the other description different?

3 Choose the best answer to these questions about the two profiles.

   a How did the father react when his son refused to apologize? (Profile A)

      1 He lost his temper.
      2 He accepted his son's refusal.
      3 He patiently repeated his request.

   b As the son left the house, what did he realize? (Profile A)

      1 That he had offended his father.
      2 That his relationship with his father would never change.
      3 That his relationship with his father would never be the same again.

   c How do the boy and his mother look at each other in the poem? (Profile B)

      1 They glance secretly at each other.
      2 They look into each other's eyes.
      3 They look shyly at each other and then look away.

A

I was about to go to college; I must have been eighteen and still living at home. I'd made some remark to my father that he wanted an apology for. He blew his top and insisted I apologize, but I didn't think I was in the wrong. A year before, I'd have done it and slunk out. I just looked at him and walked out of the house. I knew from that moment that I'd cracked it. He's never behaved like that to me again. I'd say I felt it as a mixture of freedom and pity. I was actually sorry for him – I suppose I didn't like to see him beaten. I was the last of three sons and I was leaving home. My father was a school teacher and he was very old-fashioned. The thing that irritated me a lot was how he used to shout at us children. 'I will not have you behaving in that way in my house!' It made me wonder where the rest of us lived. He also used to try and send us to our rooms when we were quite old. He just always had to be in control.

Men

B

Staring at her makes you laugh
(I don't know why!)
Our eyes are locked together
Like heat-seeking missiles and an enemy plane
Her hair is black like the deep dark night   5
Her ears are quite small like tiny little shells
Her personality changes at every time of the day
She scratches my back
(Where I can't reach)
She cares for me like a leopard and her cub   10
She's my mother and I love her.

I wrote that poem when I was nine. I'm fourteen now, and in the time that has passed I have slowly started to see my mother in a different light. As I get older she seems to get younger. We are beginning to watch and listen to the same things. I always thought she was a fountain of knowledge, perfect in every way. I suppose I saw her in the same way as any young child views his mother, but it is only now that I can look back and see how little of my mother I actually knew.

My mother can still make me laugh…   20

Sons and Mothers

Language focus: singular or plural?

1 Complete these sentences with the appropriate form of the verb in brackets.

   a *My family .... (be) very important to me.*

   b *The cabin crew .... (have) worked hard to make our flight an enjoyable experience.*

   c *My generation .... (have) very different ideas from those of our parents.*

2 What have *family*, *cabin crew*, and *generation* got in common? What other nouns can you think of like this?

3 Why are different verbs/verb forms used in these pairs of sentences with the same subjects?

   a *The government **has** announced a complete ban on smoking in public places.*
     *The government **have** been arguing for months about the best education policies.*

   b *The team **is** expected to win the World Cup this year.*
     *The team **are** all keen to show how much they have improved since last year.*

   c *A recently married couple **has** just moved into the flat next door.*
     *The couple **are** having a baby in June. They're absolutely delighted.*

4 Names of specific organizations, companies, etc. are also like this.

   a The UN **is**/**are** sending peace-keeping forces to more and more countries.

   b Ford **has**/**have** increased their share of the world car market this year.

   What other organizations like these can you think of?

Exploitation

1 Finish each of these sentences in two or three different ways. Make up sentences which are factually true, not matters of opinion.

   a In my experience, the older generation …

   b The local council …

   c My favourite football team …

   d The government in my country …

2 Work in pairs.

   a Compare your endings to sentences **1a–d**.

   b Now spend 2–3 minutes talking about each of these subjects.

     • A multi-national corporation

     • Your favourite pop group, orchestra, jazz band, etc.

     • Your English class

Speaking

Work in groups.

You are going to discuss this statement.

> Families do more harm than good.

1 Prepare for the discussion. Think about these issues:

   • the effects of parents on children and vice-versa

   • alternatives to the family as a natural social grouping

   • psychological effects of conflict

   • responsibilities for looking after elderly relatives

   • problems of inheritance.

Think of examples from real-life – you needn't refer to your own family.

2 Follow this procedure.

   a Each person in the group should make a brief opening statement.

   b The group then discusses the subject.

   c Finally, the class as a whole votes on whether they agree or disagree with the statement.

Exploring words

Conflict

1 Complete sentences 1–6 with appropriate verbs from this list. There may be more than one possible answer.

Verbs	avoid	create	crush	deal with	end	lose	quell
	reach	resolve	settle	spark off	win		

a After months of bitter arguments we'd had enough and did our best to .... a compromise.

b The demonstration led to violence and in the end the police were called in to .... the riot.

c We disagreed about almost everything, so it didn't take much to .... a row.

d Diplomats have an important role to play in .... international conflicts.

e Children often seem to want to .... arguments between their parents.

f My boyfriend hates any kind of unpleasantness – in fact he'll do anything to .... conflict.

2 a Find the conflict words and phrases in these newspaper headlines.

b Work in groups.

Who is the conflict between in each story? For example, in the second headline opposite the *soldiers* are in conflict with *civilians*. Briefly discuss the possible stories behind each headline.

c Now write the first sentences of the stories behind three of the headlines.

Example
Government soldiers last night opened fire on thousands of civilians who were rioting in protest against the recent 50% rise in petrol prices.

d Make up headlines for current news stories you know of which involve conflict.

Fight to end child labour

Soldiers fire on rioting civilians

Ex-spy to challenge secrecy laws

Spy plane row

Supermarket wins battle over cheap imports

Party leader attacks rival

US expels 10 diplomats

Top European clubs in cup clash

FURY AT RAIL FARE RISES

Language commentary

1 -ing forms

Here are some of the many uses of -ing forms.

a Part of a continuous verb form
You're **wasting** your time.

b As an adjective
That book was so **boring** that I couldn't finish it.

c As a noun
Fishing is one of the country's most popular sports.

d After certain verbs
Do you **deny stealing** my car?

e After prepositions
I can't pass my old house **without remembering** all the happy times I had there.

f In certain clauses
- As an alternative to a reason clause.
  Feeling ashamed of what I'd done, I rang my wife and told her everything. (Because I felt ashamed …)
- As an alternative to a time clause.
  Having seen the queue of cars, I turned round and went another way. (As soon as I saw …)
- As an alternative to a result clause.
  The river overflowed its banks, **causing serious flooding**. (… and so caused …)
- As an alternative to a relative clause.
  There's someone **climbing that tree**. (… someone who is climbing …)

g verb + preposition + -ing form
I thought I'd never **succeed in passing** my driving test.

Other common verbs like this
admit to   agree with   apologize for   believe in   depend on   feel like   insist on   object to   put up with   rely on   think of

Verbs with about
complain about   worry about, etc.

h verb + object + preposition + -ing form
They **accused him of shoplifting**.

Other common verbs like this
blame someone for   congratulate someone on   discourage someone from   forgive someone for   prevent someone from   stop someone from   thank someone for   use something for

i adjective + preposition + -ing form
He's **incapable of saying** anything sensible.
Who's **responsible for collecting** the money?

Other adjectives + prepositions
afraid of   ashamed of   aware of   bored with   different from   famous for   fed up with   fond of   good or bad at   guilty of   happy about   interested in   keen on   pleased about   sorry about   wrong with

2 Singular or plural?

a Groups
Singular nouns referring to groups can be followed by singular or plural verbs. When we think of the group as a body of people doing something together we are more likely to use a singular verb.
The government **is** doing its best to cut the unemployment figures.
The army urgently **needs** new recruits.

When we think of the group as a collection of individuals, a plural verb is more likely.
Throughout the flight the cabin crew **were** polite and efficient.
Without exception, the class **have** worked hard for their end-of-year exams.

b Organizations
Organizations referred to by name can also be thought of as singular or plural.
The BBC **is / are** famous for the quality of **its / their** TV and radio programmes.
Sony **is / are** opening new factories in several European countries.

c Sports teams
Singular names of sports teams are usually followed by plural verbs.
Real Madrid **look** like winning the cup for the third year running.
At half-time Brazil **were** winning 2–0.

d Special groups
These nouns, which are singular in form, are always used with plural verbs. The words or phrases for one or several of the individuals in the group are given in brackets.
police   (a police officer / six police officers)
people   (a person / 100 people)
cattle   (a cow, bull / 25 cattle)
clergy   (a member of the clergy / 25 members of the clergy)

e Spoken language
- Occasionally, especially in speech, people mistakenly use a plural verb because it sounds right. They make the verb agree with the noun closest to it.
  Not **one** of the **children have** handed in their homework.
  Paul is one of the few **people** I know who **don't** drive a car.
- In speech people commonly use plural nouns after some singular expressions:
  There's too many **people** here.
  Here's the books I borrowed from you.
  Where's my clean **clothes**?

  It would be more correct to use *There are …*, *Here are …*, *Where are …?* in these examples.

14 Work

14.1 Time management

Lead in

1 Do this quiz, then compare answers with a partner.

How good is your time management?

1	I try to do as many things at once as I can.	T/F
2	I find it hard to say 'No' when people ask me to do things.	T/F
3	I have to do everything perfectly however long it takes.	T/F
4	People often interrupt me when I'm working.	T/F
5	I always read and reply to e-mails as soon as I get them.	T/F
6	Jobs always take longer than I expect.	T/F
7	I leave difficult tasks for the next day.	T/F

2 **14.1** Listen to Lorna, a management trainer, describing the problems people come to her with.

a Which of the subjects in the quiz above does she refer to?

b **14.2** Listen to the second part of the recording. What four suggestions does Lorna make for improving time management?

c Which of her suggestions do you find the most useful? Compare ideas in pairs.

Reading

1 You are going to read an article about the way people spend their time at work. Before you read, discuss these questions, which contain key phrases from the article.

a In what situations do people need to *collect their thoughts*?

b Think of examples of *onerous tasks* at work or at home.

c How do you approach a *complex task*?

2 Read the article. Is the tone *humorous* or *serious*?

3 Match these summaries (a–e) with the appropriate paragraphs (1–5) of the article.

a Very short pauses can be useful.
b The trickiest period of time to fill usefully.
c An important quality for effective work.
d Longer pauses can be welcome.
e However well organized you are, colleagues can ruin your plans.

Close up

1.8 *Whatever* means *it doesn't matter what*. Which similar words refer to people, times, places?

1.12 When do you make mental lists?

1.16 What word could be used instead of *co-worker*?

1.22 What is the simpler, more usual term for a *beverage-assisted relaxation period*?

THE HARDEST TIME SLOT TO FILL

1 Time management is an important skill to possess in the fast-paced modern world of big business. This ability is so useful that the temporally challenged can take courses and even gain qualifications in structuring their day.

2 Every plan though has its weak points and in the case of time management, as with most other forms of planning, it lies in people. These are an ever-growing threat to the proper organization of society especially when they all take a different amount of time to do whatever you want to get done. Because of this you will frequently find yourself with a short period of time to fill between ending one task and starting another.

3 Often this pause in useful activity will be very short and will allow you to collect your thoughts, make a mental list of all the jobs you can safely put off until tomorrow or remind yourself of that television programme you plan to watch after dinner.

4 You will also encounter extended break-downs in scheduling, for instance because a co-worker found it necessary to cancel an hour-long meeting, leaving you with plenty of time to complete a complex or onerous task.

5 There is another amount of unexpected free time though. Twenty minutes. You will be unable to eat lunch in less than twenty-five minutes and a coffee break cannot be stretched beyond fifteen without the addition of another cup of coffee which will take the beverage-assisted relaxation period to twenty-three minutes or more. A brief pause could be used for a quick trip to the toilet, a long break could house a shower or even a bath, but twenty minutes offers no hope of a wash and a call of nature begins to look suspicious if it lasts for longer than six and a half minutes. If left with many hours on your hands you might be able to compose an uplifting symphony. With only three minutes you have the chance of whistling a joyful ditty to yourself but with the unholy gap of twenty minutes you can do neither.

Alex Gough

Language focus: ability and possibility

1 Which of these extracts from the article refer to abilities and which refer to possibilities?

a *... the temporally challenged can take courses and even gain qualifications ...*
b *... make a mental list of all the jobs you can safely put off until tomorrow ...*
c *... a coffee break cannot be stretched beyond fifteen (minutes) ...*
d *A brief pause could be used for a quick trip to the toilet ...*

2 Which of these sentences refer to abilities and which refer to possibilities?

a *You will be unable to eat lunch in less than twenty-five minutes.*
b *I had so many interruptions that I didn't manage to reply to your e-mail.*
c *If left with many hours on your hands, you might be able to compose an uplifting ...*
d *Eventually I succeeded in finishing the report.*

3 Which two sentences in **2a–d** can be rephrased using *can*, *can't*, or *could*? Why is this not possible for the other two sentences?

Exploitation

1 Complete this short text using as many of these alternatives as possible. You may need to use the negative.

be able to	can (could)
manage to	succeed in

I've been trying to phone my boss since 8 o'clock this morning, but unfortunately I .... (get)[1] through. He's probably got held up in traffic. He's an amazing man, my boss. He'll soon be 70 but he .... (still ride)[2] a bicycle. I hope I .... (cycle)[3] when I'm 70. Last weekend on his way to work he had a puncture. Unfortunately he didn't have his pump with him so he .... (not ride)[4] to the office. Eventually he .... (stop)[5] a passing car and persuaded the driver to take him and his bike all the way to work. He has always been a fitness fanatic. Apparently, when he was younger he .... (climb)[6] the ten storeys to his office in less time than it took to go up in the lift. I .... (do)[7] it to save my life. Another example is that he .... (still touch)[8] his toes quite easily. I .... (not / touch)[9] mine since my accident.

Speaking

Work in groups.

1 What is your idea of a well-balanced working week? Plan an ideal weekly schedule for employees working in an office in your country. Take account of these factors:

- employees' families – children, etc.
- travel to and from work
- health, earnings, morale
- the demands of employers: productivity, etc.

2 Present your ideas to the rest of the class.

14.2 The big wide world

Lead in

What are the plus and minus points of these jobs?

- Office worker
- Teacher
- Actor
- Bus or lorry driver
- Hospital nurse or doctor

Listening

1 You are going to hear four people in their early twenties discussing their future. What do you think the phrases (in *italics*) they use mean? What does the use of the verb *get* in **a–d** suggest about the speakers' feelings?

 a I don't want to *get stuck* in a boring job.
 b ... I hope I don't *get kicked out* of university ...
 c And you probably *get sucked into* a job because of the pay.
 d You might *get head-hunted* by a company on the look out for bright young graduates.
 e If you want to stay at university you'll probably have to *fund yourself*.

2 **14.3** Now listen.

 a What kinds of things worry the speakers about getting jobs?
 b What kind of job do they all seem to want?

3 Listen to the conversation again and answer these questions.

 a One of the women says *I could not work in an office*. What does she dislike about office work?
 b When one of the speakers refers to *a job in the City*, he means a well-paid job, probably in the financial sector. What do they feel about this kind of job?
 c Why would having *a good lifestyle, a nice flat, and a mobile phone* be a problem?
 d Why, according to one of the women, is it difficult or impossible to save money?
 e Why would making a lot of money quickly be particularly attractive to these young people?

Exploring natural speech

Which words could be used instead of the colloquial adjectives in **bold** in these extracts from the conversation?

 a I'll get a **great** job.
 b ... a really **nice** flat and a mobile phone ...
 c ... it's just going to be for a year or two and you've got **better** things you want to do.
 d ... going into your first real **grown-up** job ...
 e ... it's more **scary** that I'm not going into ...

React and discuss

1 Does the attitude of these young people surprise you? Do you sympathize with them?

2 Imagine you were about to start your career.

 a What kind of job would you prefer, for example manual, clerical, etc.?
 b What would be your hopes – and worst fears?

Vocabulary: phrasal verbs with *out*

Out can affect the meaning of a verb in various ways. In this extract, *out* suggests the idea of removal or exclusion.

*… my major hopes and fears are that I won't get **kicked out** of university.*

Put the verbs in sentences **1–9** into one of three meaning groups below. (There are three verbs in each group.)

A Sharing and distributing
B Coming to an end
C Removing, excluding, preventing

1 On this new diet I have to *cut out* cheese completely.
2 Who's going to *deal out* the cards?
3 No one knows quite why dinosaurs *died out*.
4 The new government is doing everything it can to *stamp out* hooliganism.
5 Soldiers have been *handing out* food rations all day.
6 During the strike the management *locked* the workers *out*.
7 I'm afraid we'll have to stop there – time has *run out*.
8 The five lottery winners *shared out* the money equally.
9 I should think the prime minister will be *voted out* at the next election.

Language focus: *someone, everybody, anything*

Something and *everyone* are 'indefinite pronouns'.

*I'll get a great job, I don't know, maybe, I don't know, **something** in theatre or TV, or **something** fun but **everyone** wants to do that.*

Check how much you know about these pronouns.

a Are these statements True or False?

1 There is no difference in meaning between *someone* and *somebody* or between *everyone* and *everybody*.
2 *Anyone* and *somebody* are followed by singular verbs.
3 *Everybody* and *everyone* are followed by plural verbs.
4 *Anyone*, *nobody*, and *everyone* can be used with the pronouns *they* and *them*.
5 *No one* and *nothing* are used with negative verbs.
6 *Anyone* and *anything*, etc. are more common in negative statements than *someone* and *something*.

b One of these sentences is not correct. Which one?

1 *Anyone can find a job if they look hard enough.*
2 *Did anything interesting happen at work today?*
3 *Everyone I know has taught themselves to use a computer.*
4 *It's been really quiet at work today. I haven't done absolutely nothing all morning.*
5 *Would you like something else to do?*

c What is the difference between *any* and *every*?

1 *You could have any job you wanted.*
2 *You could have every job you wanted.*

Exploitation

1 Complete these sentences about your family, friends, and other acquaintances, then find other students in the class with similar answers.

a Everyone in my family …
b Nobody I know …
c I've never met anyone …
d Someone in my family …
e I can't understand how anyone …

2 Now make generalizations about people of your nationality, using these phrases.

| almost everyone | hardly anyone | no one at all |

Example
Almost everyone over the age of 15 owns a mobile phone.

Compare ideas in pairs or groups.

Speaking and writing

1 What would be your ideal job? Think about:
  • type of work, location, working conditions, salary, and perks*
  • colleagues, management structure, and social aspects
  • job security and career prospects.

* a perk is a benefit an employee receives from an employer in addition to money, for example, a company car.

2 Tell a partner in detail about your ideal job.

3 Write a job description for your partner's ideal job. Include the following information.
  • Job title, location, salary, and other perks
  • A description of what the job involves (**50–75** words)
    You will spend most of your time in our London office, but will be expected to travel both in Britain and abroad several times a year.
  • A description of the kind of person who would be suitable for the job (**40–60** words)
    The ideal candidate should be between the ages of 20 and 25, have a good standard of education, and be able to speak at least one foreign language.

4 Exchange job descriptions with your partner. Read what they have written and decide whether or not you would apply for the job.

Exploring words

Euphemisms

1 A *euphemism* is a word or phrase used to avoid saying another word or phrase that is more forceful and honest but also more direct and therefore possibly more offensive or embarrassing. These 'sensitive' subjects may include

A Wealth and poverty   D Ability   G Employment
B Death, illness, etc.   E Age
C Dishonesty   F Alcohol

   a Match the euphemisms in the list below to one of the subjects **A–G** above.

> between jobs   comfortably off   from a deprived background   disinformation
> economical with the truth   economically inactive   enjoy a drink   pass away
> hard of hearing   hard-up   imaginative journalism   in your golden years   less able
> mature   slip away   have a drink problem   unwaged   visually handicapped

   b Which of these euphemisms might you use to describe the following:

      1 a politician who regularly told lies?
      2 a class of slow-learning school children?
      3 your friend who has lost his job and not found another?
      4 an acquaintance who is frequently drunk?
      5 someone who is never short of money?
      6 your 80-year-old grandfather?

2 **14.4** You are going to hear some extracts from conversations.

   a What sensitive subject is each conversation about?
   b Make a note of the euphemisms the speakers use.
   c What do you think each euphemism means?

3 Many euphemisms include a negative word. For example, you could describe an illiterate person as *not a great reader*.

   a What do you think the negative expressions in these sentences really mean?

      1 I'm afraid my brother's *no scholar*.
      2 The West should try and help the *non-industrialized* countries.
      3 You'll have to talk very slowly to her – she's *not all there* today.
      4 You'll just have to slow down a bit – don't forget you're *not as young as you were*.
      5 Didn't anyone tell you about Jack – I'm sorry but he's *no longer with us*.
      6 I find it quite difficult to talk to Richard. He's *not the most sociable of people*.

   b Try inventing some negative euphemisms of your own. Think of indirect ways of referring to the fact that someone is:

      1 unintelligent
      2 confused and irrational
      3 always drunk
      4 unemployed
      5 unfriendly
      6 ill.

4 Discuss these questions in groups.

   a When are euphemisms used in your language? What subjects do they usually refer to?
   b Are certain types or groups of people more likely to use euphemistic language than others? Why do you think this might be?
   c Do you think euphemisms are likely to cause confusion or misunderstandings?

Language commentary

1 Ability and possibility

a Physical abilities or learned skills

- *Can*, *could*, and *be able to* are used to refer to abilities and skills.
  Birds **can sleep** while they're flying.
  I **can't sleep** if there's a lot of noise.
  My sister **could read** when she was only three years old.
  I **couldn't walk** till I was nearly two.

- *Be able to* is used for all tenses.
  I've been able to play the piano since I was seven.
  If she trains hard, **she'll be able to run** in the marathon next year.
  If **he'd been able to speak,** he could have told us exactly what happened.

- The affirmative *could* is used to refer to general abilities in the past but not specific abilities.
  When I was younger I **could sleep** anywhere. (general)
  I couldn't get to sleep last night. I was worried about a problem at work. After a lot of tossing and turning, **I managed to get / succeeded in getting to sleep** at 4 o'clock. (specific: on one occasion)

b Possibilities

Can and *could* can also refer to potential or possibility.
Autumn **can** be very wet in the British Isles.
When I started smoking you **could** buy a packet of cigarettes for less than a pound. (Also **It was possible to** …)
You'd better answer the phone – it **could** be something important. (Also **it may / might** …)

c Other uses of *can* and *could*

- Permission.
  You **can't buy** alcohol until you're 18.
  Can / Could I be excused, please? I have an urgent appointment.

- Asking, offering, inviting.
  Can / Could you tell me the time please?
  Can / Could I give you a lift to the airport?
  Can you come to our village festival at the weekend?

2 Indefinite pronouns

People	someone	somebody	anyone	anybody	everyone
	everybody	no one	nobody		
Things	something	anything	everything	nothing	
Places	somewhere	anywhere	everywhere	nowhere	

a *someone (somebody), something,* and *somewhere*

These mean a particular person, thing, or place and are used in affirmative statements and some questions.
I've got **something** to tell you.
I heard **someone** on the radio explaining how they learned English.
Is there **somewhere** we can meet?

b *anyone (anybody), anything,* and *anywhere*

These mean a person, thing, or place but not a particular person, thing, or place, and are used in negative statements and most questions.
Has **anyone** seen Nick's guitar?
I haven't got **anything** to say.
I haven't got **anywhere** to hide.

c *anyone, anything,* and *anywhere* in affirmative statements

In affirmative statements these mean a person, thing, or place – it doesn't matter who/which thing or place.
Anyone can learn to ride a horse – it just takes time and practice.
I can eat **anything** if I'm hungry enough.
We can go **anywhere** you like – it really doesn't matter to me.

▶ Note The difference between *someone* and *anyone* and *something* and *anything* is similar to the difference between *some* and *any*.

d *no one (nobody), nothing,* and *nowhere*

These mean not one person, thing, or place, and are used with singular affirmative verbs.
I know **nobody** who **enjoys** going to the dentist.
Nothing succeeds like success.
There's nowhere to hide.

e *everyone (everybody), everything,* and *everywhere*

These mean every individual person, thing, and place, and are used with singular verbs.
Everyone I know was at the party.
You've taught me **everything** I know.
Everywhere seems to be busier than it was ten years ago.

f Indefinite pronouns – uses

- Followed by adjectives.
  Did you meet **anyone interesting** at the party?
  No one new has arrived since you left.
  There's **something wrong** with the car. It won't start.

- Followed by *to* + infinitive.
  I'm bored. I've got **nothing to do**.
  Can you think of **anywhere to go** this evening?

- As the object of a reduced relative clause.
  Everything I read reminds me of her. (= everything that I read)
  I'd like to tell you a story about **someone I met** on holiday last year. (= someone that I met)

15 Behaviour

15.1 Why do they do it?

Lead in

1 How competitive are you? Have you ever been the best or the worst at anything?

Compare ideas with a partner. Try to use some of the expressions from this list.

| good at | bad at | top of | number one | get to the top |

2 **15.1** Listen to four people talking about how competitive they are.

a How would you rank the speakers in order of competitiveness?
b Are any of the speakers like you?

Reading

1 Work in pairs.

Student A Turn to p.159 and read the news story.

Student B Read the news story on this page. Make a note of key facts so that you can tell your partner the story later.

a What did the person actually do?
b How would you explain their motives?

2 Tell each other about the strange behaviour described in the story you read. Try to do this from the notes you made and without referring to the story itself.

React and discuss

1 What do you think motivates the people described in the stories?

2 Would you prefer to go in for a *screaming* or a *kissing* competition? Why?

Close up

l.11   To *outscream* means to scream *louder* than someone else. What do you think these verbs mean: *outrun*? *outlive*? *outnumber*? *outplay*?

l.6 & l.12   Notice how the article refers to people's ages. How could you use the word *year* or *years* instead?

l.28   How could you start or end this sentence with the word *each*?

Test of vocal cords is a scream for Polish winner

A young Polish woman has become Europe's screaming champion for the second time, beating 300 rivals from many
5 parts of the world.
Dagmara Stanek, 25, from the Baltic resort of Sopot, emitted a scream of just over 126 decibels, equivalent to the noise
10 of a racing car travelling at top speed. She outscreamed a male rival, Pawel Dabrowski, 35, from Warsaw, who produced a five-second scream of 125.3
15 decibels, defending his 1999 title of best male screamer.
Europe's only vocal noise competition, modelled on an annual screaming festival in
20 Japan, took place in the town of Goldap in Poland's north-eastern lake district.
'We allowed them to scream greetings like 'I love you' or 'I like you', the only restriction 25 was they were not allowed to swear,' said the director, Andrzej Sokolowski. The winners each took home a colour television set. 30
The judges measured the highest scream level of each contestant with equipment normally used by environmental inspectors to 35 check noisy workplaces and neighbours. Mr Sokolowski said he hoped to persuade representatives of the Guinness Book of Records 40 to record the results at next year's competition. Mr Sokolowski is also behind Poland's first kissing championship, to be held in 45 October.

Kate Connolly, *The Guardian*

Language focus: alternatives to relative clauses

1 We tend to use relative clauses in writing more frequently than in speaking. But why do you think the newspaper stories you have read sometimes avoid using relative clauses? Compare these two sentences. (Sentence **a** is from the first story.)

   a *She outscreamed a male rival, Pawel Dabrowski, 35, from Warsaw …*

   b *She outscreamed a male rival, who was called Pawel Dabrowski, who was 35 and who came from Warsaw …*

2 Where could relative clauses have been used in these extracts from the articles?

   a *Dagmara Stanek, 25, from the Baltic resort of Sopot, emitted a scream of just over 126 decibels, equivalent to the noise of a racing car travelling at top speed.*

   b *Europe's only vocal noise competition, modelled on an annual screaming festival in Japan, took place in the town of Goldap …*

   c *The judges measured the highest scream level of each contestant with equipment normally used to check noisy workplaces and neighbours.*

   d *Mr Sokolowski is also behind Poland's first kissing championship, to be held in October.*

3 Rewrite **2a–d** using relative clauses wherever possible. What kind of relative clauses are these – defining or non-defining? (See Language commentary **2b**, p.87)

Exploitation

1 a Rewrite this story as a newspaper report, reducing it to 85 words or fewer. Change punctuation where necessary.

> John Philips, who is 37 years old and comes from the North West, said his wife, who is called Edwina, had left him because of his 10-year addiction to gambling. Philips, who works as a senior accountant with a company which is based in the centre of Manchester, appeared in court, where he was accused of dangerous driving. Colleagues and others who are close to Mr Philips say he is heart-broken. Tim Roberts, who has been a friend of Philips since the two were at school together, said he can't stop thinking about his wife. 'John's doing everything he can to win Edwina back.'

   b Now work in pairs. Your shortened version is still too long and the editor has asked you to cut it. How much shorter can you make the story without leaving out important information? You will need to use different words.

   c Compare versions with other pairs of students. Who has the shortest, most accurate version of the story?

2 Now write a story in the same style, using alternatives to relative clauses. Use one of these headlines or an idea of your own. Write about **80** words.

American couple win world kissing competition

Woman escapes from block of ice after 65-minute struggle

Silence is golden – Australian says nothing for 367 days

Speaking

Work in groups.

1 Think of some original ideas for record-breaking competitions. Try and think of ideas that are even crazier than those you've read about in this lesson.

2 Present your ideas to the rest of the class.

15.2 Honesty?

Lead in

1 Look at the pictures. What is the connection between them, do you think?

2 This is the result of a survey.

a What questions were people asked?
b Are you surprised by the results?

> Young people today are under so much pressure to succeed that some admit they would lie, cheat and sleep with the boss if it would help
> 5 them get on.
>   With surprising honesty, a substantial minority revealed just how low they would sink in pursuit of success – which to 70% of them is
> 10 defined as wealth and career.
>   Out of nearly 1,000 young people questioned, 13% said they would sleep with their boss if it might advance their prospects. Even more
> 15 – 17% – admitted they would be willing to do something ethically and morally wrong. A quarter said they would be willing to be dishonest.
>
>   *The Guardian*

3 Give examples of what you consider to be:

- being dishonest
- cheating
- doing something ethically or morally wrong.

Listening

1 **15.2** You are going to hear five people talking about cheating. Listen and match speakers 1–5 with one of these statements. (One statement does not apply to any of the speakers.)

a He/she was caught cheating at an early age. ....
b He/she never had the chance to cheat. ....
c He/she thinks that small-scale cheating is a natural part of sport. ....
d He/she had an adult motive for cheating. ....
e He/she cheated in a serious exam. ....
f He/she has always resisted the temptation to cheat at sport. ....

2 Listen again.

a How many of the speakers admit to having cheated?
b What did they do?
c Have you ever cheated in any of these ways? Talk about it with a partner.

Exploring natural speech

Look at these two extracts from the recording.

1 Why do speakers use the auxiliary verb *did* in these extracts?

… I **did** cheat once – it wasn't an exam exactly – it was a course I was doing – a sort of training course …

I think as a very young child I found it very hard to lose at Monopoly and I **did** cheat once and my family …

2 Add auxiliary verbs to these sentences. How would you say them?

a I have to confess, I took a crib sheet into the exam with me.

b I'm ashamed to say, I copied from my friend in a science test.

c I must admit, I wrote a very good essay.

d It's hard to believe, but she occasionally cheats at sport.

3 **15.3** Listen, check, and practise.

4 What do the phrases which begin sentences **2a–d** above have in common?

Language focus: fronting

1 When speaking, we can start sentences with the object or complement instead of the subject. What would be the 'normal' word order here?

a *Sports I don't want to win that badly, competitions I'm probably not competitive enough.*

b *Washing up and ironing I absolutely hate doing when I'm tired.*

c *Brilliant film that was!*

d *Eating in pubs I don't mind, but fast food restaurants I can't stand.*

2 We can also start sentences with time and place expressions. What would be the 'normal' word order of these sentences?

a *Nearly every weekend we visit friends or relatives.*

b *At the end of the road there's a bus stop.*

▶ **Note** When sentences start with negative expressions the subject and verb are inverted (see **Unit 5 Stage 2**).
Not once in all the time I was at school **did I cheat** *at anything.*

3 In the examples in **1** and **2** above, what is the effect of changing 'normal' word order by bringing information to the beginning or *front* of a sentence?

Exploitation

1 Use one of the phrases from this list to 'front' (start) sentences **a–f** below.

(an) awful accident	dates, times, and phone numbers	most of the time
opposite the library	my next-door neighbour	(the) best meal I've had for ages

a .... there are tennis courts.

b .... she sits staring into space.

c .... I saw on the way to work.

d .... I've only spoken to two three times in the last ten years.

e .... that was.

f .... I just can't remember.

2 Now make up new sentences starting with the phrases in the list above.

3 Work in pairs or groups. Ask each other these questions. When you answer, start with the information you want to emphasize.

Example
What do you think of team games like football?
Team games like football, I think are overrated.

a What do you do on Friday evenings?

b Do you like taking exams?

c What do you think of TV game shows?

d Do you enjoy writing letters?

e What do you remember about your first day at school?

f What sports do you play?

g What do you like doing on holiday?

15.3 How to skive

Lead in

1 From time to time everyone makes excuses to get out of doing something or going somewhere.

  a Think of occasions when you have made an excuse.

  b Tell a partner about the occasion and what your excuse was.

2 Compare your answers with other students. What 'best excuses' have you heard?

Reading

1 Read the first paragraph of the article opposite. What does the verb *skive* mean? Choose one of these meanings:

  • to work hard
  • to avoid work
  • to work slowly.

2 Read the rest of the article.

  a Who does it seem to be written for?

  b How would you describe the writer's tone?

Close up

l.4 & l.54 What is the difference in meaning and pronunciation between *personal* and *personnel*?

l.30 *the groundwork* is the subject of this sentence – what is the main verb?

l.83 If something is someone's *bread and butter* what does this mean? (What kind of food is bread and butter?)

How to skive

1 Skiving is a skill. The good skiver, like the competent motorist, attracts no attention. There is only the quiet personal satisfaction that comes
5 from a job not well done. Skiving can be divided into two distinct parts; skiving off work and skiving at work. Minority pursuits such as skiving at home – children 'forgetting' to tidy
10 their rooms – can safely be ignored. It is in relation to authority figures, primarily schoolteachers and employers, that skiving is most commonly practised by the British people. It is the
15 compulsory nature of the activity being avoided (work, school) that provides the environment in which skiving can flourish.

2 Skiving has a long history
20 stretching back to Homer and his skiver Thersites, who managed to bunk off the Trojan wars. Modern skiving has its roots in national service, when a generation of soldiers learned the
25 skiving skills they were to take into British industry with such spectacular results in the 1960s and 1970s. Off-work skiving is largely concerned with exploiting the sick leave system. Here
30 the groundwork done at school – where the skiver will have learned that the best illnesses to claim are those that (a) sound serious and (b) are impossible to disprove – is refined and sharpened.
35 A 'pain behind the eyes' fits the bill very well.

3 Remember, a doctor's note is no longer adequate protection against interrogation. In the 1970s, the
40 limit on days off without a doctor's note moved from two to three; by the end of that decade, only on the fourth day did the skiver need to produce a sick note. The self-certification system,
45 introduced in the early 1980s, looked at first sight like a skiver's charter.

An employee could be absent for up to eight weeks on the basis of his or her own signature. Fresh territory for the skiver had been opened up. 50

4 It was not to be. Self-certification busted the absolute authority of the doctor's note and allowed personnel officers to start questioning the skiver's 'illness'. Friendly 'bad back' 55 doctors were no longer enough to ensure trouble-free skiving, and a more creative approach was called for. Intimidation provided the key, frightening the employer off any idea 60 of questioning the 'illness'. To this end, the skiver, during any brief periods on duty, would casually mention an array of medical advisers – specialists, physiotherapists, masseurs – working on 65 various ailments. He or she would also arrange 'appointments' with them during work time, thus exploiting new skiving opportunities. The more experienced skiver will ensure that the 70 'sickie' has been flagged up well in advance, making a big deal of soldiering on during the afternoon prior to the sickie, thus softening up the employer for that all-important 75 phone call on the day itself.

5 The day of return is equally important. The skiver will creep into the office with a scarf wrapped ostentatiously around his or her neck, 80 carrying a paper bag displaying the emblem of a well-known chemist chain.

6 In-work skiving is the bread-and-butter of the skiver's life. First, ensure a tool of your trade is 85 permanently tucked under your arm. Second, walk briskly and purposefully wherever you go. Third, leave a jacket permanently slung over the back of your seat. With luck, no one will ever 90 ask you to do anything. And what more could the true skiver ask?

The Observer

3 Match each paragraph of the article with one of these summaries.

  a Skiving through the ages
  b Skivers have to develop new tricks
  c Back to work
  d Skivers look forward to a new sick leave system
  e Practical suggestions for skiving at work
  f Definitions of skiving

4 Answer these questions about each of the six paragraphs.

  a In what situations is skiving most common? (para. 1)
  b Why is a 'pain behind the eyes' one of the best illnesses? (para. 2)
  c How did the British sick note system change in the early 1980s? (para. 3)
  d Why would a skiver mention specialists, physiotherapists, and masseurs? (para. 4)
  e Why should a skiver wear a scarf and carry a paper bag when they return? (para. 5)
  f Why should an in-work skiver 'walk briskly' and leave a jacket on their seat? (para. 6)

Language focus: *-ing* forms and infinitives

1 Without looking back at the article, complete these extracts with the correct form (*-ing* form or infinitive) of the verb in brackets.

  a *... children 'forgetting' .... (tidy) their rooms ...* (l.9)
  b *... Homer and his skiver Thersites, who managed .... (bunk off) the Trojan wars.* (l.20)
  c *only on the fourth day did the skiver need .... (produce) a sick note.* (l.42)
  d *Self-certification busted the absolute authority of the doctor's note and allowed personnel officers to start .... (question) the skiver's 'illness'.* (l.51)

2 Check your answers in the article. In which extract would both the *-ing* form and the infinitive be correct?

3 Complete these general rules with *-ing form* or *infinitive* and give some more examples.

  a Modal verbs are followed by .... (*must, ..., ...*)
  b Many verbs which express likes and dislikes are followed by .... (*loathe, ..., ...*)
  c The .... is used after many phrasal verbs. (*give up, ..., ...*)
  d The .... is used after many verb + object constructions. (*teach someone, ..., ...*)

Exploitation

1 Complete these sentences so that they are true for you.

  a I wish I could afford …

  b There's no way anyone will ever persuade me …

  c I'd really like to give up …

  d I'll always be grateful that my parents taught me …

  e I'm not looking forward to …

2 a Write two or three 'things' under these headings.

  • Things I always put off doing
  • Things I've given up doing
  • Things people have encouraged me to do

  b Find other students with the same responses.

Speaking and writing

Work in groups.

1 Think of tips and suggestions on these subjects.

  • How to avoid spending money
  • How to cheat at sport
  • How to keep telephone conversations short

2 Present your ideas to the rest of the class. Use some advice expressions from the box.

Do's	Don'ts
• One thing to remember is (this) …	• Whatever you do, don't …
• The first thing to do is (this) …	• Be careful not to …
• The important point is (to) …	• Under no circumstances …
• Above all …	
• And remember …	
• Don't forget (to) …	

3 Use the ideas you have discussed in groups as the basis for a *How to …* article. Try to write in the 'tongue-in-cheek' style of the *How to skive* article. Write your article in 150–170 words.

▶ **Writing guidelines p.154**

Exploring words

Competitions

1 **15.4** Listen to the recording. What kind of competitions are the speakers talking about? Which competition is least dependent on skill or ability?

2 Complete these extracts from the recordings.

a This year's top ...., a cheque for £5,000, has .... to a first-time novelist.

b ... David Jones has .... the .... of champion jockey with 25 wins in 30 rides.

c The .... was .... after three cars skidded off the track and burst into flames.

d This year's competition was .... in Paris. ... Miss Europe was .... a modelling contract with a top agency.

e All you have to do is .... this sentence in no more than ten words ...

f ... Fifty lucky .... will .... in a series of 10 weekly programmes and the .... winner will be .... a recording contract.

g Brazil is through to the final after .... Norway 5–4 ...

h The .... yacht, ... came in nearly two days ahead of its nearest ....

3 a Complete the table. (X = no useful word of this type.)

Person	Other noun	Verb	Adjective
1 competitor	....	....	....
2	championship	X	X
3	rivalry	....	X
4 defendant	....	....	....
5 contestant	....	....	X
6	....	win	X

b How are the words in 1 and 5 pronounced?

c **15.5** Listen, check, and practise.

4 Complete this article with one of these verbs.

beat   break   hold   set   win

> Fiona Frost .... [1] a new world record yesterday when she .... [2] her closest rival by a clear five seconds. She .... [3] the existing record by 0.6 of a second. This means that Ms Frost now .... [4] seven world records. If she .... [5] tomorrow's 1500 metres final she will be regarded by many as the greatest athlete of all time.

5 Work in pairs or groups.

a Design a 'Competition with a difference'. Decide what the contestants have to do, the rules, and a prize.

b Describe your competition to the rest of the class.

Language commentary

1 Alternatives to relative clauses

The alternatives below make language more concise. [...] shows where relative clauses could be used.

a Two nouns or noun phrases

Two nouns placed next to each other separated by commas can replace non-defining relative clauses.

John, [...] **an engineer**, comes from Stoke, [...] **an industrial town** in the Midlands.

b Past participles with passive meaning

These can replace defining and non-defining relative clauses.

Anyone [...] **found** shoplifting will be prosecuted.
The getaway car, [...] **driven** at high speed for over an hour, finally ran out of petrol.

c Adjective phrases

Adjective phrases can replace defining and non-defining relative clauses.

People [...] **anxious about their relatives** should phone this number.

d Passive infinitive constructions

A passive infinitive construction can replace defining and non-defining relative clauses.

The bridge [...] **to be opened** by the President tomorrow took ten years to build.

e -ing phrases

-ing phrases can replace defining relative clauses.

The people [...] **applying** for the job are all over 25.

2 Fronting

a Uses

Changing the 'normal' word order of a sentence can give more importance or emphasis to a particular idea.

Tea I love but coffee I can't stand. (I love tea but I can't stand coffee.)

b Adverbials

Sentences can start with adverbial expressions.

Place.
Outside the flat photographers and journalists waited, hoping for a story.

Time.
On the morning of the wedding, she decided she didn't love him after all.

Manner.
Slowly and silently one of the police officers aimed his gun at the door.

Frequency.
Every week police have to deal with incidents like this.

Comment.
Amazingly, no one noticed him leave the room.

c Object

In spoken English, sentences can start with the object instead of the subject.

Tony I've hardly seen at all since the summer.

d Inversion

After adverbial expressions of place and these verbs: *stand, come, walk, lie, sit, go.*

At the door **stood a tall mysterious-looking man**.

After negative and restrictive expressions (see p.43).

Not for a moment **did I suspect** anything.

After these adverb particles; *down, in, out, along, up.*

In **came the stranger** as if he owned the place.

3 *-ing* forms and infinitives

There is a large group of verbs followed by *to* + infinitive and another group followed by the *-ing* form. Often you simply have to remember the construction that follows each verb. There are lists of some of the commonest in each group at the end of this section: **f–g**.

Sections **a–e** focus on specific groups of verbs which take the same construction.

a Modal verbs

Most modal verbs are followed by the infinitive without *to*.

You really **shouldn't smoke**.

▶ Note *Need is followed by to + infinitive*

I **need to get** more sleep.
I **don't need to tell** you how important this interview is.

but *needn't is followed by the infinitive without to*.

You **needn't tell** me if you don't want to.

Need can also be followed by an *-ing* form to give a passive meaning:

Your car **needs cleaning**. (= to be cleaned)

b verb + object + *to* + infinitive

A few important verbs are followed by this pattern. (See p.125.)

I can't **persuade her to come** to my party.

Let and *make* are followed by verb + object + infinitive without *to*.

Let me help you.   Don't **make me laugh**.

c Likes and dislikes

Most verbs which express liking and disliking are followed by the *-ing* form.

I absolutely **loathe working** in the evenings.

These verbs can be followed by *to* + infinitive or an *-ing* form: *like, prefer, hate, love.*

If they are used with *would* they are always followed by *to* + infinitive:

I'd love to spend the day with you, but I'm afraid it's out of the question.

d Changes in meaning

Some verbs can be followed by *to* + infinitive or an *-ing* form with little or no change in meaning.

I've just **started / begun to learn / learning** Greek.
I'll **continue to phone / phoning** the manager until he gives me a proper answer.

Some verbs of perception (*watch, notice, hear, listen to, feel, see*) can be followed by the infinitive without *to* or the *-ing* form with a slight difference in meaning.

I saw the **ship sink**. (from beginning to end)
I saw the **ship sinking**. (the ship was in the process of sinking when I first saw it)

Some verbs have different meanings depending on whether they are followed by *to* + infinitive or an *-ing* form.

Verb	*-ing* form	Infinitive
go on	continue	finish one thing and start another
mean	involve	intend
forget	fail to recall	not do something
regret	be sorry about the past	be sorry about something you are going to say
remember	recall	do something you have to do
stop	finish	interrupt an activity
try	experiment	attempt something difficult

e Phrasal verbs

Some phrasal verbs are followed by the *-ing* form.

I'd love to **give up smoking**.

f *to* + infinitive

Some common verbs are followed by *to* + infinitive.

afford	agree	arrange	appear	attempt	choose
decide	expect	help	hope	intend	learn	manage
offer	pretend	promise	refuse	seem	

g *-ing* form

Some common verbs are followed by the *-ing* form.

admit	appreciate	avoid	can't help	consider	delay
deny	finish	forgive	imagine	involve	keep	mind
miss	postpone	prevent	report	resist	risk	suggest

16 Processes

16.1 Getting to sleep

Lead in

Answer these questions about your sleeping habits, then compare answers with other students.

SLEEP SURVEY

TIMES

1 What time do you usually go to bed and get up?
.... / ....
2 Can you sleep at other times? (For example, in the early afternoon?) Yes / No
3 How many hours sleep do you need? .... hours minimum

PLACES

1 Which of these places and situations do you sometimes go to sleep in?
• travelling: in cars .... / on trains or buses .... / on planes ....
• relaxing: watching TV .... / at the cinema .... / at parties .... / on the beach ....
• other situations: in the classroom .... / at airports or stations ....
2 Have you ever fallen asleep in these situations? standing up .... / while talking to someone .... / while driving ....

Listening

1 **16.1** You are going to hear four people talking about their sleeping habits. Which speaker(s) does (do) these things if they can't sleep? (Some speakers mention several things.)

a listen(s) to music ....
b listen(s) to the radio ....
c read(s) a book ....
d send(s) e-mails ....
e think(s) of peaceful scenes from nature ....
f watch(es) TV ....

2 Listen again and answer these questions.

a What happens to the first speaker if he is not tired when he goes to bed? What does he have to do in this situation?
b What can keep the second speaker awake and what does she do about it?
c Why does the third speaker often have to work until late at night?
d What does the fourth speaker describe as being *bizarre*?

Exploring natural speech

Thing and *stuff* are useful 'general meaning' words which we frequently use in speech.

1 How could *thing* and *stuff* be replaced in this extract from the recording?

… I can sleep absolutely anywhere, if I'm knackered enough, but er also feel terribly vulnerable doing that and get off at wrong stops and drool* and **stuff** so try not to but if I can't sleep I can panic because I do have a **thing** about getting enough hours and it'll affect me the whole next day – so it's a psychological **thing** probably more than physical.

* *drool:* water at the mouth / salivate

2 What do *thing* and *stuff* mean in these sentences?

a Excuse me, are those your *things* over there?
b I'd love to come with you but the *thing* is I haven't got any money.
c *Things* are going brilliantly at work.
d I'm going for a shower, I've got some sticky *stuff* in my hair.
e Can you help me get my *stuff* from the car?

Language focus: habits and predictable behaviour

1 How did the speakers refer to habits or predictable behaviour in these extracts? Put the verbs in the correct form – with the words in brackets in the correct order. (They did not always use the Present simple.)

a ... *if I don't go to bed at that time, then (I actually stay) .... awake for an awful lot longer when I actually do go to bed. (I have) .... to make sure that I'm completely relaxed, and completely unwound erm before I actually go to bed, otherwise then, you know (I just lie) .... awake for ages. Erm my mind (start) .... to wander ...*

b *(I start off) .... always on my left side er but that can switch. And what (keep) .... me awake is usually either hunger or anxiety, so if I can't sleep (I either eat) .... something or (I usually e-mail) .... now actually ...*

c *If ever I can't sleep – which as I say isn't really often the case, (I often listen) .... to music to try to get to sleep or (I just sit up) .... and read a book ...*

2 Check your answers on p.148.

3 Which of these sentences refer to the future and which refer to predictable behaviour?

a If I catch the nine o'clock train, I'll probably be home by midnight.
b If I listen to the radio, the voices will often send me to sleep.
c If I have something important to do the next morning, it'll take me ages to get to sleep.
d Don't disturb them now – they'll be having their lunch.
e At weekends I'll usually have a lie in and get up at about 11 o'clock.
f Phone her in the morning – it's late now. She'll have gone to bed already.

4 The Present continuous and *tend to* can also be used to talk about habits. Which of these sentences refers to a recent or temporary habit and which refers to typical behaviour?

* *I tend to get up and read or watch TV.*
* *I'm getting much more exercise than I used to.*

Exploitation

1 Work in groups. Imagine a typical day in the life of the men and women in the photos. Because you don't know exactly who the people are or what they do, use your imagination. Use *will* and phrases from the list below.

(almost) certainly   it's quite likely that   maybe   perhaps   presumably
probably
---

2 Think about someone whose habits you know well. It could be a friend or someone in your family. Tell a partner what you imagine that person will be doing now, or will have done by now. (If you're not sure, add the words *possibly* or *probably*.)

Example
My father will probably be drinking coffee and chatting to friends at work. My mother will have taken my little sister to school – now she'll be on her way home.

Speaking

Work in groups.

1 Design a survey, similar to the *Sleep Survey* in **Lead in**, to find out about people's habits in one of these areas:
* keeping fit
* reading
* watching TV.

2 Try out your survey on other students in the class.

Reading

1 Brainstorm in groups. Make a list of things you know about the making of animated films in general or of *Chicken Run* in particular.

2 Now read the article and check your ideas.

Listening

16.2 You are going to hear a description of the modelling process. Put illustrations A–F in order, then listen and check.

Poultry in Motion

① **Appearances**
Animation is an optical illusion. Where motion pictures with live actors capture events as they happen, animated films are a series of still photographs shot in rapid succession, which, when shown at 24 frames per second, give the appearance of a
5 moving picture. Animation covers a variety of styles that have expanded in recent years with the advent of computers. Broadly speaking, though, the genre can be divided between the two-dimensional, where the effect is achieved through flat images drawn onto transparent
10 sheets, glass film or on the computer, and the three-dimensional, which involves articulated puppets or models built around a metal skeleton, known as an armature, and made of plasticine, fabric or latex.

② **Clay animation**
While technology has revolutionized
15 much of the animation industry, the time-consuming techniques of stop-motion clay animation, though refined, have remained essentially unchanged. Every detail of every frame has to be changed by
20 hand. In numerical terms, there are 24 frames per second of film time, so depending on the action in a sequence, it is possible to have 24 separate poses to shoot per character for every second in a scene, each pose
25 involving the tiniest increment of movement for body, head, arms, legs, hands, fingers, eyes, mouth, clothing and more. This needs to be repeated for every character in every scene and for any props that are also in camera.
30 While making *Chicken Run* the makers sometimes had as many as 28 sets in full operation at the same time and were still only able to complete 10 seconds of film each day.

③ **Creating movement**
Most of the principles that create a naturalistic effect, such as anticipation, momentum and acceleration and deceleration have something to do with the transfer of 35 weight and the animator's ability to make it believable. Above all, though, the movement should also give insight into what the character is thinking.

④ **Creating a storyboard**
Having created the basic look of the characters the film artist plans the film sequences of the animation through 40 storyboards illustrating key frames throughout the movie. When shown together the animators can see how the models need to move during the filming and what camera angles will be used.

⑤ **A star is born**
Once rough sketches of the character have been 45 made and it has been decided how the character will move, the modelling process begins.

John Crace, *The Guardian Education*

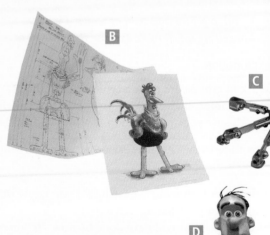

E | scene 5300 | shot 9A | DESCRIPTION 3"04 (appx)

Language focus: the passive

1 Look back at the article and find these forms of the passive.

- two infinitives (para. 2)
- the future (para. 4)
- two Present perfects (para. 5)

2 Here are some more passive verbs. What forms are they?

  a *The storyboard **is filmed** and the voices added …*

  b *In its first week, the film **was seen** by over a hundred million people worldwide.*

  c *The creators **are being praised** for their imagination and their technical abilities.*

3 Why is the passive form used in preference to the active in examples **a–c** below? Choose one or more reasons from this list.

The 'doer' of the action is
A unknown   B a secret   C obvious   D irrelevant   E not the most important element

---

  a I had this strange feeling that I *was being followed* wherever I went.

  b The government *is being accused* of widespread corruption and fraud.

  c I *was fined* £50 for speeding on the motorway.

4 In what contexts is the passive most frequently used? Where might you find these examples?

  a A man *was severely burnt* when a gas explosion ripped through his ground floor flat.

  b The technique *was invented* in about 100 BC probably in Syria. A mass of molten glass is gathered …

  c Shoplifters *will be prosecuted*.

  d The best evidence that pleasure is not the basis or the objective of consumption is that nowadays *pleasure is constrained and institutionalized*, not as a right or enjoyment, but as the citizen's duty.

    (Jean Baudrillard, *Consumer Society*)

Exploitation

1 We often use the passive to make language more 'formal' or 'official'. Transform this informal conversational language into formal (written) language using the passive.

  a You've got to wear smart formal clothes for meetings.

  b They blamed the party leader for the election defeat.

  c They opened the new town hall on 15 September 2001.

  d The judge sentenced the boy to six months in prison for 'borrowing' his father's car.

  e You can't blame the government for the recent increase in the price of petrol.

2 Work in pairs.

Describe the various stages involved in one of these everyday processes. Use your imagination if you are not sure.

- Making a film or video
- Food or drink: making bread, wine, or pasta
- Manufacturing: making cars; assembling computers

Writing

You are going to write a short report about the process you have been describing with your partner.

1 Note down the information you want to include, then organize this into appropriate sections.

2 Think of a suitable title and headings.

3 Write the report in **120–150** words. Remember to keep the style factual and fairly formal.

▶ **Writing guidelines p.155**

Speaking

Discuss these questions in groups.

1 Do you prefer cartoons or animated films to other types of film?

2 From a film-maker's point of view, what are the advantages and disadvantages of cartoons and animations?

3 Who were your favourite cartoon characters when you were a child? And now? Think about TV programmes as well as cinema films.

4 Imagine you had the money and facilities to make your own cartoon film. Who would be the characters and what situations would you put them in?

--- **Close up** ---

l.1 An *illusion* is something that is not real. What does *optical* refer to? Do you know any other words which start with *optic* …?

l.2 What kind of word is *live*? What does it mean and how is it pronounced?

l.12 What is a human *skeleton* made of?

l.19 Which single word could replace *by hand*?

16.3 Interviews

Lead in

Work in pairs. Imagine someone you know is going for a job interview.

1 Think of some advice you could give that might help them get the job. Make a list of three *Dos* and *Don'ts*.

2 What's the worst thing they could say at an interview? Compare ideas. Vote for the best 'worst thing'.

Reading

1 As you read the article think about these questions.

  a Would you consider any of these applicants for a job?

  b Who do you think makes the most serious mistake?

2 Compare your answers to questions 1a–b in pairs.

3 Which candidate, A–H

  a had done insufficient research before the interview?

  b admitted they did not have the personal qualities required for the job?

  c was incapable of speaking?

  d made an inappropriate written request?

  e had misunderstood an instruction they had been given?

  f had to be advised not to eat during the interview?

  g came to the interview inappropriately dressed?

  h made an exaggerated claim which they could not back up?

What not to say in interviews

To help new graduates on their way in the world of work, a New York research firm asked personnel executives at 200 leading companies to describe the worst blunders they had witnessed in the interview room.

A 'He had arranged for a pizza to be delivered to my office during a lunch-hour interview. I asked him not to eat it until later.'

B 'I received a résumé and a note that said the recent high-school graduate wanted to earn $25 an hour and "not a nickel less"'.

C 'On the phone I had asked the candidate to bring his résumé and a couple of references. He arrived with the résumé and two people.'

D 'When I asked the candidate to give a good example of the organizational skills she was boasting about, she said she was proud of her ability to pack her suitcase "real neat" for her vacations.'

E 'She actually showed up for an interview during the summer wearing a bathing suit. Said she didn't think I'd mind.'

F 'The interview had gone well, until he told me that he and his friends wore my company's clothing whenever they could. At which point, I had to tell him that we manufactured office products, not sportswear.'

G 'Applied for a customer-service position although, as he confided, he really wasn't a people person.'

H 'He couldn't answer any of my questions because he had just had major dental work.'

Tom Kuntz, *New York Times*

Vocabulary: applying for a job

Complete these instructions with the appropriate form of one of these words.

---
shortlist (*vb*) referee personnel interview CV candidate
application applicant

.... ¹ for this job should complete the enclosed form and return it to the .... ² manager before the end of the month. You should also enclose a full .... ³ and the names and addresses of two .... ⁴. If you are .... ⁵ for the job, you will be informed in writing and given a date and time to come for .... ⁶. The successful .... ⁷ will be expected to start work immediately.

Language focus: verb + object + *to* + infinitive

1 Various verbs can be followed by an object + *to* + infinitive. Which verbs do you think are missing from these sentences?

a I .... him not to eat the pizza until later.

b I .... the candidate to bring his résumé and a couple of references.

c It doesn't matter what you do, you won't .... me to change my mind.

d I've got a terrible memory. Can you .... me to check my e-mail before I leave work?

2 Here are some more verbs followed by this construction.

---
advise allow ask beg enable encourage forbid get
help invite order permit persuade teach tell want
wish would like

---

a List them in these meaning groups.

   A Influencing: ordering/requesting

   B Causing/helping

   C Wanting/liking

b These verbs are not the same. What constructions are they followed by?

---
discourage insist let make prevent prohibit suggest

Exploitation

Complete these sentences so that they are true for you, then compare with a partner.

a When I was a child, my parents encouraged me …

b People are always advising me …

c If I got a better job, it would enable me …

d I'd like to be able to teach …

e Unfortunately no one can help …

f If I were in a position of power, I would allow …

g When I have children, I won't permit …

Role play

Work in pairs. Read your roles and then take part in the interview.

Student A Interview candidate – turn to p.158.
Student B Interviewer – turn to p.159.

Writing

Imagine you are interested in the holiday job as a waiter. Write a letter 'selling' yourself as a suitable candidate. Your letter could be:

• an informal personal profile

   or

• a more formal letter of application.

▶ **Writing guidelines p.152**

Exploring words

American and British English

1 How much do you know about the differences between British and American English?

   a Do this quiz, then compare answers with a partner.

   b ▯16.3▯ Listen and check your answers.

A How many more speakers of American English than British English are there?

   a twice as many ▢   **b** three times as many ▢
   c four times as many ▢

B The most noticeable difference between British and American English is:

   a vocabulary ▢   **b** pronunciation ▢   **c** spelling ▢

C Where words are spelt differently in British and American English, the American spelling is usually shorter.

   True ▢ or False ▢ ?

D There are no differences in grammar between British and American English.

   True ▢ or False ▢ ?

E Words that have different spellings in American and British English usually have different pronunciations.

   True ▢ or False ▢ ?

F Most British people understand American English without any problem.

   True ▢ or False ▢ ?

2 Match these American English words with their British English equivalents.

   a ▢ *duplex*   1 rubbish
   b ▢ *line*   2 pram
   c ▢ *attorney*   3 c.v. (curriculum vitae)
   d ▢ *intersection*   4 petrol
   e ▢ *baby carriage*   5 semi-detached house
   f ▢ *eraser*   6 corpse
   g ▢ *gasoline*   7 rubber
   h ▢ *garbage*   8 crossroads / junction
   i ▢ *cadaver*   9 queue
   j ▢ *résumé*   10 lawyer

3 There are also differences between British and American spellings.

   a Complete this table which contains examples of five general differences.

British	American	Other examples
1 centre	....	....
2	rumor	....
3 offence	....	....
4	dialog	....
5 travelled	....	....

   b What other words do you know that belong to the five categories?

Speaking

Discuss these questions in groups or pairs.

1 British and American English are just two of the many forms of English. Which others do you know? Do you have a preference?

2 Why are there so many different forms?

3 Do you think English will continue to be an important world language for the foreseeable future?

Language commentary

1 Habits and predictable behaviour

a Habitual behaviour
The Present simple is used to refer to habitual behaviour.

I wake up every morning at 6.30.

An alternative to the Present simple is *will*, especially if the behaviour is so habitual that it is predictable.

When I get home in the evening, **I'll be** so hungry, **I'll eat** a whole packet of biscuits.

Notice the use of *will* in this sentence, where *if* does not express a conditional, but means *when / whenever*.

If I can't sleep **I'll** either **eat** something or **I'll usually e-mail** …

▶ **Note** This use of *will* is more common in speech.

b Expressing probability
Will be doing is also used to describe what someone is probably doing at the moment.

Don't phone him now – **he'll be having** breakfast.

Will have done is used to say what they have probably done already.

It's too late to remind them – **they'll have left** already.

c *tend to*
Tend to describes what usually happens rather than what always happens.

In the winter **I tend to read** more than in the summer.

d Present continuous
The Present continuous describes changing situations, and so is used to describe a temporary or recent habit.

I'm drinking less coffee these days.

The Present continuous with *always* means *too often* or *very often* and describes annoying habits or pleasant habits which are worthy of comment.

She's always telling me what to do. I'm fed up with it.
Tony loves his girlfriend. **He's always buying** her presents.

2 The passive
The most important reason for using the passive is to focus attention on the person or thing that is affected by an action rather than on the person or thing who performs the action. There are a number of situations in which this is necessary or desirable.

a Uses
- When the person who does the action is unknown.
  Our house **was burgled** last night.
- When the identity of the person cannot be revealed.
  I have it on good authority that **you were seen** in town at 3 a.m. in the morning last Friday. (This might be a police officer or a journalist protecting a source of information.)
- When we don't need to say who does the action because it is obvious.
  After the accident **he was banned** from driving for a year. (Judges or magistrates in courts are the only people who can ban someone from driving.)
  He was arrested for speeding. (Only the police have the power to arrest people.)

- When the person who does the action is unimportant or irrelevant.
  We were interrupted in the middle of a very intimate personal conversation.
- The passive is often used to describe technical processes.
  First the electricity **was turned off** and all wires **disconnected**.

b Agent
If we know and want to mention who or what did the action (the agent), we can include this information by adding a *by* phrase.

I was questioned **by three police officers**.

c *It* + passive
It + the passive is a way of expressing something in an impersonal or formal way.

It was agreed that wages should be cut by 10%.

3 Verb + object + *to* + infinitive
Verb + object + *to* + infinitive is a construction used with many common verbs.

Do you **want me to help** you with your homework?

The verbs that are followed by this construction can be grouped under four headings.

a Influencing: ordering or requesting

advise	allow	ask	beg	command	encourage	forbid
instruct	invite	order	persuade	recommend	remind
request	tell	urge	warn		

b Causing or helping

cause	compel	drive	enable	force	get	help
intend	permit	teach	train		

c Wanting or liking

want	wish	(would) like	(would) love	(would) prefer
(would) hate	can't bear			

d Saying or thinking

assume	believe	consider	discover	expect	feel	find
imagine	judge	know	presume	show	suppose
understand					

▶ **Note** *Consider* and *understand* are more commonly followed by a *that* clause:

We consider (that) he is the best person for the job.
I understand (that) you're interested in buying my car.

e Other patterns
Everyone tried to **discourage him from resigning** from his job.
I **insist on paying** for the meal.
Why won't you **let me help** you?
The teacher **made the students revise** for their exam.
His seat-belt **prevented him (from) being** injured.
Cyclists are **prohibited from riding** on motorways.
I **suggested going** to Brazil for our holiday.

17.1 Mr Gormley's Angel

Lead in

1 Look at the three sculptures in the photos.

a What do you think of them?

b Would you want a sculpture like this near to where you live? Why / Why not?

2 Read the factual information about one of the sculptures, *The Angel of the North*, by Antony Gormley.

a How do you think it is possible for so many people to see this sculpture?

b We find out that the Angel will last for more than 100 years. Does this seem like a long or short time? What will affect the number of years it lasts?

The facts

- It is the largest sculpture in Britain and the largest Angel sculpture in the world.
- It is seen by more than one person a second, or 33 million every year.
- It stands on a mound and is 20 metres high – the height of a five-storey building.
- Its 54-metre wingspan is almost as big as that of a jumbo jet.
- It is made of steel, weighs 200 tonnes and is built on 20-metre-deep foundations.
- It will withstand winds of 160 kph and will last for more than 100 years.
- The body of the Angel is modelled on a plaster cast of the body of the sculptor.
- The Angel cost £800,000.
- The project involved the sculptor, engineering consultants, and a steel company.

Listening

1 **17.1** Listen to Antony Gormley talking about *The Angel of the North*. Match each extract to one of these four questions.

a Is it important to you that the public may not understand your ideas?

b How do you start work on a sculpture like *The Angel of the North*?

c What ideas does the Angel represent?

d What surprised you about the location?

2 In this second extract Antony Gormley says why showing his sculptures in public is important to him.

a **17.2** As you listen, complete the extract with the words you hear.

What I'm more interested in is ....¹ people up you know on their way to the supermarket because I think that part of the problem with our ....² at the moment is that we deal in a culture of you know ....³ basically er of highly-articulated, highly-hyped, almost predigested ....⁴.

I hope the Angel makes you ....⁵ of the time of the day, the shape of the ....⁶, your speed, erm, also, even though people wouldn't recognize that perhaps as part of their response to a work. The only ....⁷ of art, I think, is as a instrument of reflexivity to make us feel more ....⁸ – there's no intrinsic value to art.

b Which of these statements best summarizes what Antony Gormley is saying in the extract you have just heard?

1 He wants to help people to understand culture.

2 He is trying to shock people.

3 He wants his art to make people think and feel.

React and discuss

Your city has decided to have a public sculpture. What kind of sculpture would you like and where would you locate it? Explain your reasons.

Language focus: dependent prepositions

1 Complete these extracts from the recording with the correct prepositions. The prepositions are dependent on the verbs, adjectives, or nouns in **bold**.

a … it's a long process, but I think it **starts** always .... the place …

b … the actual piece came about from a **conversation** that I had .... councillor Pat Murphy …

c 'Well if you're **serious** .... this Pat, it's going to have to be 65 foot tall.'

d … this **relationship** .... this mound and the road got me very intrigued …

e … each of them will have their own particular **relationship** .... this work …

2 Compare your answers in pairs and then check on p.148.

3 Some adjectives can be followed by more than one preposition. Different adjective + preposition combinations often have different meanings.

a Complete these sentences with one of the prepositions.

1 **angry** *about* / *with*
- *The car behind crashed into mine – I was really angry .... the driver.*
- *I was angry .... the length of time we were held up by the road works.*

2 **good** *at* / *for* / *with*
- *My sister is very good .... learner drivers. She's so patient.*
- *I've never been very good .... parking in small spaces.*
- *It isn't good .... you to drive too long without a break.*

3 **sorry** *about* / *for*
- *After the accident he lost his job – I feel really sorry .... him.*
- *I'm sorry .... the damage to your car – I'll pay for it of course.*

b How did you decide which preposition to use? Compare ideas with a partner.

Exploitation

1 Work in pairs or groups.

Talk about these subjects for 1–2 minutes each.

- Things I'm good and bad at
- People I'm envious of
- Things I feel angry about
- Things I can't get serious about
- Things I know are good for me – but I don't enjoy

2 Look at the lists of dependent prepositions on p.133 and test each other.

17.2 But is it art?

Lead in

1 Describe the painting opposite.

a What is the style?

b What techniques and materials did the artist use? You might find these words useful.

Styles
abstract   classical   expressionist
impressionist   modern
representational   surrealist
symbolic

Techniques and materials
brush-stroke   canvas   colour(s)
depict (vb)   draw (vb)   frame
lines   oil paint   paintbrush   paper
water colours

2 A well-known art critic described the painting as 'worthless junk'. Do you agree? Why? Why not?

Reading

1 Read the article. What do you find out about the painting?

2 Read the text again and answer these questions.

a Why have some artists been annoyed by Michael and Koko's paintings?

b In what ways are Michael and Koko's paintings different from earlier 'monkey' paintings?

c What do Michael and Koko show through sign language?

d How does Dr Patterson compare sign language and painting?

e Can you think of any reasons why the gorillas might eat the paintings?

Close up

l.4   How is *dress up* different from *dress*? What is the purpose of *dressing up*?

l.10   What does *struggling* mean here? What other meanings does it have?

l.18   What kind of animals does a *primatologist* study?

Struggling artists

There was once an artist who could not sell his work. One day, a friend paid him a visit and said, 'I know what you should do. Dress up in this 5 gorilla suit.' So he did. He created abstract pictures and became an overnight success as the original ape artist. He became rich and lived happily ever after.

10 This tale will not amuse struggling artists in California. Recently, much to their indignation, they have seen several well-publicized exhibitions of artwork by two gorillas called Michael 15 and Koko. These great apes have been raised and taught to speak using American sign language (ASL) by primatologist Dr Francine Patterson. Their paintings have achieved critical 20 acclaim many human artists only dream about.

There's nothing new about art galleries adorning their walls with monkey pictures. There was a brief 25 craze for ape art in the late 1950s when chimps were encouraged to paint by biologists trying to shed light on the origins of art. Their work was seen as a form of abstract 30 expressionism, also popular at that time, and fetched prices close to that of non-ape artists.

What is new today, however, is the representational quality of pictures 35 by apes like Michael and Koko. Instead of random brush-strokes and splattered paints, they appear able to depict objects from the world around

them. 'I noticed when they were quite young, they were doing pencil 40 drawings that were realistic,' says Patterson. 'Koko, for instance, drew a glass, a banana, a spider and a bus.' This was a first. Never before had non-humans been recorded creating 45 pictures with form.

Patterson's pioneering project with gorillas is the longest interspecies communication study ever. It began in 1972 when she started teaching 50 ASL to Koko, then a one-year-old living at San Francisco Zoo.

At three years of age, Koko began to draw using pens and pencils placed in her environment. By then 55 she had learnt about 70 signs. 'This seemed quite natural,' Patterson remembers. 'But she was private about her pictures and did not want me to look at them.' After the Gorilla 60 Foundation was set up in 1976, Michael was adopted from Vienna Zoo. He hasn't learnt as many signs but prefers to express himself through painting. 65

Through sign language, the gorillas display an incredible array of human characteristics. They joke, lie and get embarrassed, but perhaps the greatest proof of their insight is they 70 give their artwork titles. One of Michael's pictures was inspired by a bouquet of flowers. When asked afterwards what he'd call the painting, he signed 'Stink Gorilla 75 More', 'stink' being gorilla-speak for

'flowers'. Could it be that language acquisition has moulded the apes' ability to create form in their paintings? 'It's possible,' says Patterson. 'Language and art are both examples of symbolic representation so the two may be paired. But I think all apes have the capacity to do representational art on some level whether they can speak or not.' But is it really art? 85

Studies show that primates do have an aesthetic sense. Patterson herself is convinced Koko has a judgement of beauty and ugliness that's virtually the same as ours. But it's clear that Michael and Koko do not create their paintings to have a lasting presence. After laying their paintbrushes down, they like to eat their works of art. 100

Emma Bayley, *Focus*

Language focus: reference words (2)

When we speak or write, we use a variety of words and phrases which refer to something we have already mentioned.

What do the reference words in **bold** in these extracts from the article refer to?

a *This tale* will not amuse struggling artists in California. Recently, much to **their** indignation, **they** have seen several well-publicized exhibitions of artwork by two gorillas called Michael and Koko. **These great apes** have been raised and taught to speak …

b *There was a brief craze for ape art in the late 1950s* **when** *chimps were encouraged to paint by biologists trying to shed light on the origins of art.* **Their** *work was seen as a form of abstract expressionism, also popular* **at that time,** *and fetched prices close to* **that** *of non-ape artists.*

c *Koko, for instance, drew a glass, a banana, a spider and a bus.* **This** *was a first.*

d *At three years of age, Koko began to draw using pens and pencils placed in her environment.* **By then** *she had learnt about 70 signs.*

Exploitation

Complete the article with reference words or phrases from this list.

she	something	the same	their	them	them
these similarities	they	they	this	who	

Perhaps it doesn't matter that these apes eat their paintings. It's remarkable enough ....[1] create ....[2] in the first place. Most extraordinary are the pictures ....[3] made to illustrate emotions. Koko chose red and pink to paint love; green and brown for hate. 80–90 per cent of the colours Koko chose to represent emotional states were ....[4] as a human would select. As Patterson says, ...[5] shows an incredible similarity in the way brains process information.

Sadly, we may not have much longer to study ....[6]. There are only 600 mountain gorillas and a few thousand lowland gorillas left in the world. Patterson is working hard to raise money to move ....[7] to a reserve in Hawaii. Top priority will be encouraging Koko to have a baby. Could Koko teach her baby how to sign? 'Yes, because ....[8] teaches her dolls', says Patterson. She takes ....[9] hands and makes the sign.' Gorillas are born with a knowledge of communicative gestures, ...[10] first realized by Patterson when studying video footage of gorillas, ...[10] had never been taught to sign.

Emma Bayley, *Focus*

Speaking

Work in groups.

1 Is there any value in animal experiments like the ones involving Koko and Michael?

2 For what purposes do you think humans should experiment on animals?

17.3 Women in the arts

Lead in

1 Think of two famous people in each of these branches of the arts:
- writing: novels, poetry, or plays
- music: composers, instrumentalists, or singers
- visual arts: painters, sculptors, or film-makers.

2 How many of the people you thought of:
- are still alive?
- are women?

3 What branch of the arts do you associate with these people?
- Pablo Picasso and Berthe Morisot
- Clara Schumann and Mozart
- Charles Dickens and Jane Austen

4 What, if anything, do you know about these men and women? Exchange ideas, then check on p.158.

Mozart

Jane Austen

Berthe Morisot

Picasso

Clara Schumann

Dickens

Listening

1 **17.3** You are going to hear a group of people talking about men and women in the arts.
  a Which art forms and artists do they mention?
  b Why do they think women in the past were less likely than men to be involved in the arts?

2 Explain what the speakers mean by these statements.
  a *They (women classical painters) may have been edited.*
  b *Women had to put a male pseudonym on their books.*

3 **17.4** Now listen to another group of people talking about the same subject.
  a Which art forms and artists do they mention?
  b What comparison is made between the world of art and the world of business?

4 Explain what the speakers mean by these statements.
  a *There are a lot more women who have risen to the top …*
  b *No one is that high profile …*

React and discuss

1 How many famous women artists can you think of? Include as many different 'arts' as you can.

2 How would you explain the fact that, historically speaking, there are more prominent men than women in the arts?

Exploring natural speech

Look at these extracts from the recordings. What do the words and expressions in **bold** mean?

a **W1** But, you know, it's a question of if you ask, are there more famous men in the arts than women – famous in the sense that we probably know about more men than women in the arts, **do you know what I'm saying**?

  M Well as far as classical painters, you know, you certainly don't think of women.

  W1 That's true, but does that mean they didn't exist?

  W2 **Good point** …

b **M** Well, look at authors like Georges Sand – women traditionally for a good number of years had to put a male pseudonym on their books (**Right, exactly, yes**) or they were not going to sell.

  W2 **Smart women** who did that, boy.

c **W2** I think more and more although I heard a statistic in this documentary that, I think last year, out of the 200 or so sort of feature films, you know big feature films not independent films that were made, maybe 20 of them were directed by women.

  W1 **Wow!**

Vocabulary: male and female words

Certain words used to have male and female forms. For example *poet* (*m*) and *poetess* (*f*). A few pairs of words like this are still in common use, for example *waiter/waitress*. Now, we tend to use one word to refer to both men and women, for example *manager*. Similarly, we used to use the suffixes -*man*/-*woman*, for example *spokesman/spokeswoman*, whereas now we use -*person*, as in *spokesperson*. The distinctions are now regarded as sexist and possibly insulting, so we avoid them where possible. If we need to make a distinction, we can use the words *male* or *female* with a neutral noun, for example *female film producer*.

1 Which words could you use instead of these 'old-fashioned' words?

a barmaid b chairman c authoress d fireman e policewoman f businessman
g headmistress h cameraman i air hostess j statesman

2 There are also alternatives to other words which include the word *man*. Replace the words in **bold** in these sentences with the appropriate forms of non-sexist equivalents from this list, making any other necessary changes.

artificial   human being   people   staff (n)   staff (vb)

a ***Man** is the only living creature to use highly-developed language.*
b *Despite high unemployment, some industries are suffering from **manpower** shortages.*
c *There's a huge **man-made** lake near here where you can go sailing or wind-surfing.*
d ***Mankind** has always been interested in scientific progress.*
e *Our phone lines are **manned** twenty-four hours a day, seven days a week.*

Exploitation

Rewrite these news reports replacing any sexist language with acceptable alternatives.

1 Two policemen and two policewomen went to a club in central London last night after a barmaid had phoned to report a disturbance.

2 A meeting took place yesterday between a group of air stewards and stewardesses and representatives of the management. The chairman reported that there was overmanning in the company and that redundancies were inevitable.

3 Before leaving, the manageress of the shop made a thorough search of the burning building to check that all the staff were safely out. Firemen who attended the blaze praised her for her bravery. A spokesman said, 'Lives could so easily have been lost.'

Speaking

1 In your country, which of these jobs are more likely to be done by women and which by men? Compare your ideas in groups.

accountant   doctor   hairdresser   managing director of a company   nurse   politician
primary school teacher   social worker   soldier   train driver   vet

2 Discuss these statements. Present your conclusions to the rest of the class.

- Men are better at practical, manual work than women.
- Women are better than men when it comes to working with people.
- I don't mind whether my doctor is a man or a woman.
- If women become soldiers, they should be able to train and fight alongside men.
- Women are more naturally creative than men.

Exploring words

Metaphorical language

A metaphor is the imaginative use of a word or phrase to describe something else. Words and phrases can have both literal and metaphorical meanings.

Oops!

1 Work in pairs.

Talking about his art, Antony Gormley used several metaphors. He talked about:

- **tripping** people **up** on the way to the supermarket
- a culture of **snacking**.

What are the literal 'normal' meanings of the words in **bold**?

2 a These sentences all contain commonly-used metaphors related to *fire*. Identify the metaphor in each sentence.

1 After a month of peace, violence flared up again last night between the two communities.
2 In my opinion this new first novel will set the literary world alight.
3 The world's most popular footballer arrived yesterday in a blaze of publicity.
4 When I was a teenager, my burning ambition was to become an airline pilot.
5 The rise in the price of bread was enough to spark off a weekend of rioting.
6 Tim and Ella never have blazing rows but there's always an atmosphere of smouldering discontent in their house.

b Decide the metaphorical meanings of the words and phrases. Then choose three of the metaphors and use them to refer to different situations.

Example
He's quite an interesting politician but this speech is not going to set the election campaign alight.

3 a The words and phrases in *italics* in these extracts from newspaper stories are metaphors. What do you think they mean?

1 The *poaching* of nurses from developing countries *to shore up* Britain's *crumbling* health service has been condemned at a national conference of nurses.

2 The government's record on education *was savaged* yesterday by the head of one of the country's top schools.

3 A murder inquiry has been *launched* after a man died following a knife attack outside his home.

4 In a *feverish* day of electioneering yesterday, the opposition party *turned the spotlight* on Labour, claiming there was a £10 billion hole in their finances.

5 Farmers in the north are being urged not *to drop their guard* against foot-and-mouth disease after two new cases were discovered.

b Work with a partner. Rewrite the extracts, replacing the metaphorical language with 'normal' words or phrases.
c How do the two versions compare? What is the effect of using metaphorical language?

4 a **17.5** You are going to hear five extracts of conversation. Identify the metaphors.
b Discuss their meanings with a partner.
c What is the effect of using these metaphors? What literal words and phrases could be used instead?

Language commentary

1 Dependent prepositions

a Verb + preposition + noun / Verb + object + preposition + noun

(Verbs marked * can also be followed by -ing forms.)

at: aim (something) at*   point at   point (something) at

for: apologize for*   apply for   hope for   send for
arrest someone for*   blame someone for *
criticize someone for*   exchange one thing for another
praise someone for *   thank someone for*

from: refrain from*   suffer from   borrow something from
discourage someone from*   learn something from*
save someone from*

in: believe in*   participate in   succeed in*   invest money in

of: consist of*   dispose of   accuse someone of*

on: concentrate on*   decide on   depend on*   insist on*
rely on*   spend money on*   congratulate someone on*

to: admit to*   belong to   happen to   object to*
occur to   refer to   resort to*   invite someone to
compare something to (or with)   lend something to someone
prefer* one thing to another

with: collide with   cope with*   deal with*   interfere with
start with   replace one thing with another thing
share something with someone

b Noun + preposition

between: a contrast between   a difference between
a link between

for: time for lunch   no room for you   the reason for the
delay   no need for rudeness   a desire for peace
a substitute for tobacco   respect for the police

in: pride in my country   an increase / a rise in employment
a decrease / fall in interest rates   belief in democracy

of: a good example of modern art

to: an alternative to walking   the answer / solution to the
problem   your attitude to children   my reaction to the
situation

with: the trouble with   problem with motorways
What's the matter with you?   a conversation with a friend

c Adjective + preposition

absent from   accustomed to   afraid / frightened of
ashamed of   aware / conscious of   bored / fed up with
confident of   curious about   dependent on   different
from / to   excited about   famous for   fond of   guilty of
harmful to   involved in   jealous / envious of   kind to
late for   made of   nervous of   popular with   present at
proud of   safe from   serious about   short of   similar to
successful in   suitable for   superior / inferior to
sure / certain of   surprised by / at   tired of   typical of
wrong with

d Adjectives which can be followed by more than one preposition

afraid of / for
I'm afraid **of** dogs. (= frightened of)
I'm afraid **for** the future. (= worried about)

angry with / about
I'm angry **with** her. (= anger at a person)
I'm angry **about** poverty. (= to direct anger at the cause
of a problem)

good with / at / for
She's good **with** people. (= capable of dealing effectively with)
He's good **at** maths. (= to do something well)
Exercise is good **for** you. (= beneficial for)

grateful to / for
I'm grateful **to** you. (= to a person)
I'm grateful **for** the present. (= for a thing)

pleased with / about
I'm pleased **with** my new car. (= personally satisfied with
something that has to do with me)
I'm pleased **about** the improvement in the economy. (= happy
about a general situation)

responsible to / for
I'm responsible **to** the Managing Director. (= to a person)
I'm responsible **for** internal security. (= it's my job)

sorry for / about
I'm sorry **for** you. (= feel sympathy)
I'm sorry **about** the delay. (= regret)

2 Reference words and phrases

a Use

Reference words and phrases refer to something in
another part of a conversation or a text. Some references
are backwards, to something already mentioned; some
are forwards, to something to be mentioned.
We decided to spend the day in London. We went **there** by
train. (**there** = to London)
You know my address. **This** is my phone number: 0293 453465.
(**This** = the phone number which follows)

b Pronouns as reference

I've just bought a new computer. **It** cost less than £1,000.
(**It** = the computer)
I've just seen Elaine. I told **her** I couldn't go to her party.
(**her** = Elaine)
That's not your coffee. It's **mine**. (**mine** = my coffee)
She's giving me a lift to work tomorrow, **which** is fantastic.
(**which** = the fact that she's giving me a lift)
I'm sorry I woke you up so early. **That** wasn't what I intended.
(**That** = to wake you up early)
My sister has just had a baby. **Both** are doing well. (**Both** =
my sister and her baby)

c Time and place words as reference

My grandparents were born in the 1920s. At **that time** hardly
anyone owned a car. (**that time** = in the 1920s)
They're upstairs having a rest. They only got **here** ten
minutes ago. (**here** = to this place)

18.1 Infamy

Vocabulary

1 a Look at these abstract nouns. Do they have positive, negative, or neutral meanings?

| celebrity fame glory heroism infamy notoriety |
| renown reputation villainy |

b Which three words have similar meanings?
c Find two words with opposite meanings.
d What are the adjectives formed from these nouns?

2 Who do you particularly associate with the idea of *infamy*?

Reading

1 Read the title and subtitle of the article. Why might the writer not want to give the killers notoriety?

2 Now read the article and check if your ideas were correct.

3 Answer these questions.

a Which of these sentences best summarizes the writer's ideas?

1 We should publicize the names of criminals so as to deter other people from committing crimes.
2 Denying criminals the possibility of winning fame and glory may help to reduce crime.
3 Most serious criminals would prefer to remain anonymous.

b Why does the writer mention Buford Furrow, Theodor Kaczynski, and Kevin Mitnick? What do they have in common?

c In what way is Erastratos similar to these three men? How is he different?

Close up

l.3 What is the meaning of *fair* in this context?

l.29 What does *toxic* mean? What effect might a *toxic idea* have?

l.47 If you are *teetering in indecision*, have you made up your mind about what to do or not?

Names that live in infamy

Killers want notoriety. Let's not give it to them.

Now it's 'Buford Furrow,' another name we'd much rather not know. By firing 70 bullets toward a bunch of defenseless children, he seized our attention and far more than his fair share of our collective memories.

5 In the recent spate of highly visible hate crimes the emerging pattern seems to be less about specific hates than frenzied tantrums staged by a string of losers with a common goal – to grab headlines. 'The reason they are doing this is for their moment of glory,' says Marvin Hier, who has studied the
10 subject intensely, 'when they feel the whole world is stopping to take notice of them.'

It's an all-too-familiar pattern. The Oklahoma City terrorists, cyber-vandal Kevin Mitnick and Unabomber Theodor Kaczynski all showed a yearning for attention, both in
15 the headline-grabbing nature of their crimes and after capture.

Society appears to be trapped, obliged to pay madmen the attention they crave, in direct proportion to the hurt they do.

This is not a new problem. Two millennia ago, in Ancient Greece, a young man torched one of the seven wonders of the
20 ancient world – the Temple of Diana at Ephesus. When caught and asked why, he then admitted that he really wanted to make a mark, to be remembered. Since he wasn't a great warrior, or creative person, his best chance was to gain infamy by destroying something.

25 Conditions are ripe for more of this. Not only has fame itself been made sacred, but films and novels feed a culture of resentment by extolling the image of romantic loners battling vile institutions. When exaggerated, it becomes one of the most toxic of all modern clichés – preaching contempt for all
30 institutions.

Language focus: sentence structure

The article contains many complex sentences.

1 What is the main difference between a complex sentence, a compound sentence, and a simple sentence? What are the structural differences between these three sentences?

  a Simple   *This is not a new problem.*

  b Compound *This is not a new problem and it is not easy to solve.*

  c Complex   *This is not a new problem although people have not thought about it seriously before.*

2 Underline the main clauses in these complex sentences from the article. (The main clause is the part of the sentence which can stand alone. It makes sense without the other clause or clauses.)

  a *Since he wasn't a great warrior, or creative person, his best chance was to gain infamy by destroying something.*

  b *To punish his selfish act and deter others, the city banned speaking of him.*

  c *By harming innocents, you're only destroying your own name.*

  d *Some of those angry ones out there, who are teetering in indecision with each desperate day, may even decide that it's better to help lay a few bricks.*

  e *If they choose to join us, we should try to welcome them.*

3 How could you describe the other clauses – the parts which are dependent on the main clause and make no sense on their own? Choose one of these descriptions for each dependent clause.

  a a relative clause

  b a clause introduced by a participle expression

  c a conditional clause

  d an adverb clause expressing reason

  e an infinitive clause

We just don't need this trend further reinforced by the seductive lure of renown. Are there solutions?

One answer is suggested by that fellow who burned the temple at Ephesus. He is often called Erastratos. But in fact, many scholars think that is a made-up name, used to replace his true 35 identity. To punish his selfish act and deter others, the city banned speaking of him.

Were the ancients on to something? If people are attracted to villainy partly because they are hoping for celebrity, an 'Erastratos law' might take away some of the allure, by ensuring the opposite. 40

However it's done, won't it make sense for ridicule to replace the fashionableness that's now attached to terror? It would reflect society's determination to allocate fame to those who earn it. We would be saying – 'You can't win celebrity this way. By harming innocents, you're only destroying your own name.' 45

Who knows? Some of those angry ones out there, who are teetering in indecision with each desperate day, may even decide that it's better to help lay a few bricks, alongside the rest of us, than to claw after infamy by tearing the walls down.

If they do – if they choose to join us – we should try to 50 welcome them. And learn their names.   David Brin, *salon.com*

Exploitation

Rewrite these profiles of famous film villains in complex sentences. Try to tell each story in one or two complex sentences. You can change some of the words and the order of the information.

1 **Catwoman from *Batman***
This feline queen of crime is protected by her nine lives. The sexy cat constantly has her evil eye on Batman. She tries to get him to turn to crime. Then he will be hers forever!

2 **Cruella De Vil in Disney's *101 Dalmatians***
Cruella De Vil always gets what she wants. She lies, cheats, and steals for it. She wants the fur of Dalmatian puppies! The puppies' owners, Roger and Anita, say the pups are not for sale. Cruella is angry and swears she will get her hands on the dogs somehow.

Speaking and writing

Work in groups.

1 Tell each other about your favourite villains. They can be real people, still alive or dead, or fictional characters from books, films, TV programmes, etc.

2 Write a profile of one of the villains you have talked about. Use complex sentences where possible. Write your profile in **40–60** words.

▶ **Writing guidelines p.150**

18.2 A year in the public eye

Lead in

Imagine you saw this advertisement in a magazine or newspaper. Would you be interested in taking part? Why? Why not?

Listening

1 **18.1** You are going to hear a group of people discussing the *Castaway* project. First they give their initial reactions.

   a Are their general reactions positive or negative?
   b What are their main objections to the idea?

2 Next the group discussed what skills they have.

   a **18.2** Listen to the recording. What skills do they mention?
   b Which of these skills do you think is the most useful? Rank the skills mentioned in order of importance.

3 Finally the speakers think about the problems of organizing a group of people on an island.

   a Before you listen, think about how you would do this. Do you think you would need to have a leader? If so, how would you decide who should be leader?
   b **18.3** Now listen. How would the speakers solve this problem?

Exploring natural speech

1 When we express opinions which other people might not agree with, we may want to sound tentative and not too forceful.

   Look at this extract from the recording and complete it with tentative words and phrases from this list.

| certain   don't you think?   I don't know   I mean   maybe (x 2) |
| perhaps   sort of |

R So, if we're on the island – we're all faced with having to deal with new people and we all are faced with the fact that we're going to be with these people for the next, ...**1** six months, where do you start? ....**2** how do you, how do you put everyone into their, into their ....**3** hierarchal positions, and, and does it happen by itself or do you think it ...?

K I don't like the sound of hierarchical – I think that would be one of the things you'd want to try and avoid, ...**4**? To try and find some sort of er some sort of society that isn't built on hierarchy – that's built on skill ....**5**.

R Yeah – I suppose that's, that's an ideal, but ....**6** things would just happen.

P I think they would. I think the idea would be to ....**7** all sit down, have a meeting and I suppose talk about what skills you have and try and share out ....**8** responsibilities based on that.

2 **18.4** Now listen again and check your answers.

Castaway

WANTED
Robinson Crusoes and Swiss Family Robinsons

Sick of the City? Want out of the rat race?
In need of adventure and a challenge?

Castaway 2000 is an experiment to examine what aspects of life are really important in society at the start of the new century and what aspects could be disposed of. Do we work too hard? Are we defined by our jobs too much? Are our children getting the right kind of education? What luxuries are actually essentials and what essentials are actually unnecessary? Is there a difference between the priorities of the old and younger generations? How will a range of people who previously didn't know each other, and perhaps wouldn't choose to be together in normal circumstances, get on together when they have to depend on each other?

Contact BBC TV.

HEBRIDES

Language focus: *get*

Get is one of the most useful verbs in English. How much do you know about its uses?

1 In the advertisement for *Castaway*, the producer wrote

a *Are our children **getting** the right kind of education?*
b *How will a range of people who previously didn't know each other … **get on** together …?*

What do *get* and *get on* mean in these two extracts?

2 *Get* as a main verb

Match the uses of *get* in these sentences with meanings in this list.

achieve   arrive   become   bring or fetch   buy   catch (x2)
understand

a *Our cat seems to be **getting** thinner – I hope it's not ill.*
b *My grandmother's in hospital – she **got** flu on holiday.*
c *What time did you **get** home last night?*
d *Can you **get** my glasses for me? – I left them on the desk.*
e *I **got** a first-class degree from Southampton University.*
f *I've decided to **get** my mother a parrot for her birthday.*
g *We had to run, but luckily we managed to **get** the last train.*
h *I don't quite **get** what you mean. Can you explain again?*

3 *Get* + past participle in causative constructions

What is the difference in meaning between these sets of sentences?

a *My jacket's filthy. I'll have to **get** it cleaned.*
My jacket's filthy. I'll have to clean it.
My jacket's filthy. I'll have to have it cleaned.

b *I've **got** an essay to write. I must finish it by tomorrow.*
*I've **got** an essay to write. I must **get** it finished by tomorrow.*

c *I **got** my finger trapped in the car door.*
My finger was trapped in the car door.

4 *Get* as a phrasal verb

Replace the phrases in *italics* in these sentences with the correct form of one of the phrasal verbs from this list. (You may need to make other changes to the original sentences.)

get at   get by   get on   get out of   get round to   get up to

a *I'm enjoying my new job but I don't have a very good relationship with my boss.*
b *I wish you'd stop criticizing me. I'm doing the best I can.*
c *The children have been very quiet all morning – I don't know what they're doing that they shouldn't be doing.*
d *Since my dad lost his job, life hasn't been easy. But we've managed to survive.*
e *It took me a week to find the time to answer her phone call.*
f *When I was at school, I did everything I could to avoid doing athletics.*

Speaking

Work in groups.

1 You have been given the job of suggesting a new reality TV programme. Decide on the following points.

• What is the basic situation? Is the programme located in a particular place?
• Who is involved? How will you attract the people you need for the programme?
• What have they got to do?
• Will the TV audience get involved in any way in the programme?
• How does the programme end – or what happens at the end of the programme?

2 When you have thought out your programme, present your ideas to the rest of the class.

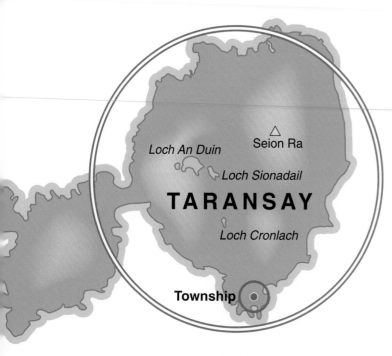

Exploring words

Getting away from it all

1 a Which of these words and phrases do you personally associate with city life and which with rural life? Some could be associated with either.

---

backward   bad transport   bright   bustling   close to nature
conservative   cut off   dangerous at night   dull   exciting
isolated   lonely   no nightlife   noisy   overcrowded
peaceful   polluted   poor public services   poverty   relaxed
secure   stressful   traffic   tranquil   uncrowded   unpolluted
unreliable public transport

---

b Which words on your two lists have positive and which have negative meanings?

c Find as many pairs of opposites in the list of words as you can.

d Compare lists with a partner. How similar are your lists?

2 a Match a word or phrase from **A** with another from **B** to make noun phrases which are places found in the city or the country.

A		B	
1	agricultural	a	blocks
2	farming	b	car parks
3	high-rise	c	communities
4	multi-storey	d	congestion
5	narrow	e	land
6	one-way	f	lanes
7	open	g	malls
8	parking	h	restrictions
9	shopping	i	fields
10	traffic	j	systems

b Where would you be more likely to find each place, in the city or the country?

3 Talk about the main differences between living in the city and living in the country. Here are some points to consider:

- the quality of life
- the environment
- financial considerations
- social life
- entertainment
- transport
- job opportunities
- facilities: schools, hospitals, etc.

4 Work in groups.

The college or school where you learn English has decided to move to a new location. You are on a student committee that has been asked to recommend a suitable place. Two options are under consideration.

- A high-rise block in the heart of the capital city
- A brand-new site in parkland 50 km from the capital but 20 minutes away from an international airport and convenient for motorways and railways

a Discuss the options.

b Present your recommendations, with reasons, to the class.

Language commentary

1 Sentence structure

There are three main types of sentence.

a Simple sentences

These consist of a single clause with one main verb.

5,000 people **applied** for the job.

b Compound sentences

These consist of at least two clauses which make sense on their own. They are independent of each other.

Clauses in compound sentences can be joined by these conjunctions: *and* (*then*), *but, either / or, neither / nor, or, so, yet.*

The radio crackled **and then** (it) went quiet.

The castaways have to be as self-sufficient as possible, **so** they grow their own vegetables and keep farm animals.

c Complex sentences

These consist of more than one clause. One of these is the main clause; other(s) are dependent on (or subordinate to) the main clause.

He worked as a spy until the mid-1950s when, realizing that the authorities suspected him, he fled to the West.

This sentence has three clauses.

He worked as a spy until the mid-1950s	= main clause
when he fled to the West.	= dependent clause
realizing that the authorities suspected him	= dependent clause

d Subordinate clauses in complex sentences

There are many kinds of subordinate or dependent clauses in complex sentences.

- Conditional clauses.
  If they choose to join us, we should welcome them.
- Relative clauses.
  Firemen **who attended the blaze** praised her for her bravery.
- Adverbial clauses.
  When he saw what he'd done, he apologized immediately.
  As he knew everyone there, he felt quite confident.
- Infinitive clauses.
  To make up for his mistake, he took everyone to the theatre.
- Clauses introduced by a participle.
  Seeing me on the television news, he thought I must have done something terrible.

2 *get*

a As a main verb – meanings

Get is a very useful verb because it has many different meanings, although some native speakers of English prefer to avoid it by using more specific verbs instead.

achieve
My sister **got** 95% in her English exam.

arrive
We **got** home at 3 o'clock in the morning.

become
I'm **getting** hungry – it must be nearly lunchtime.

bring / fetch
Shall I **get** you a cup of coffee?

buy
I'm going to **get** a new car next year.

catch
My friend **got** the 10 o'clock bus into town.
I hope I don't **get** a cold this winter.

prepare
Shall I **get** dinner tonight?

receive
He **got** a car for his eighteenth birthday.

understand / hear
I didn't **get** that. Can you say it again – more slowly this time?

b *get something done* – causative use

This is an alternative to *have something done*. Both *have something done* and *get something done* are used to refer to actions that the subject initiates, or causes to be done, but does not do personally.

I'll have to **get my shoes repaired** soon.

c *get something done* – non-causative use

In these examples something unfortunate happens to the subjects – through no fault of their own.

He **got stuck** in a traffic jam on the way home.
They **got** their new car **stolen**.

In these examples *get* is used informally to mean 'do something that has to be done'.

We'd better **get** the flat **cleaned** and **tidied**.
I can't **get** my work **done** – it's too noisy in here.

d Other expressions with *get*

It takes me about 10 minutes **to get washed and dressed**.

get changed   get shaved   get undressed

Last year I **got divorced** – next year I'm **getting married** again.

e Phrasal verbs with *get*

Stop **getting at** me. (= criticize)
We're not rich but we **get by**. (= survive)
Do you and your brother **get on**? (= have a good relationship)
I'll do everything I can to **get out of** going to the dentist. (= avoid)
I don't know when I'll **get round to** writing back. (= find the time to)
It's about time we **got down to** business. (= start doing seriously)
He's managed to **get in with** all the right people. (= become friendly with someone because you think they may help you)
Can we just **get** the interview **over with**? (= complete something unpleasant that has to be done)
I've tried explaining but I just can't **get through to** him. (= communicate, make someone understand)

Tapescripts

1.1

Speaker 1
For me the key event of the 20th century would have to be the erm, the coming down of the Berlin Wall. ...

Worst idea of the 20th century must be the the motor car, I think.

Speaker 2
I think the most important event of the 20th century was the er breaking down of the Berlin Wall and the er union of the two Germanies and the integration of the ex-Communist countries into the erm shall we say 'free world'? And I think one of the worst ideas of the 20th century was beside Cold War was Communism, state socialism.

Speaker 3
Erm I would say some of the key events of the 20th century would be erm, the first things that spring to mind are the wars, so the First World War and the Second World War and the Vietnam War erm, man on the moon, and scientific advances, the discovery of DNA which has huge implications now ...

Erm I don't I don't know if I'd call it really the worst idea of the 20th century but but I think possibly cars or or motorized transport would come fairly close ...

Speaker 4
... I think I would list all the wars – the First World War, the Second World War, Vietnam, I think all the wars. Erm ...

Intertwined with the hundred key events, cos although er the First World War the Second World War were key events, they were also bad ideas, er Hitler's idea to eliminate the Jews, for example, would be one of the worst ideas ...

1.2

Speaker 1
I'd say one person that really influenced me when I was growing up was erm a teacher. Now I I'd moved schools at a time when not many children were moving across to to a new school – it was sort of in the middle of a, in the middle of a term, I think it was and erm, I didn't know anyone obviously and I was feeling a little bit unsure of myself and er the physical education teacher was called Ralph which is my name and er he was very popular – he was a really sort of tall guy, you know, er he was er ranked in the in the country for his tennis playing and I loved tennis and I really sort of admired him and because I had the s..., the same name I thought that there may be some connection and erm you know, I sort of you know would watch him and see what he was up to and then he actually took me under his wing a little bit and gave me some extra coaching, tennis coaching, and erm it was great, but it taught me a lot about sportsmanship and a lot of values and things that were to do with with sport and sport-related which was you know something I was very much into when I was a child and er it was really useful and very beneficial even now.

Speaker 2
... erm well, I'm influenced I suppose by by my parents and friends and stuff and I base, well my role model might be, I think probably my brother because he's he's always erm really confident and relaxed and I seem to get a bit stressed and I dunno, tied up and he'll come home and watch TV and phone up his friends and stuff and if he's got an exam he won't really care – he'll just go out and enjoy himself and I'm a bit more conscientious so I sort of look up to him and I I see that he's always enjoying himself – but he's still got time to, you know he still does well, and he he's got a good job and he he works hard, so he he is probably the person that I look up to most ...

Speaker 3
I'd have to say er one of the people who has has had a great influence on me would be Barbara Walters, believe it or not. Erm I just remember as a little girl er turning on the TV and there not being a whole lot of women er giving the news, I mean hard-hitting news, and I remember watching Barbara Walters be right up there with all the the other male news anchors and thinking 'Wow if she can do it then then I can definitely do it!' and er I just always loved er watching her stories and the questions that she would ask and for me she was just a smart woman erm that I could you know flip on the TV and see her and she was a real inspiration and made me feel like as a woman as a young girl I could really do whatever I wanted to do – so she was a role model for me in that way.

1.4

1
W1 Well, I'd like to think that I'm a quite strong person, would you say?
W2 Yeah, yeah, you know your own mind.
W1 Good, I'm glad you agree with me on that. Erm I have been accused of being I suppose, a bit self-centred sometimes.
W2 Everyone's like that though. OK.
W1 OK. Erm, the last two.
W2 Ah, you're dependable.
W1 Yeah. I'd say (definitely). I'm always there on time, aren't I?
W2 Yeah.
W1 Yeah, dependable.

2
M Er, I'd say, I'm I'm quite an excitable person actually.
W Definitely, you do get a bit overexcited at times.
M I do, I do get a bit carried away. I'm maybe I should try some meditation to calm down.
W Maybe, what about, what about the second two?
M Oh all right, erm ...
W You're quite easy-going, though.
M I'm very easy-going ...
W Quite laid back.
M Yeah very laid back. I I should learn to be more difficult, really. I (should) go to difficult classes or something.
W Erm.
M I'd like to be more passionate about things. (Yeah, yeah) I think, erm I think more oomph ...
W Yeah, you lack a bit of passion. Bit of ambition.
M I'm a bit too cautious perhaps.
W So, I suppose cautious will do.
M Yeah. I am cautious.

3
W1 Erm ...
W2 Well, I think that's answered it really.
W1 What? Timid?
W2 Yes. Timid, definitely. We'll choose timid.
W1 Timid. And – er oh, I'm not gloomy.
W2 No, definitely not, you're always in a good mood.
W1 So ...
W2 Sunny.
W1 Sunny.
W2 Definitely, yeah.
W1 OK.
W2 And, agreeable or moody?
W1 Do you think I'm moody?
W2 Not at all, no.
W1 Really? I'm not moody, am I?
W2 No.
W1 No, I think I'm quite agreeable.
W2 Definitely.
W1 OK.

4
W So, what sort of mood are you in then?
M I am in a good mood.
W Good.
M Definitely in a good mood.
W OK.
M I have a smile on my face.
W Right, and are you, do you think you're in a carefree mood or a thoughtful mood?
M I would edge towards carefree, but ...
W Right.
M ... that sounds a bit lacksadaisical, but no I do, I'm not feeling terribly pensive or thoughtful.
W OK.
M And ...
W And well obviously if you're in a good mood, you're probably feeling optimistic.
M I am ...
W Yeah.
M No definitely feeling optimistic. It's it's the middle of the week, there's lots of things happening. It's good.
W Good.

2.1

Speaker 1
Erm computers really equal work in my mind, erm. That's not to say I don't like them. I do. I love, love using them and I can't believe the sort of progress I personally have made in my use of it in the last, well, two years, since working here. Erm, I would like one at home in some ways, I mean, mainly just as an information source, rather than having to make phone calls all the time – I'd much rather be on e-mail or Internet, erm – I really like using the Internet actually and would like to to do it more erm. I wonder what else I'd use it for if I had one at home. I probably would end up working at home which is not a good thing in my mind – so not in that sense erm, but yeah, I'm not really into computer games or anything like that, but I guess I could be converted.

Speaker 2
Computers – incredibly important for work erm – where I just completely take them for granted – if one went wrong I wouldn't know what to do with it at all erm, but basically I just use it as a sort of glorified typewriter erm and for sending e-mails to friends erm and I have got a computer at home which probably hasn't been turned on, I would guess for at least a year now erm and is under a blanket.

Speaker 3
I suppose the most of the contact I have with computers is at work. Erm and they are vital for for the kind of work I do – erm communication between different people via e-mail, erm writing up documents, erm and researching on the Internet – I suppose these are, are the main uses. I really only use Word erm when I'm creating a document myself because I'm not, I'm not a computer wizard. Erm at home I do have a computer but I use it very little erm, I suppose erm the most it's used for at home is is games and I'm not very good at them, so so I don't play.

Speaker 4
Computers are very important to me, cos I couldn't do my job without one really – I'm a designer and I basically sit in front of a computer for most of my working day and then I haven't got my own computer at home but my housemates do and I have used them at home as well, so my life is erm pretty much revolving round computers some of the time but I could live

without one and erm maybe I quite appreciate living without one some of the time.

Speaker 5
I'm not sure how important computers are to me really. I think I need to use one at work but only really for for word-processing. I tend not to use one at home although we've got one. E-mail clearly is a very important part of what you can do with a computer at the moment and I must say that I think it's a wonderful invention, but if we didn't have e-mail then I'm sure I'd go back to communicating in the ways we used to and in fact I think in a way it would almost be good if if I did and chose to write letters to people and telephone people rather than rely on e-mail which is very easy in a way – it's it's a very good thing to have but it also makes you fairly lazy, I think.

3.1

W   Oh I know I got absolutely soaked – I wish I'd brought my umbrella – I can't believe it, but I …
M1 Oh – what this morning?
W   Yeah yeah – but it occurred to me actually – cos I was running down the street to try and get into the office and erm, as I say, I arrived drenched but erm someone said to me – when I got into the office – was saying oh well, you know, I mean you don't achieve anything more by by running cos you're still going to get just as wet …
M2 Yes.
M1 Well it's about a ten-minute walk isn't it, so …
W   Well, no no, that's not the …
M1 … by running you'll do it in five, so you're not going to achieve anything – you're still going to be wet.
M2 Yeah.
W   Yeah, but no the idea that, you know, you're by running in it you're, you're still – as much rain is falling on you as if you were walking – mind you it would have gone totally against the grain just to have strolled down the road.

3.2

Speaker 1
First of all, I'd like to go back to around the turn of the century, 1900 I'm thinking – 1899–1900 in England cos I'd really like to see what it was like before the First World War, before things really started to go wrong.

Speaker 2
I'm very curious about the very very early time of the sort of the beginnings of humans when we first came down from the trees, if if that's how we started, so I'd be very curious to see what … how we lived …

Speaker 3
Perhaps the time of the the pharaohs in a in a sort of Egyptian – yes I I quite fancy the idea of being an Egyptian.

Speaker 4
I think I would go back to the time of Jesus, I think – first century Palestine …

Speaker 5
Erm, I dunno, I think the Renaissance would just be absolutely amazing – to go to Florence and sort of walk through those narrow streets and see the workshops, hear hear the noise of people working on these huge canvases and furniture and stuff, I think that would be great.

3.3

M1 The problem with making choices about time travel is you have to lay down the ground rule of 'Can I change things?' – (Oh) or do you have to

leave everything – tell people not to get on the *Titanic* or yeah, … (Right, yeah) and can I make bets on, you know, can I sell short on Wall Street just before the Crash? If you can't it's not worth bothering to go back …
W1 Oh no, but I think it'd be interesting to go back and just sort of be a fly on the wall, cos it's one thing to read it, but it's another thing to actually be there and see it and smell it and (Yeah) taste it, you know.
M1 And yeah, you wouldn't realize like if you went back in time in New York and you're so used to New York now that first of all there's going to be horse dung everywhere, you know and multitudes of flies and it must smell and the the noises the sounds you hear are not horns – it's clip-clop, clip-clop. (Right) Things you don't necessarily think of – you just look at photographs and you don't get that sense of like smell and hearing. (Yeah)
W2 Oh that's true and also on a much more personal level, I would love to go back and see my parents as children – see what their lives were like – see how they interacted with their family.
W2 That's a scary thought to me.
M1 No, that's too personal, I wanna go back and look at strangers at a time before anybody I know existed.
M2 I I think it might be more fun to project a thousand years into the future.
W1 You would, you'd want to go ahead?
M2 Yeah because we have books and movies to … you know and now the Internet is like a library in your home, you know to to explore the past, but er (To go into the future) the absolute unknowable …
W1 What would it be like to come back? You know to go somewhere and find out – yeah all this stuff to come back – do you think you'd be able to live in today's world knowing how much it's … I mean I assume it's going to change a great deal.
M1 Well, if I had no choice I – would I want to come back? I don't know till I go into the future.
M2 Yeah, it might be great there. (Yeah)
W1 Or, you know what – it might not exist.
M1 That's the thing that I'd fear, (That's scary) like – or the world ended ten minutes (Yes) before the time I decided to visit.

4.1

M1 … late at night on the motorway when I was, erm, I was driving home from London to Oxford, erm about, I don't know, about 11 o'clock at night or something like that on a Saturday night and the motorway was quite deserted – it was a very clear night, very good visibility and I noticed these lights coming up very very fast behind me …
M2 UFO!
M1 Well, it wasn't, it wasn't. I only wish it had been erm and er we were approaching a junction and I thought well this car's coming up very close behind me obviously he's going to go off up the slip road to the junction but he didn't – he came right up behind me and at the last minute swerved out to overtake me, hit the back of my car erm but not enough to to to send either of us off course, and sped off up the motorway, so I thought well, you know, I'm not having this, so I chased him and flashed him and he pulled over on to the side of the road erm when I caught up with him and and I pulled in behind.
M2 Do you think he hadn't noticed or something?
M1 Er well, it's difficult to imagine he couldn't have noticed cos there was a big bang and there was actually quite a lot of damage to both cars when

we actually got out and had a look, but I got out of the car erm and of course I could see the car in front in my headlights and erm both doors opened … (Ah) … and two very large guys in baseball caps and big Puffa jackets got out …
M2 Oh no, big Puffa jackets is fine though, T-shirts would be more dangerous …
M1 … all right well, there were two two big guys in baseball caps and I suddenly realized that I was completely alone on this motorway, it was just me and them and they looked extremely …

4.2

M1 And er I suddenly realized that I was completely alone on this motorway, it was just me and them and they looked extremely intimidating …
M2 Sorry were you still in your car at this stage?
M1 No no, I was out of my car but I was wishing I was back in the car.
M2 No baseball cap I presume?
M1 No baseball cap. No baseball bat – anything like that. Erm, and they they sort of approached me, one from either side of the car erm and there were a couple of minutes when I thought mm yeah this was a bad idea – I really wish I was anywhere but here, erm but in fact they were very apologetic and and said sorry we didn't realize you were going so slowly, erm but it's OK – here's our insurance details and sorry about the damage to your car and everything was fine, but just for those two seconds, you know …

4.3

W   … it was in Italy and I went to erm this er station which was well outside the city and erm the friend that I'd met there took me to the station and I missed the train before last back so I was, I had to catch a very late train back – there were two people on the platform and when I got into the carriage there was only one other person in there and there were about eight stops on the train, erm and halfway through the journey the other person in the train got out so I was on my own in this train late at night …
M   With the lights on?
W   With the lights on, with the lights on, but erm I was thinking to myself, well this is all right because when I get to the end when I get to the station it'll be fine because I can just jump out and get into a taxi and I'll be back in the hotel and everything'll be fine. Erm, when I got to the end of the, when I got to the station, erm because it was the last train, everybody had gone home there was nobody there, it was virtually deserted erm and I grabbed this person I said 'Where's the taxi rank?' and they pointed over to this sort of clump of trees in the middle of this sort of like very dark patch …

4.4

M   My only experiences of road rage or potential road rage have been with me on a bicycle and other people in cars which instantly puts you at a fairly large disadvantage erm …
W   Have you been knocked off?
M   I've never been knocked off, no, no. I made an angry gesture at a car driver once …
W   Oh did you?
M   Yes, cos I was sort of cycling along as I thought I was in the right as cyclists always are, (Yes, definitely) erm and he didn't think I was in the right and he opened his window and shouted abuse at me, (Yeah) erm so I made an angry gesture as they call it in the newspapers (Uhuh) erm and he actually

followed me (Oh) and erm pulled alongside and stuck his head out of the sunroof while driving along which was slightly odd, stuck his head out of the sunroof and and (He was big enough to do that) basically said you know if you do that again I'm going to knock your head off – he was just absolutely furious, so I said I was sorry erm …

W Like you do.

M Like you do, yes, erm and he drove off and he scowled at me in a very nasty way. But it was quite unsettling.

5.1

P All right. I have another e-mail here. This one's from Jo. Er, let's see what you think of this. She says that somebody she sits near at work is always on the phone – he has a very loud voice and she can hear everything he says. Now she wants to know, does she treat his conversations as public property? You know passing on bits of gossip or even interrupt his conversations – adding her own comments, you know. So, what do you think she should do about that?

W I don't think she has the right, I'm afraid, I just don't think she has the right – she has to put up with it. She's got to concentrate on what she's doing and erm let him get on with it – maybe talk to him about it, but it's absolutely not her right to get involved.

M I completely disagree. I think that erm if he is going to be so rude as to, you know, have conversations like that – at that tone and interfere with her work – there's no way that he can expect her to to not take what he's been saying and erm and use it or to to refer to it. I think it's it's the most annoying thing to be in a work environment and have someone shouting down the phone to them so …, you know to to whoever.

W I agree, but why not rise above it? Why sink to their level?

P I would imagine it would be very distracting. What do … when you say rise above it, what do you think she could do to sort that out?

W Possibly try and talk to him about it, but to start gossiping and using his conversations as public property is being absolutely no better than what he's doing – erm I think that would be an appalling way to behave.

M But perhaps by doing that he would stop, he would get the hint. He'd start maybe being a little more considerate with his conversations.

W But why not simply talk to him in an adult manner?

M Yeah, you're probably right. That's probably the first thing that she should do, but erm I think that she should definitely confront it, either by speaking to him or by just making it completely obvious that she's heard everything he's said.

P Well, Jo, hopefully you're listening and hopefully that can be of some help.

5.2

P Well, let's move on to our next e-mail from someone in London. They don't give us their name and we don't know if they're a man or a woman, so we'll call them Sam. Let's hear what Sam says. 'My boss has asked me to book him a double room at a hotel for a conference. The thing is he's not taking his wife with him. I feel like protesting – but I know that if I do he'll just tell me to mind my own business.' So, do we have any advice for Sam?

M Well Sam, erm, I think this might be a case of jumping to conclusions because erm …

5.5

M Have you read about the progress they're making with the whole mapping of the of the genes for for for humans?

W No, I mean a little bit about that it could help them solve some er diseases and things like that or understand them …

M Right, that's the good part …

W … which I think is great yeah.

M Sure, I mean I guess probably like most people I have incredible ambivalence about this, because you know we we, no matter what your religious faith is, you know, we move into sort of playing God if we can actually pinpoint, you know what that gene in the body does what in effect …

W Definitely, and then if we start to choose 'Well we want this or we want that', it's I think you're right, I think the whole issue of God and erm creation really comes into play and I think it's actually a scary area, I think as as far as, you know, helping the medical field, I think that's wonderful, (Sure) but when we get into actually changing things (Right) – that's a little scary to me.

M Right – well I'm a Star Trek fan (yeah) and that's always amazing when one of the crew people, you know, are are sent to the erm, you know, the doctor and they just do a (Noise) you know …

W Right right and they're all better right.

M Right, and and they're they've been scanned and you know and somehow they're they're better within seconds usually, you know. (Right) So in terms of eradicating disease, you know, that's that's a wonderful thing, although I guess if we all lived to two hundred years old because so many natural cause diseases, if you will, have been eradicated (Right) – that cause a natural death is what I'm trying to say (Right), then then we have economic issues to deal with, you know.

W Well, right and I guess what, what scares me is where does it all end? (Sure) You know where does it stop and how do we control it (Right) and I really don't know how we do. Who in the end says 'OK, enough,' or you know, what can actually happen in these labs? What what can they create?

M Right, right and er the expense of all of it is just astronomical and er it it could be very exciting to finally find cures for cancer and to and to be able to pluck out those genes or modify them so so that people don't have these horrible diseases …

W Right, but I think choosing whether your child has blue eyes or brown eyes, whether it's male or female I, I really, I don't agree with that personally. I think you know, I think that should be left up to God.

M I agree.

6.1

Speaker 1
Yes, wordgames, I'm quite good at, I'm quite quick about words and visually, I'm good at crosswords and I can spot an anagram very very quickly – and I always impress the children with these quiz games on the television where you have a couple of letters and and you have to think of the word or the phrase and I always get it straightaway and they, they're open-mouthed in amazement and tell me I ought to go on the telly.

Speaker 2
A natural asset I have which I didn't realize I had until relatively recently is incredibly good eyesight. Erm, I haven't had my eyes tested for about 20 years,

probably more, erm but I was driving along with a friend one day, who's got particularly bad eyesight and we were doing the kind of the classic driving-test test, where you to read somebody's number plate from, I dunno, X metres behind you erm and I could see, sort of four or five cars in front on the motorway and this friend of mine was completely astonished and then she was testing me all the rest of the the weekend as to what I could see and what I couldn't see.

Speaker 3
Yes, bizarrely enough, I do have this ability to remember things like phone numbers and birthdays and dates of all kinds – erm I've no idea where the ability comes from – er it's not something I cultivate consciously erm but I don't actually need to carry people's phone numbers around with me – I've got them in my head.

Speaker 4
Erm I've always been, I've always been fiendishly fiendishly good at mental arithmetic erm, which goes back an awfully long way, erm I mean even when I was at at primary school at the age of eight I used to come erm sort of top in the mental arithmetic tests, which were probably, just things like you know eight plus seven and you'd have a roomful of seven-year-olds scratching their heads and I would get 15 straightaway.

6.2

W1 Oh gosh there are all kind of gifts that people can be born with – you know mental gifts, intelligence, physical attributes – beauty – strength

W2 Definitely, yeah. Talent …

W1 Talent absolutely, musical inclination.

W2 And I definitely believe that people are born with certain talents – I think that they can can also, er you know they can grow depending on the environment that they're in, but …

W1 Yeah, but I think you either have an affinity for something or you don't.

W2 Definitely.

W1 Two children take piano lessons – one's going to be amazing and the other …

W2 … the other is just OK, I agree and I …

W1 Do you think it comes from the parents?

W2 I think, you know, maybe partly, like I said, I think that it can influence a talent, but I think er I think some people are born with certain talents and some people aren't.

W1 And the people that are born with it, is it because their parents, like were their parents musically gifted so they have an inclination?

W2 I think so, yeah …

7.1

M1 Well now, you see, the thing, what I think is, is the reason that the five senses are called senses is because they are in effect tangible in that there's something that we can either agree on or disagree on – if you start talking about erm intuition or instinct as a sense, you're into a vaguer area, you know – your instincts – your both your instincts are different to mine, whereas if I say 'Do you think this feels like cat's fur or whatever', then there's there's a point that we can agree on – we can use our tangible senses, but I I don't think instinct and intuition is something that's – I think some people have more intuition than …

W I was going to say – there does seem to be, which is is peculiar, I mean why that should be.

M2 There's a heck of lot that we don't know about the human mind though, isn't there, (Yeah) when you you go into the situation where you think 'I've been here before, I know I've been and I know what's going to happen next.' How can you explain that?

M1 Well exactly – it's a vague area. I mean it's it's the way I always feel about, you know, psychology and therapy and psychiatry because, you know, you're supposed to be dealing with something that is tangible or recognizable, but there's nothing to go on and I think instinct and intuition is much the same thing – it's different for all of us, you know.

W Would you agree that there is such a thing as female intuition?

M2 We know there is.

M1 Well if I do, I could only take that, I could only accept it as a female point of view, so we could, yeah, we could debate that all night. I mean, yes, I'm prepared … Convince me.

W Well, I have to say I feel that there is, but erm I might just be just a little bit biased.

7.3

Number 1 is false. Paying someone to do something they already like to do will not lead them to enjoy the task more.

Number 2 is false, too. The majority of employees prefer non-challenging jobs that allow them to socialize.

Number 3. Again, this is false. Most people get upset about inequity in pay rather than their own low pay. People can be happy with low pay when everyone in the company is the same.

Number 4. False again. It is better to start with the most extreme position you can take. Most negotiations end up in the middle of where the two parties started. The more extreme your starting point the more likely you are to end up with the better side of the bargain.

Number 5. This is true. The essence of leadership is sticking to a position despite appearances. By changing their position too often, leaders create confusion in the organization.

Number 6. True again. Groups do not bring out the best in people unless they are well-structured and individual contributions are clear. Most people, it seems, need to be held accountable.

Number 7. False. The data does not support the idea that happy workers are necessarily better, more productive workers. Unfortunately, while angry workers may be unproductive, satisfied workers are not necessarily productive.

Number 8. Once more, this is false. Employees do better when they are told what is expected.

Number 9. False again. All the data shows that groups can make more extreme and less accurate decisions than individuals.

Number 10. This one's true. Give your feedback immediately. Don't wait. This has been shown on mice and men alike. Tell them what's wrong right away.

8.2

Presenter
Gun control is a subject which concerns most people in the United States – whether they want to defend their right to own and use weapons – or whether they see them as the curse of modern America. And it's easy to see why it's such an emotive issue when you study the statistics. Each year half a million gun-related crimes are committed in the US – including thirteen thousand murders. And with nearly two hundred and fifty million firearms in circulation it's clearly not an easy task to keep track of who has a gun and why they want to keep it.

[Radio extract The Million Mom March flooded the national mall today with a call for tougher gun control. 'I was eight years old when my father …']

Presenter
The Million Mothers March, when tens of thousands of people converged on Washington to call for tighter gun laws, was an example of how strongly many campaigners feel about the issue. But while tragedies like Colombine – when two teenagers shot dead twelve of their classmates and a teacher – have heightened public concern about guns, many people want to keep their right to own one. Trish Gregory is a member of the NRA – the National Rifle Association.

Trish Gregory
I am a law-abiding American – I've never broken a law. I'm a single woman who lives alone and I feel like I have a right to defend myself. For instance if someone was stalking me or I was fearful about myself or my family, I have a right to own a firearm.

Presenter
The gun lobby argues that the second amendment gives everyone the right to carry a firearm. But as with most things to do with the gun debate, it's not that simple. The amendment is actually open to a variety of interpretations – as Yan Vernick, the Assistant Director of the Centre for Gun Control in Baltimore, explains.

Yan Vernick
One of the primary controversies is whether the second amendment protects an individual right to own a gun, or whether, instead, the second amendment protects only a collective right, that's closely related to the old-fashioned idea of state militias – groups of citizens who collectively were there to help to keep the peace.

Presenter
And while campaigners on both sides of the argument will continue to put as much pressure on politicians as possible, the battle is increasingly being fought in the courts. Not only are people testing out what the second amendment actually means, but more than thirty cities and states are trying to sue gun manufacturers for medical costs that stem from the misuse of firearms. Barbara Holt of the group New Yorkers against Gun Violence explains the basis of the cases being brought.

Barbara Holt
When you are making and distributing a product that is particularly dangerous, you have a duty as a manufacturer to take particular care in how you distribute it – whose hands it gets into. And **what they're arguing is that the gun manufacturers have not taken care.**

Presenter
While similar law suits have been successful against other industries, it's far from clear what the results of the ones against the gun manufacturers will be. **What is certain is that the process is being watched closely by campaigners** and politicians alike, to see what it will mean for the future of gun law in America.

8.4

Speaker 1
The rubbish in my house consists of food, packaging, paper, cardboard, plastic, newspapers, bottles, that kind of thing. Erm, I don't really sort it into different types, I'm afraid. I'm not a very green person – I try to put the bottles in the bottle bank er when I've got the energy and I do put the newspapers into a a collection box that we have for newspapers, but apart from that I don't sort the rubbish. Erm I use about one large plastic bag a week, not very much, because I live by myself, and the local council takes the rubbish away. I don't know where it goes. I presume it goes to a local rubbish dump. Erm, I presume that when it gets there – I hope they sort the newspapers and the bottles and things like they say they do, but I'm not convinced and

I think the rest of the rubbish just goes to erm fill in the land.

Speaker 2
Rubbish that we regularly get rid of in our household, erm is normally paper, erm paper packaging and plastic packaging for food, cardboard, newspapers, bottles, tins, and we do sort them into different types. Erm we sort out the bottles and the paper which we leave out for recycling and that's collected once a week. We probably use about three to five bags a week, I should say, for getting rid of actual rubbish, er but that obviously depends – over Christmas we certainly got rid of a lot more. The rubbish is taken away by the local council refuse collectors or dustmen, whatever you like to call them, and the recycling is also taken away on a weekly basis by the same council. I would imagine that the rubbish goes to landfill sites and is buried there and the bottles and the paper are taken away and recycled into some other form.

9.2

Speaker 1
I have quite specific music tastes. If I'm working, I have to listen to classical music because if … anything with words I start singing along and then I can't work. So I like Fauré's Requiem and Mozart's Requiem and depressing things like that – a bit of Debussy. Er, otherwise I like acoustic rock, as everybody laughs at me. I like acoustic guitars and Jeff Buckley and Tom Waites because it's fairly depressing but very soothing kind of music. I like Radiohead, makes me quite mellow cos otherwise I am quite an intense person. So my music calms me down.

Speaker 2
I've always loved Michael Jackson music and sort of really poppy stuff – everything that's in the charts. I know that it's cheesy but it's erm, I don't know, it's fun to dance to and it's catchy – you you hear it once and I dunno next time you hear it, you sort of know know the lyrics and you want to sing along erm. And then when you go to night clubs or wherever, it's fun to dance to. Erm, but more serious stuff, I, I really like Ella Fitzgerald and jazzy stuff but yeah, that's about it.

Speaker 3
Well I'm actually a bit of a classical music buff myself and I like all the Classic FM Standards by sort of Mozart and Elgar, and people like that. The really sort of clichéd ones. I think my favourite piece of music is probably Bach's Brandenburg Concertos. Erm, I like listening to that and it helps me unwind and relax at the end of a day, something like that. Erm, I also quite like erm, erm classical music when it's adapted in films, I particularly like the way someone like Stanley Kubrick uses it sort of in an undermining way, sort of, in *A Clockwork Orange* – the Beethoven scenes in that, I think that there … that's very clever and very moving and erm, yeah.

Speaker 4
Erm, my favourite music is kind of older music. The sort of erm, the sort of standards, I think they're called – jazz standards, which are sung by people like Ella Fitzgerald and er people like that. I like it because erm, I like singing it myself. Erm, I used to sing in a band where we did a lot of stuff like that. Erm, I find it very relaxing, erm and it's just very calming music. It's it's something that you can just sort of lie down and listen to. Erm I like having it on in the car cos I sing in the car a lot which is quite embarrassing at traffic lights because it's quite obvious that I'm singing very loudly. Erm and er it's just nice – it's nice music to go to sleep to, it's nice music to sort of just relax to, it's nice music to drive to, erm and they're just they're they're classic pieces, they're sort of classic melodies.

W1 Right, well. I've got to have my boys – my Back Street Boys.

M Oh no.

W2 Oh Ellie.

W1 We've got to have some pop in the car to sing along with.

M OK, but just short bursts of that, please.

W1 Oh all right. Well what do you want?

W2 Well, I like to sing in the car …

W1 Exactly!

W2 So, I think some sort of, I dunno, girl with a guitar, some Joni Mitchell, Suzanne Vega.

W1 Yeah but nobody knows them.

W2 I know it.

W1 God, Mum and Dad'll probably know that more than you.

W2 Shut up. It's better than Back Street Boys.

M I definitely want … I want some quite chilled-out stuff, some instrumentally kind of trip-hoppy stuff, so when we've got the nice vistas, the nice things to look at through the window …

W1/2 All right. OK

M … we can all feel very relaxed.

W1 Well Back Street Boys do a really chilled-out one on their album.

W2 No.

M Leave the Back Street Boys, honestly.

W1 OK.

W2 You wanna bring Kylie as well, don't you?

W1 No.

W2 You did last time.

W1 That was last year.

M Do we want any rock?

W2 Yeah.

W1 Really?

M So we can rock out …

W2 Yeah, maybe some classics.

W1 Yeah maybe a bit of Queen classics. What else?

W2 How about some classical stuff?

M/W1 Hmm.

W2 OK. Write that off. That says it all.

M Not too sure. Maybe.

W1 Erm.

W2 How about some songs from the musicals? Come on we all love that …

W1/M No, No.

W2 … we can all sing …

W1 No we don't want …

W2 Pleeese.

M1 We should have some Motown.

W1 Yeah, definitely.

W2 Some Diana Ross, some Stevie Wonder, …

M Stevie Wonder, yeah stuff like that.

W1 Jackson Five, we'll have some of the old …

M Ah, (I) like (the) Jackson Five, very good.

W1 Yeah, definitely.

M That'll keep us awake.

W1 Sing along with that.

W2 Yeah, sing along with Stevie, that would be good …

W1 … show off your musical voice.

W2 It passes the time, doesn't it?

W1 All right, OK what else, what have we got here?

W2 Eminem?

W1 Could have a bit of that.

W2 Yeah, we like that.

W1 Yeah.

W2 You don't like that, do you?

M Well, no, it's all right. I don't mind.

W1 You'll just start getting all political, and contro…, d'you know what I mean?

M I'll bite my tongue.

W1 Controversial.

M It's fine.

W2 So, so far we've got Joni Mitchell, the Back Street Boys …

M Yeah.

W1 All right.

W2 Some chill-out stuff,

M Yeah.

W2 Some Queen …

M Some Queen, some Motown …

9.5

Speaker 1

(A) piece of music that I was actually given, not a piece of music that I bought recently erm was a CD by someone called Badly Drawn Boy, which I'd heard of but I assumed that I wouldn't like and in fact it's one of the best CDs that I've heard in a very long time – and the reason why I like it is that it's got some excellent tunes and some very sensible and meaningful lyrics which I think is quite a rarity nowadays and since we were given it at Christmas we've played it non-stop, so we obviously like it very much.

Speaker 2

I went to this concert in Oxford a couple of months ago. It was Elgar's the Dream of Gerontius, which is a choral piece and I'm not a big fan of choral music but it surprised me. It was fantastic. It had some really really surprising stuff in it that I didn't expect – it sounded like erm a movie soundtrack …

Speaker 3

I went to a concert last year which I thought was really fantastic, erm it was a violinist who I'm quite keen on in any case and it was just really good to see him perform. He was conducting the orchestra as well so as well as seeing him perform I can't remember what piece he did, erm as well as seeing him perform that, we were able to get an idea of how he felt erm music should be interpreted. The atmosphere was really nice erm it was at the Albert Hall which is, er, an interesting place to go to a concert – although the acoustics aren't that good the actual atmosphere in the audience is is excellent.

10.1

Presenter

You work hard all year and your few weeks of holiday are precious – so surely the last thing you'd want to do during them would be to give up your creature comforts? But in fact that's exactly what a growing number of people are choosing to do. Travel companies which specialize in anything from deep-sea diving or trekking to camel-riding are reporting a year on year growth in customers. Michelle Cook, who's worked as a tour leader with an adventure holiday firm for more than ten years, says the interest doesn't just come from students or twenty-somethings.

Michelle Cook

We actually take people from fourteen to seventy-nine years old. In the past I've led tours with people in their eighties and they've been the life and soul of the group. And the people that travel with us are people that have the right attitude, a sense of adventure, a sense of humour – they're people that want to go on holiday, have some fun, but they also want to learn about the country they're travelling in. They really are all different types of people, from different backgrounds, different nationalities, all ages.

Presenter

Michelle's company regularly holds information evenings for people who want to find out more about their holidays. Some of the potential clients explained why they were interested in trying out something different.

Woman 1

I think because I want to be a traveller rather than a tourist – or I want to believe that I am and I want to understand a bit about the culture and where I'm going to – and lying on a beach is kind of boring by comparison.

Woman 2

I'm just really interested in getting to know exactly what's going on in the country and really seeing the place rather than going out and just having a relaxing time. I just think this gives a more comprehensive look at a country rather than just going to relax really.

Man

You're not staying in a you know always a British or in an American mentality, I mean anyone can be a tourist – see all the pictures you know when you get home, but to really experience the food, and the experience and and the way they dress and how they treat one another …

Woman 3

Cos life's too safe at times. I'm mean not going to be doing anything very adventurous but I think riding a donkey is going to be adventurous for me and for the donkey so um I think it's a challenge cos, yeah, we live very safe lives, and it keeps you lively if you try something new.

Presenter

And as tour leader Peter Crane points out, this trend towards adventurous holidays is likely to continue. As people's disposable incomes increase, more are encouraged to experiment with their holidays – just as with the first foreign holidays a generation ago.

Peter Crane

The beach holiday in itself is a relatively new phenomenon – it began in the nineteen sixties with the advent of air travel. It may be the case that after a generation of beach holidays people are just finally getting a little bit bored with lying on beaches. It's not as fulfilling and as exciting as erm as many people want their holidays to be. They want to know what happens away from the tourist hotels, how the local people live their lives, where the children go to school – really just understanding the real country as opposed to the tourist version of it.

Presenter

So it looks as if the quest for challenge and excitement and the desire to be a traveller rather than a tourist, will continue to shape the kind of holiday many people decide to take.

11.1

B OK, so what are your earliest memories?

G Erm, well, I think probably one of my very earliest memories was when I was in Canada. Erm, I must have been about five or six years old at the time …

B Right OK …

G … and erm, basically, I was on a family holiday with my mum, my dad and my brother and we were staying with erm my uncle and his wife and they erm had some very strange rules of their house that you had to abide by if you stayed with them, and I was quite sort of fussy as a kid. Anyway, they had these rules and we had to stick to them, as we were staying there, and we sat down to dinner one one night and one of his rules was that you had to eat everything that was on your plate …

B No.

G Yeah, you had to completely finish your food.

B What if you didn't like it?

G Well, you weren't allowed to not like it, basically.

B OK …

G Erm, and anyway I was quite fussy and my mother made sure that he did make something that I liked, so I had this hamburger. Anyway, I was talking to my uncle, telling some kind of story and basically I was putting ketchup on my hamburger and I was talking and I didn't basically realize how long I was talking for, and turned to look at my meal and there was ketchup everywhere all over my plate.

B Oh no!

G And, basically, I had to eat everything that was on my plate and my uncle, cruelly, actually made me sit there and finish it, and I was sick afterwards for about two days.

B Oh my.

G So, yes, that's mine …

B Well, let me see.

G … not a pleasant one.

B No, I don't think mine was good either, erm.

G Go on then.

B I can only have been about four, maybe slightly older.

G Yeah.

B And, er, I was in my mum and dad's house and I was messing about on the stairs and of course my mum was, like, you know 'Be careful, you'll fall down the stairs' (Yeah). But I didn't really listen to her, and of course I did, fell down the stairs and tumbled all the way down the stairs and cracked my head open on the radiator at the bottom of the stairs.

G Oh dear.

B Yep. So of course I was crying and screaming …

G Did you go to hospital?

B Yeah, my head was bleeding and I had to go to hospital and have thirteen stitches.

G Err!

B 'Unlucky for some,' my mum said. So that's another bad memory as well.

G Yeah.

B Can you think of any …

G good ones?

B Erm, not …

G So we've both had really bad childhoods.

B I think I think you tend to remember the bad things, more than the good things.

G Yeah.

11.3

Speaker 1
I think I'm at the age when I'm starting to for… realize that I'm forgetting more things than I used to. Erm, I cert…, I've always found it very difficult to remember directions how to get to places. Erm, but I've now, I've had to start to use a diary which is an admission I think that I'm forgetting more than, than I used to or maybe I'm just doing more things, erm, so using a diary really is how I try to remember things as much as possible – maybe repeating things to myself that are very important just so I realize how important they are.

Speaker 2
I'm very good actually. I don't forget many things – I'm one of these people that's quite good at remembering birthdays, anniversaries, friends and family. I tend to remember most things and I remember because I am a compulsive list-writer, which is very tragic in my life …

Speaker 3
I'm quite proud of never forgetting anything – erm I have a system erm which revolves around post-it notes erm which, depending on what I have to remember, I'll write it down on a post-it note and stick it to the inside of my front door, erm so I never forget anything – amazing.

Speaker 4
I always forget when I have to pay my bills, and I always forget to water the plants. With bills I have to leave them sitting in front of me so that I actually remember to pay them, but most other things, birthdays, names, phone numbers, useful things I can remember, but just not the bills, the serious stuff.

Speaker 5
My memory's getting worse and worse and worse and it's very difficult to say what kind of things I forget because I forget everything, erm I used to have an extremely good memory for numbers and faces and dates and people and general information and now that's just got worse and worse and because it is something that I didn't use to have problems with, I actually find it quite difficult to find a good way to remember things. I, I write lists and keep books and leave myself notes, but none of those works as well as actually having a memory that works and unfortunately mine doesn't do it so well any more.

11.4

a After the performance the star was presented with an enormous bouquet of roses. **bouquet**
b Many of the friends I was at university with now live very bourgeois lives. **bourgeois**
c It took undercover police officers three months to find the terrorists' cache of weapons. **cache**
d The televised debate between the two presidential candidates was full of political clichés. **cliché**
e It's very convenient – they're going to start a new crèche at the place where I work. **crèche**
f People like living in cul-de-sacs because they're usually quiet and traffic-free. **cul-de-sac**
g We have two duvets – a light one for the summer and a heavier one for the winter. **duvet**
h Paul Getty was one of the twentieth century's most successful entrepreneurs. **entrepreneur**
i I'd love a slice of that chocolate gateau. **gateau**
j Novels and poems belong to different literary genres. **genre**

12.1

Speaker 1
When I was a girl I suppose I was completely ballet-mad – erm I used to go to ballet classes two or three times a week, erm used to get books about ballet from the library, used to read novels about ballet and always wanted to be a ballerina and of course never managed to do that – but I was absolutely obsessed with ballet and all my friends were as well.

Speaker 2
Actually one time, I had a birthday party and I invited about twenty kids and I told them all what I wanted was a stuffed animal and every single one of them got me a stuffed animal and my mother was so mad and it was like 'What are you doing?'

Speaker 3
Slightly embarrassing childhood, not exactly an obsession, but I used to be a great fan of heavy metal music erm which now seems incredibly embarrassing – I was about 14 years old and wore blue jeans and a sort of blue anorak with a grey rabbit fur hood and went around listening to what now seems to be the most awful music in the world …

Speaker 4
When I was really young I was really keen on playing with Lego® and I had to have every set and I really wanted to go to Legoland in Denmark, but never made it and then I was too old and when it came over here and there was one in Windsor, but erm I was a member of the Lego® club and I had lots of sets and I

used to play for hours and hours with it making different buildings and houses and cars …

Speaker 5
I think probably from about the age of 7 or 8 until 11 or 12, I was completely obsessed with football – erm all my spare time was spent playing football with friends. Every break time every lunchtime at school we would play football in the playground. Erm it had a disastrous effect on my shoes – my mother was having to buy me shoes, I remember, every, every three or four months or so cos I wore them out so quickly erm I used to buy regularly a football magazine which I would read avidly every Saturday morning – I knew the names of all the teams in the football league, I knew their grounds, I knew their colours, I knew the names of most of the players in all the teams – it was a complete obsession and the odd thing is that now I have absolutely no interest in football whatsoever …

12.2

I think in the past obviously classic films, things like *Casablanca*, things that have endured over the years, but I think also films in the past that were popular were very strict to their genre, things like Westerns, which had a very strict set of rules that were always followed. They were based around the same thing – that actually have a fairly universal appeal. I think a western is actually an example of sort of myth, a legend, almost like a fairy tale – the good guy and the good guy always wins, and the bad guy. But the good guy never quite integrates into society – the good guy always goes off riding into the sunset and these rules are very very strict, but I think that that's part of the appeal, but that that genre really, I think, has had its day, erm I think it's being eclipsed by other things and I think an example of that is *Crouching Tiger, Hidden Dragon*, which is a similar sort of thing actually, in some ways.

Looking at things in the cinema at present and I think there's the two main types of film erm there's blockbusters, box-office smash films, romantic comedy, there's, you know, things, I don't know, any Julia Roberts films, anything, you know, some of the Michael Douglas films, whatever, erm and then there's the big action films, things like *Braveheart*.

12.3

As for where films are going, I think the idea that the genre is no longer applied as strictly as it was once that erm genre is something which is increasingly you know that and a good example of that is *Crouching Tiger, Hidden Dragon*, that what kind of movie is it? Well it's a feminist, art house, martial arts movie – very very difficult to pigeonhole. It comes across much more like something like a computer game than a film in some ways, the fighting scenes and the flying scenes and the treetops and the canopy of the forest, you know it's an incredible mixture of of different influences and yet it's got this nineteenth century China, star-crossed lovers erm, and the honour code and you know this this amazing story behind it that it's a really interesting film and I think what's interesting about it is that it doesn't fit into the rules of any one genre.

I think that actually is the key to what makes a good film is if it really carries you into that film and involves you in it and has you somewhere else for two hours and I think that's what film does probably better than any other art form. A book does but you're still having to read it and yeah I love books, don't get me wrong erm, but I I feel that a film really can do that – it transports you it's the, the whole atmosphere, the music and that especially when you see it at the cinema and you have to go and make an effort to go see it, erm and you sit there in the dark and this massive movie is is playing – and you know there's the music and the effects and the sound and the pictures and it's just the whole experience.

I really think that's the essence of a good movie is a movie that carries you away that takes you from your normal life for a couple of hours – it's an escapist thing.

12.4

T There's that bit in *Psycho* when I think there's a girl hiding under the staircase, isn't there, and whoever it is, is coming in, he runs up the stairs and you're you're not quite sure if he's noticed her or not and he's sort of looking around the house and you know that he's about to come down and find her and then obviously the shower scene.

R Hitchcock is always good for suspense really.

K Definitely.

R I love the bit in I think it's *Misery*, is it called *Misery*? with Kathy Bates (Yes) where where she's gone out for a drive and he's in the house and he has to try and get out of the room which she's locked him in and, you know, he gets all the way …

K (Does it) with hairpins or something? He finds …

R Yeah, he has to unlock all sorts of doors and of course he's wheelchair-bound as well and then she … you see the car coming back and the camera keeps cutting to the car coming back and he's got to get back into the position that she expects to find him in.

J And obviously, he just makes it.

R Just in the nick of time.

J In an amazingly short period of time. Apart from the fact that when she comes back in, one of her china erm ornaments is the wrong way round.

R That's right, she notices something's just slightly been moved.

J Total psychopath because she's noticed that.

R Picks up the sledge hammer and breaks his legs.

J That is an absolutely horrible scene.

12.5

1

M1 This looks kind of office wear.

W1 Quite conservative, isn't it?

W2 Yeah. It's a bit sensible.

M1 I like her red dress though.

W2 Really?

W1 Yeah, but you wouldn't actually wear it. I wouldn't.

W2 Remind me not to go shopping with you.

M1 No I wouldn't wear it either, actually, funnily enough.

M2 I prefer the one in the middle – she looks kind of …

W2 Yeah, she's a bit more snazzy.

M2 Yeah, definitely.

W1 Yeah, OK.

M2 Whereas the one on the right – not very flattering.

W2 No.

M1 Well, she's chosen pale colours, hasn't she, …

2

W2 Right what about him? Now that's very office.

M2 Very office.

M1 But it's kind of casual office.

W1 It works.

W2 It's kind of special, but in a stylish way.

W1 I think he looks neat.

M1 Nice tie.

M2 Presentable.

W2 Definitely – if you're going for an interview, you know – it's fine.

W1 You could take him home to your mum …

3

W1 Ooh look at her!

M1 Now that's saucy secretary, isn't it?

W2 That's kind of air hostess actually, isn't it?

W1 It's quite scaring.

M2 She looks quite powerful – you know bit of a power suit there, powerful suit …

W2 It is powerful definitely – yep, she knows where she's going – she knows what she's doing …

4

W2 So, what about this guy?

W1 Hello.

W2 No, he does look pretty fit, do you know what I mean?

W1 Yeah, but what about the clothes?

W2 OK, let's look at the clothes.

M2 That's classic.

M1 Chinos, black T-shirt.

M2 Yeah.

W2 Casual again.

W1 Quite neutral.

W2 Yes.

M2 Uncomplicated.

W2 Definitely.

M1 Smart.

W2 Classic.

W1 Yeah.

M1 That's it, really, isn't it?

W2 Yeah.

M1 And I think everyone likes it.

W2 You could wear that anywhere, really, couldn't you?

5

W2 OK, let's move on to her.

W1 Oooh.

M2 Right. Action.

W1 I like the colour.

M2 It's bright.

W1 I know.

M1 It's sporty-ish.

M2 Yeah. That's what I'm thi… I'm thinking outdoor wear.

All Yeah / Definitely.

M1 Could be good snowboarding …

W2 All weather, all weather.

M2 Yeah it's kind of got that snowboard look, hasn't it, it's sort of …

W1 Yeah – it's still trendy, it's cool.

M2 Yeah.

W2 Like the boots.

M2 Yeah good boots.

W1 Hiking.

M1 Sturdy boots. She's got sunglasses on her head, as well.

W2 Has she?

M1 Yeah. I think she's thinking she's …

W1 She's quite trendy.

M2 She could be going sailing. …

13.1

Speaker 1

Well it's very different in personal and professional, but erm I think I probably find it easier to deal in a professional context because you have some sort of structure that you can you have recourse to, but in personal life I find it very stressful.

Speaker 2

Conflict – I'm getting better at it – much better than I used to be, but it's not enjoyable, it's never enjoyable having to deal with conflict, erm but I can stay much calmer now than I used to be in those kinds of situations, which always helps, because then you can step back from it and decide what's really happening

without getting upset or excited or angry or any of those things.

Speaker 3

Absolutely impossible I would always avoid conflict whenever I possibly could, which I think is always, if if you want to avoid conflict badly enough you can avoid it. Which is cowardly I know, and I see it as a a failing I think, because I think some people can make something constructive out of conflict but I can't. I don't like it at all.

Speaker 4

In my personal life I find it erm probably a bit easier than in my professional life. I would say that, erm I like to deal with it absolutely immediately and er can't rest until it is dealt with whereas professionally although I would like to do that it's not quite as easy to do that.

Speaker 5

I find it very difficult, but you need to be able to deal with conflict in order to to progress.

So how do you approach it – what do you do about it?

You've got to be sure of your facts before you start, and I think you've also got to be aware of some position of compromise.

Speaker 6

… I feel professionally I deal with it pretty well, but personally that's a whole nother ball-game for me – I really have a problem with it personally – when someone yells at me, even if it's totally unjust, rather than argue back or yell back, I cry which isn't very helpful in resolving the conflict, but I just, I get so upset I …

Speaker 7

Well conflict – I'd rather not talk about it, that's basically how I deal with conflict. I'm I'm very uncomfortable with conflict quite honestly and – personally and professionally – and I'll do just about anything to avoid it. I like to be an easy-going laid-back kind of person and it really takes a lot for me to confront someone on something even if they've treated me badly – it's actually an area that I'd like to get better at, but erm I have a boyfriend who is, loves conflict so we actually make a great pair because …

13.2

M1 What do you think you're doing?

M2 I was following you. I wasn't that, I wasn't that far behind – you stalled …

M1 You, yeah, you wait till I move off, right? The lights turned green. You are behind me and you wait till I've moved off.

M2 Yeah, all right, all right.

M1 Look at this.

M2 I know, well look at my headlight mate.

M1 Well look at my rear lig… They're not even working.

M2 All right. We're not going to get anywhere by shouting, are we? (I've got to go) We're not going to get anywhere by shouting.

M1 I've got to go and pick my kids up and it's getting dark.

M2 All right. You gonna get, all right look I've got a mobile phone if you wanna use it. It's fine, you can call, you can tell em you're gonna be late.

M1 I don't believe this.

M2 Look there's no point getting upset. Look – you've lost a bit out the back. I've lost me headlight. It's fine. It's not serious. It's absolutely not serious. If you've got your insurance …

M1 It's your fault mate.

M2 I don't …

W Excuse me.

M2 I don't think it's right to start blaming people.

M1 It is.
M2 I mean this is, this is it's easily remediable.
W Look, excuse me, but you're really causing quite a tailback, back here.
M1 What's it got to do with you?

13.3

Speaker 1
Mess, I think is the biggest cause of arguments in our house, erm, who made it, whose turn is it to clear it up, who makes more mess, who clears up more mess, erm, can't think we argue about anything else really, just general tidiness, organization and mess.

Speaker 2
Me and my family have argued about very few things really. Erm, I mean, I suppose the only things I can remember would be playing Scrabble and arguing over whether a word was actually a word, but that's always sorted out by getting the dictionary, and occasionally what to watch on TV, but that's pretty much it really.

Speaker 3
Erm – my family and I have argued a lot about food, erm. My mother likes meat and my sister's a vegetarian so often we have to cook more than one meal – causes a lot of problems.

Speaker 4
We tend to argue about really silly things, I think. It's very often something and nothing and the argument is is basically simply because somebody feels in a bad mood and just needs to have the release of possibly picking a fight of some kind, so erm we can argue about anything and everything. It really is impossible to say whether there is anything specific that we we argue about.

Speaker 5
My family always argue about holidays. My mum always wants to go abroad, but my dad doesn't like to fly, so he always wants to stay in the country. My brother and sister like a seaside-type holiday, but my mum likes to do sightseeing and I always argue, because I never get an opinion.

14.1

I think one of the most common problems people have is that they simply just try to do too much. They have too many tasks on the go at once. Rather than concentrate on one task at a time. So at the start of the day they might have several things on their 'to do' list but they'll try and do a bit of everything all in one go. So they'll try and be writing a report and answering the phone and talking to people at the same time. Secondly I think we tend to take on too much in the first place because we are not very good at saying no to other people. Particularly it is hard to say no if it's our boss or other managers asking us to do a task and that doesn't help because we're too quick to give their task priority over our own. Thirdly I think interruptions are a big time management problem for people. There's two types of interruptions, firstly, interruptions caused by other people either dropping in for a chat or dropping in to get some information, or ringing you up to see if you've got their e-mail. And the second type of interruption is the interruptions that we cause ourself, so procrastination, which is the art of putting off till tomorrow the things that we should be doing today. And we are our own worst enemy because we tend to put off particularly large or difficult tasks and instead we do easy short tasks to avoid doing the long ones.

14.2

What would be your top tips for improving time management?
Well I think leading on from what I was just saying about using your time well, is first of all to be really clear about what it is you want to achieve. Not only at work but in your home life as well. And then focus your time and effort on those things. The principle being that if you don't know what you want to achieve, it's much more easy to get side-tracked. Secondly I think, be realistic about how long things really take. When we're planning tasks I think we assume that they'll only take an hour or two hours, when in reality, once you have been interrupted several times they might actually take three or four hours. And then, once you have decided how long tasks really will take, put them in your diary, and I think people could use their diaries more effectively to make appointments with their tasks not just appointments with other people. And my last tip I think, is to break down big tasks into manageable chunks. It makes it much more easy to get started if you if you break it down into short steps and then start with an easy one to get the ball rolling.

14.3

T I'm just worried that I'll get stuck in some sort of boring job or that I won't get a job and I won't have enough money and that I'll have to pay off my student debts and it will be impossible and stuff like that. Hopefully something more exciting will happen.
K Meaning what?
T I'll get a great job, I don't know, maybe, I don't know something in theatre or TV, or something fun but everyone wants to do that.
R Everyone's dream.
T Totally.
K It's everyone's real hope, isn't it? To be able to be paid for something that they really enjoy doing.
K Yeah.
T A hobby.
K Yeah.
J I can't work in an office. I mean at the moment my major hopes and fears are that I won't get kicked out of university but beyond that, I could not work in an office. (Yeah)
K You might have to.
J I have to do something where I stand up.
K Where you stand up?
J Or move around at least.
T You are allowed to move around in an office, you can go to the photocopier, get some tea.
J Yeah, (four walls) it is those first sort of couple of years of making tea, isn't it that just seem a bit …
R It's just immediately what you are going to do once you leave university really, what really scares me – the big wide world.
K I work in a café – I make coffee all the time.
J You make coffee all the time?
T We keep on getting leaflets at college or posters and things saying wouldn't you just love a job in the City? – which is not what you want at all.
K Well, (It's a lot of money) everyone I know who's started working in the City within a year they absolutely hate it.
J But it's the kind of thing that you don't need to really love, I mean it would be amazing to do it for a year. It, it's hard work but it's an awful lot of money.
T But once you start having that sort of lifestyle, like a really nice flat and a mobile phone and everything then you want to keep it.
R And you probably get sucked into it, don't you?

K Yeah, you stay there for two or three years.
J Everybody says that and maybe it's just very naïve of me not to believe it but why can't you just save?
K Because you are so miserable, your work makes you so miserable that you you are desperate to go out.
J Because it's the perfect way, yeah but you can go out I mean it's not as if anyone's saying that you can't spend any money. You've got double the amount of money that you'd have in any other job.
T I think that if you tell yourself that it's just going to be for a year or two and that you've got better things you want to do.
K Yeah.
J Everybody says that, though, don't they?
T It's dangerous.
J And then stays there.
R And then you get head-hunted. (Yeah)
J Yeah, and that's probably very flattering but it's the perfect way to make a lot of money and then go and be an actor. Do you know what I mean? Because, you know … (You make it sound so …)
K Yeah, and then I'm going to go and be an actor.
J No, but you, but you've sorted out enough money to …
R Fund yourself.
J Yeah, to be able to maybe go to drama school or to not have to worry about things.
K Yeah. Someone said to me a couple of months ago, 'Oh isn't it so scary you know going out and going into your first real grown-up job in a couple of months' – and I was … 'Well it's actually more scary that I'm not going into my first adult grown-up job in two months because I don't have a job at all.'
J What are you gonna do?
R What are you doing at the moment?
K Well, I am working at the moment but I'm saving up to go away over the summer. (On holiday) Yeah. Six weeks in China.
All Wow!
K That's what I am hoping to do.

14.4

1 A If anything happens to me, I'd like you to take over the business.
  B I'm sure everything will be OK – it's only a minor operation.
2 A The papers accuse you of being tired and emotional after the party, Minister. Is that true?
  B No, certainly not.
3 A The figures clearly show that the economy is doing very well. Incomes are up and inflation is down.
  B Yes, but everyone knows that figures can prove anything. Our party thinks the government has been involved in creative accounting here.
4 A I was sorry to hear about your grandmother. Had she been ill long?
  B No, only a couple of weeks – she's always been very healthy.
5 A You wanted to see me, Mr Birch.
  B Yes, John. I'm afraid your work has not been satisfactory recently. We're going to have to let you go at the end of the month.

15.1

Speaker 1
I don't think I'm a particularly competitive person. I suppose like most people I don't like it if I feel something good or worthwhile that I've done hasn't been recognized, but I'm not actually competitive, I'm not particularly bothered about being the best or being number one or getting to the top, being the star and being the boss and all those sorts of things …

Speaker 2

I don't think I'm very competitive, although I find lately that in some ways I am, but I never did any sports.I never got into the habit of beating other people or being defeated. I always just try to achieve things or be good at what I do on my own and not compete with others.

Speaker 3

I'm very, very, very competitive – having an older brother definitely is why, erm. We had a pool table – it was my brother's and he could always beat me – he's three years older. I thought 'Right! I'm going to beat him,' and I used to practise on the pool table, for like, three hours a day and I beat him finally – it was brilliant and now I'm quite good at pool actually.

Speaker 4

I wouldn't say I'm particularly competitive – only at things like games and quizzes where I do like to win, but that's just showing off …

15.2

Speaker 1

Yeah, I did cheat once – it wasn't an exam exactly – it was a course I was doing – a sort of training course where in preparation for the exam we had to do a timed essay – like a like a little mock exam and we had one hour to do this timed essay and I wasn't very well prepared for it and I decided that I would get more out of it if, instead of writing an essay that was complete rubbish – because I hadn't particularly studied the topic we were writing about – if I took a little crib sheet in with me and wrote a very good essay – and so that's what I did – I mean it was one of these subjects where there are basically ten major points, so rather than desperately try to remember them in the two minutes before the exam, I just wrote them down on a little piece of paper about the size of cigarette packet and took it in – it wasn't it wasn't sort of (a) sneaky childhood thing – I was probably in my mid-twenties and and cheated in a very sort of mature kind of a way and wrote quite a good essay – not surprisingly …

Speaker 2

Cheating, erm, have I ever cheated in anything? I think as a very young child I found it very hard to lose at Monopoly and I did cheat once and my family has never forgotten erm – they mistakenly put me in the bank and I must have been about seven and I thought the bank was there to give me money and erm I took it. I think apart from that I'm too cowardly to cheat in an exam I was given a very stern warning at age seven that my exam would go in the bin if I smiled or talked to the person next to me and since then I, I haven't risked it. Sports I don't want to win that badly and competitions I'm probably not competitive enough.

Speaker 3

I haven't actually cheated in anything that I can remember – the only very very small thing I did was in the first year there used to be about four of us who sat round a table and we had a science test – and (we'd) all sort of copy each other, sort of – that's the only sort of thing I can remember but erm, no I've never tripped anybody up in a sports event or anything – would have liked to, would have broken my ankle or something.

Speaker 4

I haven't ever cheated in an exam or any other kind of competition and I think the main reason for that is that I haven't really had an opportunity to do that but I probably wouldn't if it came to the crunch.

Speaker 5

I've never cheated in an examination and never would erm but that I think is to do with the fear of being found out as much as anything else. I occasionally

slightly cheat at sport, I think, and in fact I don't know anybody who doesn't, so when you're playing a game where it's a very close decision where something is 'in' or 'out' – depending on how I'm feeling and whether we're winning or losing – I might say something was 'in' when it was 'out' or vice versa, but not very often – maybe once in every five or six games and it doesn't worry me at all – I think it's part of the game.

16.1

Speaker 1

If I don't go bed when I'm completely and utterly exhausted like when your head is about to, you know, just drop off regardless of where you are – **if I don't go to bed at that time, then I will actually stay awake for an awful lot longer when I actually do go to bed. I have to make sure that I'm completely relaxed, and completely unwound before I actually go to bed, otherwise then, you know I'll just be lying awake for ages. Erm my mind starts to wander** and I start thinking about all the things that I haven't done or that I've got to do, so I have to sit in front of the television for an hour or something or two hours and er just make sure that I'm completely exhausted and completely tired and my eyes are closing before going to bed, otherwise I just stay awake for hours. In terms of position, well, I mean, if I'm that tired I, I just go to bed in any position and I probably sleep anywhere when I get to that stage – on a bus on a train, you, you name it erm and if I can't get to sleep, well, I dunno I try all sorts of things of, try to think of erm, relaxing thoughts of you know waterfalls and fields …

Speaker 2

I don't have a fixed routine of going to bed – I panic if I'm going to get less than about eight hours – I always have done and always will. I sleep always on my left side – **I start off always on my left side er but that can switch. And what keeps me awake is usually either hunger or anxiety, so if I can't sleep I'll either eat something or I'll usually e-mail now actually** which'll, which is very bad because then I definitely get at least an hour less sleep than I should have, but I'm addicted to it, or I'll read a novel or listen to Radio 4 and yes I can sleep absolutely anywhere, if I'm knackered enough, but er also feel terribly, terribly vulnerable doing that and get off at wrong stops and drool and stuff so try not to but er if I can't sleep I can panic because I do have a thing about getting enough hours – and it'll affect me the whole next day – so it's a psychological thing probably more than a physical.

Speaker 3

To be honest, being an English student sleep isn't really much of a problem for me – I spend a lot of time sleeping. Erm I often lie in till about 2 o'clock in the afternoon when I'm supposed to be writing an essay or making notes or something and then just end up working really late – so get into sort of bad patterns anyway. **If ever I can't sleep – which as I say isn't really often the case, I often listen to music to try to get to sleep or I'll just sit up and read a book if,** basically if I can't sleep, then I don't try.

Speaker 4

I tend to drink quite a lot of coffee, so sleeping is often quite difficult, and it drives me mad. If I can't sleep I tend to get up and read or watch TV. Some nights I just don't go to sleep at all, which is very bizarre and then just continue the next day as if I have been to sleep, cos once it gets light then can't get back to sleep – like I went to a ball the other day and we didn't go to sleep all night and then by nine o'clock the next morning as far as I was concerned it was the next day so I just carried on which is quite bizarre.

16.2

So, once rough sketches of the character have been made and it's been decided how the character will move, the modelling process begins.

First of all a detailed drawing is made showing the model's armature or skeleton.

Then the armature is made using twisted wire or ball and socket joints.

This enables a basic clay model to be created and this in turn becomes the finished character.

Next the storyboard is filmed and the voices are added, allowing the director to check that the scenes, and the movie as a whole, work. This stage is followed by a very simple animation known as a 'blocking rehearsal' where the director checks characters' movements and how they look on set.

Once the voices of the characters have been recorded the animators are able to match the shape of the mouth to the dialogue. The mouth forms different shapes depending on what sound is coming from the character. This process is called lipsynch.

Then finally there's the actual filming of the movie. This is a painstaking process. The final action may be fast and furious but *Chicken Run* took four years to make. Every aspect of the character has to be carefully adjusted for each frame, 1,400 times to produce one minute of film time. This means that actions like the blinking of an eye can take hours to film.

16.3

OK, here are the answers to the quiz. Give yourself a point for each correct answer.

A. How many more speakers of American English than British English are there?

The answer is C – there are actually four times as many speakers of American English.

B. The most noticeable difference between British and American English is in fact B – pronunciation. There are relatively few differences in spelling and vocabulary.

C. The statement 'Where words are spelt differently in British and American English, the American spelling is usually shorter', is true.

D. The statement 'There are no differences in grammar between British and American English', is false. But there are only a few, for example in American English it is possible to use the time adverbs *already* and *yet* with the Simple past.

E. This statement is false. Pairs of words with different spellings in British and American English are usually pronounced in the same way.

And finally F. It is true that most British people understand American English without any problem. This is probably because British people are used to seeing lots of American films and TV programmes.

17.1

Extract 1

Well it's a long process, but I think it starts always **with** the place, the location. The actual piece came about from a conversation that I had **with** councillor Pat Murphy who had been a miner himself – he was Irish – and er he said 'What we need Mr Gormley is is one of your angels,' and I said 'Well if you're serious **about** this, Pat, it's going to have to be 65 foot tall,' and that was the beginning of the whole thing.

Extract 2

I had told the people that I wasn't interested in making motorway art erm rather snobbishly – but, as it turned, out this relationship **between** this mound and the road got me very intrigued. There is always cars on it and we know that 90,000 motorists pass that point a day.

Extract 3

You would expect a work of that scale to perhaps express some heroic ideal or anyway monumental certainty and it doesn't – I think it expresses as much anxiety as it does succour.

Extract 4

Not at all. Couldn't matter less. I mean I think these are the, these are the thoughts and feelings that I had in the process of making it, having made it er looking at it as a work amongst my other works erm, but for the average person I wouldn't even imagine they would begin to think in these terms, so that you know an ex-ship builder or an ex-miner or a housewife or the train driver or the schoolboy that passes every day – each of them will have their own particular relationship **with** this with this work.

17.2

What I'm more interested in is tripping people up you know on their way to the supermarket because I think that part of the problem with our culture at the moment is that we deal in a culture of you know snacking basically, er of highly-articulated highly-hyped, almost predigested experience. I hope the Angel makes you aware of the time of the day, of the shape of the landscape, your speed, erm, also, even though people wouldn't recognize that perhaps as part of their response to a work. The only value of art, I think, is as a instrument of reflexivity to make us feel more alive – there's no intrinsic value to art.

17.3

W1 But, you know, it's a question of if you ask, are there more famous men in the arts than women – famous in the sense that we probably know about more men than women in the arts, do you know what I'm saying?

M Well as far as classical painters, you know, you certainly don't think of women.

W1 (That's true,) but does that mean they didn't exist?

W2 Good point.

M They may have been edited, who knows?

W2 … or not had, you know, the kind of exposure that a male painter had.

M Well, look at authors like Georges Sand – women traditionally for a good number of years had to put a male pseudonym on their books (Right, exactly, yes) or they were not going to sell.

W2 Smart women who did that, boy.

M Yeah, also women were not historically given the educational advantages that men were – women were, you know, to grow up and marry off and men were sent to the universities where they were exposed to art. (Right)

W Do you think it's changing, now? Do you think more women are getting positions of prominence in the arts?

M Not in the business of art.

W2 Yeah, I mean what do you mean – in what field of art are you talking about?

W1 Well all different fields – let's talk about the media – what do you think about like film and TV? Do you think more and more women are …

W2 I think more and more although I heard a statistic in this documentary that, I think last year, out of the 200 or so sort of feature films, you know big feature films not independent films that were made, maybe 20 of them were directed by women.

W1 Wow!

17.4

J It's funny, though. If you look at say, composers, directors, theatre directors, film directors, how many of those could you name who are women?

K You mean the people who are in charge?

J Yeah. How many female composers? There are, I would say there are less female …

R (I can) Think of a few directors, a few producers.

J There are very few female, well-known female theatre directors or film directors.

R Oh yeah, comparatively.

J Comparatively.

R Of course you're right.

J Which is bizarre, because that is nothing that need be dominated by men, (No) but it just is. And I mean, even I feel that …

R But that's you … There's a parallel there with sort of I don't know, sort of business as well, do you know what I mean?

J Except that busi…

R Like the director is sort of the head of the theatre business in a sense, or the director and the producer.

J But that's become quite controversial and there are therefore a lot more women who have risen to the top because a few years ago there were a lot of people who made a lot of fuss about women being on average being paid less, and a lot of women did go to the top of businesses. But going back to art, er musicians, what about musicians? How many famous female musicians do you know?

T There are just thousands. Do you mean …?

J Of female?

T Umm.

J Female famous musicians?

R That can play instruments or singers?

K Classical musicians?

J Classical musicians …

K Well it's interesting, isn't it because …

J … or jazz musicians.

K Well I don't know I think classical music is always perhaps, well not always but is rather more balanced. It's just no one is that high profile. I mean I could, you could name classical musicians, you could name Vanessa Mae, you could name Jacqueline Du Pré, you could name, you know, there are quite a lot of people.

18.1

P So what did you think about that Castaway 2000 documentary – have you seen anything of it?

R Yeah – it was scary.

K I think it's awful.

J Yeah, I couldn't do that.

K No way!

J Never! Just to be thrown on to an island in the cold north of Scotland with a whole group of people that you don't know.

K Awful people, though, awful people!

P Is it the idea of being filmed? Is that the problem? Or, or just the experience?

J It's the fact that you can't choose who you're who you're spending time with – I think that's what I would find difficult.

K Then it's too late because you're stuck there – and there's no going back – and it's such a risk.

18.2

R I did two years of agriculture at my school.

K Did you?

R Because the choice was agriculture or Latin.

K Wow!

R And my father said in his very practical Dutch way 'You'll never learn …, need to learn Latin – why learn Latin – learn about sheep.'

J So can you, do you know about farming? – I mean would you know how …

R I did then.

K But I'm sure that must still be there.

R Yeah, I'm sure it's all there, yeah.

K I think we need a therapist as well – a group therapist. (Yes)

R And do you think that you could bring that to the group?

K That would be a laugh, I'd love to try that, yes absolutely.

R I think you'd need one.

K I think definitely – definitely something.

R So we've got farming, we've got therapy covered.

J I'm very good at DIY.

P Yeah, me too.

K/R Well, that's fantastic! / Great!

R So we don't eat anything, though at this stage.

J Eat?

R Mmm. (Can) anyone cook?

K Oh yeah, yeah, cooking – I'm sure we can all cook, can't we, I can cook, (Yeah) yeah. Grow things, I mean grow vegetables and – (Yeah) we could do that.

P Did they … Did they have to do that? Grow their own food?

K I think so, I'm sure.

R/J I don't know.

K I'm sure they did.

18.3

R So, if we're on the island – we're all faced with having to deal with new people and we all are faced with the fact that we're going to be with these people for the next, I don't know, six months, where do you start? I mean how do you, how do you put everyone into their, into their sort of hierarchal positions, and, and does it happen by itself or do you think it …?

K I don't like the sound of hierarchical – I think that would be one of the things you'd want to try and avoid, don't you think? To try and find some sort of er some sort of society that isn't built on hierarchy – that's built on skill maybe.

R Yeah – I suppose that's, that's an ideal, but maybe things would just happen.

P I think they would. I think the idea would be to perhaps all sit down, have a meeting and I suppose talk about what skills you have and try and share out certain responsibilities based on that.

J Yes.

K And there are natural leaders and natural followers which would inevitably happen – and some people might not like that, they might not like being a follower or …

J … or being led by somebody that they don't particularly like.

K Absolutely and how many leaders do you have? And … that could be very difficult.

R But what if you were in a situation where there were, you know, six people – three people considered themselves or felt that they were natural leaders, I mean, there's immediately a conflict there with the three of them and three people underneath not really knowing what to do, I mean – in some ways it's almost better to say 'OK – you're our spokesman or spokeswoman'.

P What elect somebody?

R Yeah …

Writing guidelines

Personal profiles are written for a variety of purposes. They could be

- an informal description of someone in a letter to a friend
- a formal character reference in support of someone's application for a job or an education course
- a biography or an obituary
- a profile of yourself, for example as part of a letter of application.

Analysis

Read the extracts from four profiles and answer these questions about each one.

1 Where do you think it comes from? (Where might you read it?)
2 Why was it written?
3 Who do you think wrote it?
4 Who might read it?

A

She is a highly-motivated student who participates in class discussions and regularly produces written homework of an excellent standard.

Although she is rather quiet and reserved, her spoken English is fluent and colloquial. This enables her to communicate effectively in a range of situations. She has worked hard on her pronunciation and the slight accent which remains does not interfere with her ability to communicate. She has a wide vocabulary and makes few errors.

She is an excellent student in every way and I can recommend her for the course at your college.

B

I've never met anyone like him before. He's nothing special to look at – tall and slim with short dark hair – but he's got such a lovely personality. He's just so kind and he makes me laugh. I can't believe I've only known him since last week.

We actually met at the station last Friday morning. The train was late as usual and this guy asked me if I had the time. We got talking and spent the whole train journey telling each other our life stories. It was amazing.

C

PERSONAL PROFILE

Reliable, enthusiastic, committed, with a wide range of skills. I am conscientious and can work to deadlines. I work well as part of a team and am keen to learn from others.

D

TURNEY was a professional musician all his working life. His polished musicianship ensured that he was rarely out of work, but it was not until his forties, when he had moved permanently to New York, that his name became known to the wider jazz public.

Norris William Turney was born at Wilmington, Ohio, on September 8 1921. He showed early promise in music and longed to learn an instrument. 'Back in those days, no black person ever had music lessons in high school. There were good athletes, football and basketball players, but no musicians.'

His father bought him a second-hand saxophone ...

Electronic Telegraph

Useful language

Read the extracts again, and underline or make a note of any words or phrases you may find useful in your own writing. Look particularly for descriptive words and phrases.

Checklist

Ask yourself these questions when you are planning a profile.

1 What is the appropriate balance of fact and opinion? Are your feelings and opinions about the person relevant?
2 How much detail is necessary? Is it important to include detailed facts or are approximations acceptable? (Could you use 'vague language'?)
3 How important are these aspects of the person?
   - their physical appearance
   - their character and behaviour
   - their background and experience.
4 Is it important to mention your own relationship with the person? What information should you include?
   - How long have you known the person?
   - What is the nature of your relationship – intimate? personal? professional?
   - Has this person had an influence on you (or vice versa)?
5 What style is appropriate?
   - What is the context of the profile?
   - Who is it for?
   - Is there a standard format for the kind of profile you are writing?
   - Are you writing as a friend, a colleague, a teacher, an employer?
   - Who is going to read the profile?

Generally speaking, the more public the profile, the more formal the style should be.

Stories and narratives include not only fictional writing – novels, short stories, etc. – but accounts of events that actually happened. They could, for example, be part of a letter or an e-mail.

Analysis

Read the extracts from three different narratives and answer these questions.

1 Which extract(s) is/are probably fictional? What evidence is there for this?

2 Where do you think the other extract(s) is/are from?

3 Which extract includes descriptions of people and locations? What effect do these descriptions have?

4 How does the writer of extract **B** convey his excitement?

A

IT WAS JUNE 1976. My wife and I were staying in Rosas on Spain's Costa Brava. Driving along a coast road we passed a black Cadillac with black windows. Was it the local Mafia, I joked to our English friend, who lived locally. No, it was Salvador Dali's chauffeur-driven car – 'He lives a few miles from here in Port Lligat.'

Next morning, of course, we set off for the fishing village of Port Lligat. The Dalis' villa, screened by a high wall, was dominated by four enormous shapes on the rooftop: two white eggs and two metallic-grey human heads, both bald. Suddenly two bodyguard types came out of the house. Then the great surrealist himself emerged wearing a wide-brimmed straw sunhat, pale blue bathrobe and sandals …

B

You probably won't believe this, but I jumped out of a perfectly operational plane at 12,000ft above Lake Taupo!!! The view was fantastic. Mountains all around and the lake right below us. We were in freefall for about 45 secs and going at 200 kmph. Then the chute opened up and we had a nice journey down to the ground. I even landed on my feet. The worst bit was leaving the plane. I have to admit that I closed my eyes and just let the instructor jump. I opened them once we were out though, and it was absolutely fantastic.

C

There was no point in writing letters; he was too busy to answer them, except by occasional postcards that arrived without stamps.

'Surely it's nicer to talk to each other properly?' he said, and made sure she had extra pocket money to pay for the calls.

'It's not talking properly,' she protested. 'It's just noises that sound like us.'

During the first weeks at school she had rung her father every evening, weeping into the receiver and begging to be fetched home again. Now the telephone was ringing in Richmond instead of Balham. He did not answer the summons instantly, as her mother would have done …

Useful language

Read the extracts again, then underline or make a note of words or phrases you may be able to use in your own writing. Look particularly for language used to show how events are sequenced or structured.

Checklist

Ask yourself these questions when you are planning a story or narrative.

1 Who will read your story? What will your reader(s) find interesting?

2 What are the central event(s) you want to describe?

3 Who are the people or characters involved? How much do readers need to know about their personalities, behaviour, and background?

4 How important is background information? Should you include the time and place when the action takes place? If you are writing a detective story, for example, a detailed description of the location may be essential.

5 How will you structure your narrative?
 - How could you lead up to and follow on from the central event(s)? How could you start and finish the story effectively?
 - How could you link the events in an interesting way?

6 What style is appropriate?
 - If the story is fictional, are you going to write in the third person or could the first person make the story more immediate?
 - Can you use direct speech, rather than reported speech, to bring your story alive?

Analysis

Read these examples of four different kinds of letter and answer these questions.

1 Why was each letter written?

2 Who do you think wrote each letter? Who was it written to?

3 Which is the most formal letter and which is the least formal?

4 Answer the questions after each letter.

A

Hi Matt,

We spoke on the phone a couple of days ago, so I haven't really got much news, but your friend Tina rang me last night to ask if there was anything I wanted her to take to give you when she went to see you in Australia next week – very kind of her. We've arranged to meet outside the Playhouse today. I said she could recognize me by my yellow gloves. 'Cool,' she said.

Did I tell you we were thinking of moving again? We haven't actually seen anything we fancy yet but we're looking. There are loads of fantastic big houses, but they all cost a fortune. Val quite likes the idea of getting out of town, not too far, just a place we can park the car and have a bit of peace and quiet.

Better stop now. Becky's just rung to say her car's broken down. I've said I'll go and help her out.

- What do you think is the relationship between the writer of this letter and Matt, Tina, Val and Becky?
- What ending would you use for a letter of this kind?

B

Dear Sir,

We are writing to comment on our stay in your hotel last weekend.

My wife and I decided to have dinner in the restaurant on the Friday evening. Although the food and service were satisfactory, the music coming from the karaoke bar made normal conversation quite impossible. There was apparently no way of keeping this noise out. What was worse, there was no quiet area away from the restaurant where we could spend the rest of the evening.

Breakfast the following morning looked very appealing, but the food was almost cold; the bacon was so overcooked that it was almost impossible to eat. We had to wait for nearly twenty minutes for our coffee and toast.

In addition to this, there were problems in our bedroom. It was impossible to close one of the windows, which made the room cold and noisy. Also, it was very difficult to control the temperature of the water in the shower.

We will be very interested to hear your response to our comments.

- What are the purposes of the first and last paragraphs of this letter?
- What ending would you use for a letter of this kind?

C

Dear _____

In response to the advertisement in last week's local newspaper, I wish to apply for a place on the Jazz Improvisation course to be held on the weekend of 20–21 January.

As an amateur jazz musician I am very interested in joining this course. I play the piano in a modern jazz group called *The Big Six*, which performs in jazz clubs locally and occasionally at national festivals. My group plays a mixture of standards and our own compositions.

I was trained as a classical pianist and achieved Grade 8 when I was 14 years old. Until the age of 22, I played in orchestras and smaller groups. I became interested in jazz quite recently and now play very little classical music. One of the things that attracts me most to modern jazz is improvising, although at the moment I am limited in what I can do.

If accepted on the course I would be a committed and enthusiastic participant. I work well with other people and hope I would be able to contribute to the success of the course.

I hope you will consider my application favourably and look forward to hearing from you.

Yours sincerely,

- What are the different topics or purposes of each of the five paragraphs of this letter?
- How might this letter begin?

D

Dear Shaun,

It was good to hear from you after what seems like a very long time. We often wonder what happens to our ex-students.

We were interested to hear too that you have been making use of the training you received here; the work you've been doing in South America sounds most challenging.

In answer to your request, I'm afraid we can't be much help. There is actually very little in the way of freely available material of the sort you require. You could try the regional tourist boards or travel companies. The other obvious source of relevant information is the Internet.

Life is as hectic as ever at the university. We have an inspection coming up next week, so we're all on our best behaviour.

Anyway, good luck with your project. Everyone sends their regards.

Keep in touch.

- What ending would you use for a letter of this kind?

Useful language

Read the letters again and underline or make a note of any words or phrases you may find useful in your own writing. Look particularly for words and phrases which give the letters their formal or informal style, and that you could use to close a letter.

Checklist

Think about these points when you are planning formal or informal letters.

1 What format and layout is appropriate? What details (addresses, date, etc.) do you have to include?

2 What is the appropriate way to begin? If it's a formal letter, do you know the name of the person you are writing to? If you do, then use it.

3 How do you end a formal letter that begins with someone's name? What if you don't know the name? How does this type of letter begin and end?

4 What phrase or phrases could you use to finish the last paragraph of the letter?

5 In a formal letter, what should your first sentence do? And the last?

Analysis

Read the beginnings of four articles **A**, **B**, **C**, and **D**, and answer these questions.

1 What is the subject matter of each article? What kind of reader is it aimed at?

2 Which subject do **you** know most about already? Which is the most relevant to you?

3 Which article, **A**, **B**, or **C**, has the most effective title? What makes it effective?

4 How does the writer of each article try to capture and keep the reader's attention?

5 Extract **E** is the last paragraph of one of the beginnings **A–D**. Which? What makes this an effective ending?

A

Is this paradise or a hell of a challenge?

WITH Cambridgeshire woman Joleene Drage appearing on our television screens trying to survive the jungles of Peru, reporter JO KOWALSKI takes a look at why we suddenly seem to be so keen to get close to Mother Nature.

I am definitely a four-star hotel kind of girl who cannot do without the latest conveniences and luxuries of modern living.

Having been forced to camp out on the side of a Welsh mountainside as part of a team-building exercise at school, I have come face-to-face with the elements and hated it.

But if the recent glut of television survival programmes is anything to go by, there is a growing appetite among people to pit their wits against the wilds.

Cambridge News

B

Are we really about to die?

by David Rowan

If you've read this far, the huge tidal wave that will flatten Britain has, mercifully, spared us for another day. But don't relax too much: according to headlines yesterday, the 'mega-tsunami' due to hit us from the Canary Islands will get us sooner or later, destroying everything in its 500 mph path. According to scientists at University College London, there's no question that the tidal wave will wreak devastation – it's simply a matter of when.

London Evening Standard online © Associated Newspapers Ltd

C

Fishing around for Mr Right

I HAVE never been a Brad Pitt, Tom Cruise or Pierce Brosnan type of girl. Don't ask me why, but pretty boys just don't do it for me.

On the other hand I've always found the French actor Gerard Depardieu thrillingly attractive. Yes, that's right, the big fat guy who looks like he's been beaten about the head with a bag of baguettes.

The Sunday Mail, online © 2001 Queensland Newspapers

D

Sooner or later you're going to encounter a problem with your iMac. It could be a system freeze, a crash or other unexpected behaviour that makes you think: 'Uh-oh, trouble.' This isn't unusual and it certainly isn't something to panic about. It's probably not your fault, and it's most likely that it will be fixable.

Your iMac Magazine

E

'These global geophysical events are real,' he says. 'They're going to happen, and are not necessarily a long way in the future. Maybe a thousand years away – or maybe tomorrow.

'Though,' he admits, 'I don't lie awake thinking about it.'

Useful language

Read the extracts again and underline or make a note of any words, phrases, or techniques you think you may find useful in your own writing. Look particularly for ways the writers keep your attention as a reader.

Checklist

Think about these points when you are planning an article.

1 Who are the readers? What will interest them?

2 What title can you use to attract the reader's attention? Could you use sub-headings to help readers see at a glance what topics are covered in the article? Could you use an introductory paragraph to summarize the article?

3 Think about using one of these ways of starting your article:
- an unusual or surprising fact
- a provocative statement: the writer's opinion
- a question to involve the reader in the topic.

4 Bring the article to a definite conclusion. You could:
- summarize the main points of the article
- give a final personal opinion on the topic
- leave the reader with something to think about.

5 The content, tone, and style of writing should suit the likely readers of the article.
- How much are readers likely to know about the topic?
- Are opinions as well as facts appropriate in the article?
- What are the appropriate style and tone for the topic and the readers: formal or informal? serious or humorous?

Answer these questions by looking at the report below – do not read it yet.

- How does a report differ from an article or a narrative?
- What are you going to find out by reading this report?

Analysis

Now read the report.

1 What is the purpose of the report? Who do you think wrote it? Who might it have been written for?

2 Think of a suitable heading for the third section.

3 What personal comments does the writer make? Where do they come in the report?

Report on college eating facilities

This report outlines the results of a recent survey of student attitudes towards the canteen and restaurant facilities at this college. We asked a sample of 250 students, of different ages and on a variety of courses, just three questions. Do you think the food available at the college is reasonably priced? Is there sufficient variety? Can you suggest any improvements?

Price

On the whole the students thought the food available was good value for money. However, there were exceptions to this. Firstly, they felt that the hot drinks, particularly coffee, were overpriced. Secondly some of the snack foods, such as sandwiches, available at lunchtime cost more than many students were prepared to pay on a regular basis.

The majority of students were satisfied with the variety of hot meals available at lunchtime, although over 25% said that they would like this range of food to be available in the evening as well. Sandwiches were criticized for their unimaginative fillings. Ham, cheese, and prawns, although firm favourites with well over half the students, were felt to be rather dull. There was support for the idea of more vegetarian fillings.

Improvements

Although most students would prefer to pay less for their food, price was not a major concern. What worried many students was the fact that there were frequently long queues at lunchtime. Many reported that they regularly had to wait for more than 15 minutes to get their food, and suggested that the college might have different lunchtimes for different groups of students.

Conclusion

Overall, it seems that students are happy with most aspects of the food available at the college. There is a widespread feeling that coffee is too expensive and that sandwich fillings could be more interesting. In addition, I suggest that the college management find a way of reducing the overcrowding which occurs in the canteen between 12.30 and 1.00 on weekdays.

Useful language

Read the report again, then underline or make a note of any words or phrases you may find useful in your own writing. Look particularly for examples of formal language.

Checklist

Think about these points when you are planning a report.

1 Use a title and subheadings to give your report clear focus and purpose. Use the first sentence to give a clear statement of intent, and the introduction to make the overall scope of the report clear.

2 In the final section you should:
   - summarize briefly the information contained in the report and/or
   - make clear recommendations or suggestions.

3 The layout of the report should help the reader to see at a glance the areas covered. Reports can look quite different from other types of writing, like letters, articles, etc. You can use separate sections with headings instead of conventional paragraphs.

4 Reports are impersonal presentations of factual information, so they are usually written in formal language. If you include personal comments, write them in a relatively impersonal or detached style.

Analysis

1 Read the three reviews below and answer these questions.

   a Which review contains the most factual information?

   b Which expresses strong personal opinions?

   c Which do you think is the most balanced?

   d Which review is the most formal? How could you describe the style of review A?

2 If you have actually heard the CD, seen the film or read the book, do you agree with the reviewer's opinions? Would you take any notice of reviews like these?

A

Kid A   (CD)   Radiohead
KKKKK

Well, what can I say? Just when I was beginning to get bored of all that guitar band release-the-same-thing-over-and-over-again nonsense, *Radiohead* come along with something completely new and magnificent. I firmly believe that this is one of the best albums ever released, so if you haven't bought it yet, then you should. And if you have bought it but don't like it, then listen to it again. I can't work out exactly what about the album makes it so good; my favourite track changes on every listen. The only bad thing about it is that it's not long enough! I love the variations in time signature, and the overlapping rhythms. If you liked the mini-album *'Airbag/How am I Driving'* then you'll love *'Kid A'*. I just can't wait for their next album.

Tom Price

B

Titanic   (James Cameron, 1997, US)
Leonardo diCaprio, Kate Winslet   195 mins

Despite the enormous cost of making this film – $200m – *Titanic* is a disappointment. The main problems are the characterization and the structure. Too much time is spent on the romance between the upper-class Rose (Kate Winslet) and the poor artist Jack (Leonardo diCaprio). What the audience really wants to see is the collision between the world's greatest ship and the iceberg. Having said that, once the ship starts to break up and sink the special effects are incredible and certainly kept me on the edge of my seat. Unlike the ship, this film will not sink – it will go on making millions at the cinema and on video. Go and see it – if only to try to work out how they spent that $200m.

C

Harry Potter and the Chamber of Secrets, J.K. Rowling, Bloomsbury   (Ages 9 to Adult)

J. K. Rowling's sequel to *Harry Potter and the Philosopher's Stone* carries on where the original left off. Harry is returning to Hogwarts School of Witchcraft and Wizardry after the summer holidays and, right from the start, things are not straightforward.

Unable to board the Hogwarts Express, Harry and his friends break all the rules and make their way to the school in a magical flying car. From this point on, incredible events happen to Harry and his friends – Harry hears evil voices and someone, or something, is attacking the pupils. Can Harry get to the bottom of the mystery before it's too late?

As with its predecessor, *Harry Potter and the Chamber of Secrets* is a highly readable and imaginative adventure story with real, fallible characters, plenty of humour and, of course, loads of magic and spells. There is no need to have read *Harry Potter and the Philosopher's Stone* to enjoy this book. However, if you have read it, this is the book you have been waiting for.

Philippa Reece

Useful language

Read the reviews again, then underline or make a note of any words or phrases you think you may find useful in your own writing. Look particularly for language which expresses positive and negative opinions.

Checklist

Think about these points when you are planning a review.

1 Who will read your review? What style is appropriate for your readers?

2 Is your main purpose to provide factual information or to express personal opinions? Or do you want to combine these two purposes?

3 Which of these factual details do you need to include?
   • the title of the book, film, CD, concert, etc.
   • the type of book, film, CD, etc, for example, love story, thriller, Rock 'n' Roll
   • the intended audience, for example adults, teenagers
   • the author, director, main actors, singer, group, etc.
   • the publisher, cinema, channel, label, venue, etc.
   • the price.

4 Will you give a summary first, or will you simply give your opinions? When you give your opinions, support them with clear examples.

   To make your review balanced, you could include *good points* (What I liked) and *bad points* (What I disliked).

5 Make your recommendation clear in the final sentence or paragraph.

Interaction and check

Student A

1 You are a time traveller who has just returned to the present after a visit to the future. You have agreed to give an interview about your experience to a journalist.

2 Prepare for the interview.

Note down some details of your journey to the future. You know that many people will not believe your story, so try to think of evidence that will convince the interviewer that your story is true.

Here are some of the subjects the journalist may ask about

a the time and place you travelled to
b your method of travelling
c the length of your stay and what happened to you
d the people you met and what they were like.

Student A

You are passionate about wildlife conservation.

An isolated wooded area on the island is the nesting place for a small colony of birds which are native to the island. Without active support and protection this type of bird will become extinct within five years. There is strong international support for this project and the possibility of financial aid from other countries.

More information

• The farmer had frequently been burgled in the past. He kept three large dogs in a nearby cottage and had built lookout posts around his property. He kept a loaded shot gun in his house. (He had no licence for this gun.)
• At no time did the farmer warn the intruders or give them a chance to surrender.
• The boy who was killed was a serial offender. He had previously been in court many times for crimes that included theft, offences against property, and public disorder.
• The law states that every citizen has the right to use reasonable force to prevent crime.
• The farmer received massive support from local people who had been complaining for some time about the lack of effective policing in remote rural areas.

Student B

You are an expert on the history of the island.

One of the original languages spoken on the island is on the brink of extinction. The language is still spoken by the older people in three villages in a poor area. Without a special education programme, the language will die out within 20 years. There is widespread support among islanders for saving the language, but the younger generation in the two villages prefer to use the dominant language.

Student B

Johnny explains why he is a virus writer

'Why do I write viruses? Why do I spend nights without sleep, fuelled by caffeine, cigarettes and sugar? Why do I buy, borrow and read technical manuals that the average person would classify as boring? Or even consider doing
5 something that can result in the loss of a job or an investigation by the police? Well, here are my philosophical reasons for writing viruses. It allows me to play god in my own little microcosm. I can pretend to be a dark villain, or some sort of cyber-terrorist. Not that
10 I'd seriously pose as one. Oh, and for the record, I'm not antisocial, nor do I wear centimetre-thick glasses.

How about ethics then? Aesthetically, a virus can be a piece of art. Think of graffiti. You can use it as a means to send some sort of message to the world. Like guns,
15 viruses are fun to play with. In irresponsible hands they can be dangerous.

I will make this clear though – I don't believe that the average person does deserve to lose data. So, I've never written a destructive virus, nor have I ever intentionally
20 spread one.

Those are my thoughts if anyone cares.'

Johnny The Homicidal Maniac

The Guardian

Close up

1.3 A *manual* is a handbook, but what does the adjective *manual* mean in phrases like *manual work* or a *manual typewriter*?

1.8 A *microcosm* is a small-scale society or situation. What other words start with the prefix *micro-*?

1.12 *Ethics* is a singular word which means the study of moral principles. What other singular study words do you know with this ending?

■ Unit 3 ████████████████ Exploring words p.26

The farmer was found guilty of murder and sentenced to life imprisonment. On appeal his conviction was reduced to manslaughter.

■ Unit 4 ████████████████████ Stage 3 p.33

Student A

Read this e-mail from the Head of English at a language school. Imagine it is your school.

> To   All students
> From   Director of the English Department
> Subject Fun
>
> I have recently received a number of complaints about the behaviour of certain students in the Advanced English classes. It seems that a small proportion of you have been enjoying your English lessons. This unrepresentative minority is making it difficult for other, more serious students to concentrate on their lessons.
>
> It has even been suggested that some of the teachers have been making their lessons interesting. Obviously this situation cannot continue.
>
> In the next few days, I will be visiting classes to make sure that there is no unnecessary fun.

■ Unit 5 ████████████████ Exploring words p.42

We could not let this death threat affect our judgement, however, and we decided to publish. After the story appeared, the public supported Tim and was very critical of me and my newspaper. Tim lost his job and went to work for his mother's business in another town. He didn't commit suicide.

■ Unit 9 ████████████████████ Stage 2 p.69

Student A

1 Rewrite this story in a more formal style. Incorporate some of the features listed in the Language commentary on p73.

> We got to the concert hall about two minutes before they opened the doors. There was a massive queue all down the main street. So, Maria got out of the car and stood in the queue. I went to find somewhere to leave the car.

2 Rewrite this continuation of the same story in a more informal, conversational style.

> Owing to the fact that we were late, all the seats were occupied and we were obliged to remain standing throughout the performance. But, having come to hear the music, which was brilliant, this did not worry me in the slightest.

■ Unit 3 ████████████████████ Stage 3 p.25

Student C

You are the owner of an important tourist hotel.

An ancient monument in the island's capital town has been damaged by the weather over the centuries and is now in danger of collapsing. The monument has religious and cultural significance to the islanders and is an important tourist attraction. (Tourists are essential to the economy of the island.) It will not be possible to repair the monument if it collapses.

■ Unit 16 ████████████████████ Stage 3 p.123

Student A: Interview candidate

* You have applied for a holiday job as a waiter at a local fast food restaurant. You are well qualified for the job and have some experience of this kind of work.

* Soon after the interview has begun, you change your mind about the job. You decide you're no longer interested.

* Do and say whatever is necessary to make sure you do NOT get the job.

■ Unit 17 ████████████████████ Stage 3 p.130

Jane Austen (1775–1817)
English novelist. Famous for *Pride and Prejudice*, *Emma*, *Sense and Sensibility*.

Charles Dickens (1812–1870)
English novelist. Famous for *Oliver Twist*, *Great Expectations*, *David Copperfield*, *A Tale of Two Cities*.

Berthe Morisot (1841–1895)
French impressionist painter. Famous for her paintings of women in domestic and social settings.

Wolfgang Amadeus Mozart (1756–1791)
Austrian composer. Famous for his symphonies and operas.

Pablo Picasso (1881–1973)
Spanish painter. Famous for his cubist style and Spanish Civil War painting *Guernica*.

Clara Schumann (1819–1896)
German composer. Famous mainly as an international pianist.

Unit 3 ━━━━━━━━━━━━━ Stage 3 p.25

Student D

You are a patriotic islander, but have no strong views yet.

This is all you know about the three projects:

Project 1   to save a colony of rare birds from extinction.

Project 2   to teach young people one of the island's minority languages.

Project 3   to repair a monument in the capital that has been damaged by the weather.

Unit 15 ━━━━━━━━━━━━━ Stage 1 p.110

Student A

Read the news story below. Make a note of key facts so that you can tell your partner the story later.

a   What did the person actually do?

b   How would you explain their motives?

Buried alive for five months

Geoff Smith was buried alive for five months in a wooden box in the back garden of a pub. It had been his ambition to get the family name back in the Guinness Book of Records after his mother – who was buried for
5 101 days in 1968 – lost the record to an American.

Geoff tells his story. 'What they actually did was they lowered the box into the hole, I climbed into it and they put the lid on, screwed it down and covered me in. It didn't bother me when they first buried me because it's
10 what I expected. I had a little television, a CD and radio and a mobile phone. I'd got enough room to turn round in it and do basic exercises. I got a lot of different reactions from people. Some were 100% behind me. Some called me a lunatic. It was a fantastic feeling when
15 they did actually take the lid off. I could see the sky, … it was an unbelievable feeling.'

Geoff was buried for 147 days, and took the record, only to discover that the Guinness Book of Records had removed the human endurance category for safety
20 reasons.

The Guardian

Close up

1.2   What is the name for the wooden box that people are buried in when they are dead?

1.13   What is the meaning of *behind* here?

1.14   A *lunatic* is a person. What related noun means the condition a *lunatic* suffers from?

Unit 4 ━━━━━━━━━━━━━ Stage 3 p.33

Student B

Read this e-mail from the Head of an English Department.

To   All staff and students
From   Director of the English Department
Subject   Spelling / Grammar

I am pleased to tell you that I have just received a letter from the British Government detailing some official changes to the English language. The most important changes will be:

1   All verbs will be regular with the exception of *to be*. (So instead of *drink, drank, drunk*, the verb will be *drink, drinked, drinked*.)

2   All words will be spelt in the same way as they are pronounced. For example: *enough* will be spelt *innuf*.

3   All question tags will be replaced by a single new tag: *innit?*

These changes will come into effect from January 1st.

Unit 9 ━━━━━━━━━━━━━ Stage 2 p.69

Student B

1   Rewrite this formal story in an informal, conversational style.

We arrived at the concert hall approximately two minutes before the doors were opened. There was a long queue of people stretching the length of the main street. So, while Maria got out of the car and joined the queue, I went to find a car park.

2   Rewrite this continuation of the same story in a more formal style. Incorporate some of the features listed in the Language commentary on p73.

Because we were late, all the seats in the hall were taken and we had to stand right through the show. It didn't really bother me – I mean, I'd come to hear the music and that was brilliant.

Unit 16 ━━━━━━━━━━━━━ Stage 3 p.123

Student B: Interviewer

• You are interviewing applicants for a job in your fast food restaurant. You have interviewed several people already, but found no one suitable.

• Soon after the beginning of the interview with A, you decide he/she is the right person for the job.

• Do everything possible to make the interview a success.

OXFORD
UNIVERSITY PRESS

Great Clarendon Street, Oxford OX2 6DP

Oxford University Press is a department of the University of Oxford. It furthers the University's objective of excellence in research, scholarship, and education by publishing worldwide in

Oxford New York

Auckland Bangkok Buenos Aires Cape Town Chennai
Dar es Salaam Delhi Hong Kong Istanbul Karachi Kolkata
Kuala Lumpur Madrid Melbourne Mexico City Mumbai
Nairobi São Paulo Shanghai Taipei Tokyo Toronto

OXFORD and OXFORD ENGLISH are registered trade marks of Oxford University Press in the UK and in certain other countries

© Oxford University Press 2002

The moral rights of the author have been asserted

Database right Oxford University Press (maker)

First published 2002

2008 2007 2006 2005 2004

10 9 8 7 6 5 4 3

No unauthorized photocopying

All rights reserved. No part of this publication may be reproduced, stored in a retrieval system, or transmitted, in any form or by any means, without the prior permission in writing of Oxford University Press, or as expressly permitted by law, or under terms agreed with the appropriate reprographics rights organization. Enquiries concerning reproduction outside the scope of the above should be sent to the ELT Rights Department, Oxford University Press, at the address above

You must not circulate this book in any other binding or cover and you must impose this same condition on any acquirer

Any websites referred to in this publication are in the public domain and their addresses are provided by Oxford University Press for information only. Oxford University Press disclaims any responsibility for the content

ISBN 0 19 437960 4

Printed in China

ACKNOWLEDGEMENTS

The author and publisher are very grateful to the following for piloting the course: Carole Patilla and Jon Midmer, Aspect Covent Garden Language Centre, London; Éva Rózsa and 3a group, Leőwey Klára Gimnázium, Pécs; Amanda Smith, King Street College, London; Siobhán O'Connor and CPE Class 06.00, Aspect, Dublin; Joanne Savage, Bell Schools of English, Budapest; Gareth Taylor, CCIV (Montigny-le-Bretonneux); Rory Power; Francesca Horta, Sociedade Brasiliera de Cultura Inglesa, Belo Horizonte; Litany Pires Ribeiro, Sociedade Brasiliera de Cultura Inglesa, Belo Horizonte; Marcia do Amaral Prudêncio; Rachel Allan, Aspect, Dublin; John Haagensen, Eurocentre Victoria, London; Felix Mathez, Kantonsschule Solothurn; Joanna Sosnowska, I LO im. St Dubois, Koszalin; Pedro Pascual-Zahinos, Escuela Oficial de Idiomas de Huelva; Krystyna Paszkowska-Hoppe, Centre for Foreign Language teaching, University of Warsaw; Frances Mosimann, Swiss Post; Julie Anne Smith, British Council, Madrid; William Stone; ASC/International House, Geneva; Haydée Elena, Sta Brigida, Profesorado del Consuedec 'Septimio Walsh'; Christiane Khatchadourian, Cultura Inglesa, São Paulo; Rosana Nucci, Cultura Inglesa, São Paulo; Ali Işik; Aydan Ersöz, Neslihan Özkan, Gülsen Altuntas.

We would also like to thank the following for their comments on various drafts of the material: Jane Hudson; Rachel Allan; Rory Power; Luiz Otávio de Barros Souza; Matthew Moody; Joanna Sosnowska; Brian Brennan; Josephine Rudland; Magdalena Junkieles. The author would also like to thank everybody who contributed to the recordings.

The author and publisher are grateful to those who have given permission to reproduce the following extracts and adaptations of copyright material: p.6 'Response to Time 100 (Why this site?)' by Cliff Ruesch. Reproduced by permission of Cliff Ruesch; p.10 Extracts from *The ISM Book* by Peter Saint-Andre. Reproduced by permission of Peter Saint-Andre; p.14 'If only everything in life was as reliable as a computer' from www.bloor.co.uk. Reproduced by permission of Bloor Research Ltd; p.18 'Big brother is watching you' by Nick Paton-Walsh, © *The Observer* 18 July 1999. Reproduced by permission of Guardian Newspapers Ltd; p.20 'Scientists rule out running from the rain' by Roger Highfield, *The Daily Telegraph* 1987. Reproduced by permission of Telegraph Group Ltd; p.24 'This man is worth £100,000 a year' by David Crystal, *High Life* June 2000. Reproduced by permission of David Crystal; p.32 'Melissa creator pleads guilty' from www.reuters.com 1999. Reproduced by permission of Reuters Ltd; p.38 'It's an everyday dilemma ...' by Nicholas Whittaker, *The Daily Mail* 17 November 1995. Reproduced by permission of Nicholas Whittaker; p.46 Extract from 'Outlasting the Dinosaurs'

interview with Dr. James Perran Ross from Nova 'Crocodiles!' website. Reproduced by permission of NOVA/WGBH Boston; p.48 'Face it – they're perfect' by Maureen Freely, *The Observer* 12 March 2000. Reproduced by permission of Maureen Freely; p.52 'What are you looking at?' by Robert Matthews, *The Daily Telegraph* February 1998. Reproduced by permission of Telegraph Group Ltd; p.58 'Escape from the family hothouse' by Deborah Orr, *The Independent* 7 July 2000. Reproduced by permission of Independent Newspapers (UK) Ltd; p.62. 'Waste that we want not' by Sasha Norris, *The Guardian* 16 August 2000. Reproduced by permission of Sasha Norris; p.68 Extract from *The Piano* by Jane Campion and Kate Pullinger. Reproduced by permission of Bloomsbury Publishers; p.71 'Genesis: Earl's Court review' by Adam Sweeting, © *The Guardian* 26 November 1992. Reproduced by permission of Guardian Newspapers Ltd; p.71 'Top of the world. El Hadj N'Diaye' review by Katharina Lobeck, *Songlines* Spring/Summer 2000. Reproduced by permission of Songlines; p.76 Extract from *Pole to Pole* by Michael Palin © 1994 Michael Palin. Reproduced by permission of BBC Worldwide Limited; p.80 Extract from *Letters Home* by Fergal Keane, Penguin Books 1999 copyright © Fergal Keane, 1999. Reproduced by permission of The Penguin Group (UK); p.82 Adapted extracts from: *From Brains to Consciousness* by Stephen Rose. Reproduced by permission of Stephen Rose; p.90 'How we learned to love the Big Mac' © John Sutherland, *The Guardian* 6 November 2000. Reproduced by permission of Guardian Newspapers Ltd; p.98 'In praise of danger' by Ros Coward, *The Guardian* 7 July 1999. Reproduced by permission of Ros Coward; p.99 'Stories from up high' by Elliot Neal, *The Guardian* 30 April 2000. Reproduced by permission of Guardian Newspapers Ltd; p.100 Extract from *Men* by Anna Ford © Anna Ford 1985, Published by Weidenfeld & Nicolson. Reproduced by permission of The Orion Publishing Group Ltd; p.100 Extract from 'My Mum' by Phineas Foster in *Sons and Mothers* edited by Victoria Glendinning and Matthew Glendinning. Reproduced by permission of Little, Brown and Company (UK); p.105 Extracts from 'Twenty Minutes' by Alex Gough from www.galacticguide.com. Reproduced by permission of Alex Gough; p.110 'Cheating, lying and sleeping with the boss' by Sarah Bosely © *The Guardian* 14 July 2000. Reproduced by permission of Guardian Newspapers Ltd; p.112 'How to skive' © *The Observer* 3 October 1993. Reproduced by permission of Guardian Newspapers Ltd; p.118 'Poultry in motion' by John Crace, *The Guardian* 27 June 2000. Reproduced by permission of John Crace; p.120 'What not to say in interviews' by Tom Kuntz, *The New York Times Week in Review* 24 January 2000. © The New York Times Company. Reproduced by permission; p.126 'Palette of the Apes' by Emma Bayley, *Focus* August 1999. © National Magazine Company. Reproduced by permission; p.132 'Names that live in infamy' by David Brin from www.salon.com. Reproduced by permission of Salon.com; p.134 Extract from 'Introduction to Castaway 2000' by Jeremy Mills, Lion Television. Reproduced by permission of Lion Television; p.150 Norris Turney Obituary, *Electronic Telegraph* 22 January 2001 © Telegraph Group Limited 2001. Reproduced by permission of Telegraph Group Limited; p.151 'First Person Singular' by Tony Wilmot, *Cover Magazine* October 1998. Reprinted by permission of The Oldie; p.151 Extract from *Posts and Telecommunications* by Jan Mark © 1983 Jan Mark. Reproduced by permission of David Higham Associates; p.156 Review of *Harry Potter and the Chamber of Secrets* by Philippa Reece from www.amazon.co.uk. Reproduced by permission of Amazon.co.uk; p.156 Review of Radiohead 'Kid A' CD by Tom Price. Reproduced by permission of Tom Price; p.157 'The webslingers' by Simon Waldman © *The Guardian* 15 July 1999. Reproduced by permission of Guardian Newspapers Ltd; p.159 'Buried alive for five months' © *The Guardian* 28 May 1999. Reproduced by permission of Guardian Newspapers Ltd.

Although every effort has been made to trace and contact copyright holders before publication, this has not been possible in some cases. We apologize for any apparent infringement of copyright and if notified, the publisher will be pleased to rectify any errors or omissions at the earliest opportunity.

The publisher would like to thank the following for their kind permission to reproduce photographs and other copyright material: © 2000 DreamWorks, Pathé and Aardmann pp.118 (filming), 120; Action Images p.96 (T.O'Brien/footballers); Action Plus pp.8 (N.Tingle/ football fan), 102 (M. Clarke/football); Agence France Presse p.21; AKG London pp.6 (L.Jacobi/Einstein), (Freud), (Picasso), 22 (Egyptian Pharaoh), 130 (Gesellschaft der Musikfreunde/Mozart), (Private Collection/Austen), (Historisches Museum der Stadt Wien/Clara Schumann), (Morisot); Allsport pp.58 (Williams family), 112 (Ben Johnson, Seoul Olympics); Courtesy of Antony Gormley p.127 (*Iron Man* © Antony Gormley 1993); BBC Picture Archives pp.134 & 137 (group.of people in front of pods), 134, 136; Courtesy of Braun p.14 (food processor); The Bridgeman Art Library pp.22 (painting by Abraham Solomon, *First Class – The Meeting,* National Railway Museum, York/Victorian time); Bryan and Cherry Alexander/www.arcticphoto.co.uk pp.74 (penguins), 76; Bubbles Photo Library p.8 (J.Woodcock/boy in his room); © Dr. Ronald H. Cohn/Gorilla Foundation/Koko.org pp.128–129; Collections pp.80 (M.Diggin/landscape), 89 (P.Wright/teddy bears), 106 (G.Wright/actors), 138 (S.Warner/village); Comstock p.106 (office worker); Corbis p.6 (J.Cooke/Pelé), 112 (Georges de

la Tour, *The Cheat with the Ace of Clubs,* c.1630, Kimbell Art Museum); Eyewire pp.14 (fax), 36 (floppy disc); Courtesy of Ford Motor Company p.14 (car); Gateshead Council/C.Cuthbert p.126 (*The Angel of the North,* © Antony Gormley 1998); GettyOne Image Bank pp.36 (B.Erlanson/eating), 56 (television), 90 (R.Lockyer/ woman eating), 96 (L.D/Gordon/couple arguing), (H.Sims/two businessmen), 104 (S.Murez/desk and clock), 119 (Bokelberg/ cinematographer), 122 (Morrell/Infoc/interview), 124 (J.Silva/ yellow cab); GettyOne Stone pp.6 & 9 (ED-PT/teacher and boys), 10 (H.Sitton), 14 (A.Meshkinyar/TV & video), 14 & 16 (J.Turner/laptop), 28 (H.R.Johnstone/sea), (P.Chelsey/ disco), (D.Hiser/jungle), 31 (W.Scholz/caravan), 36 (B.Ayres/man at work), 66 (Z.Kaluzny/gospel choir), (T.Raymond/ Tennessee folk band), (S.Grandadam/saxophonist), 74 (E.Collacott/ice climber), (B.Bailey/woman climber), (D.Torckler/ diver), 78 (H.Sitton), 96–97 (N.Dolding/couple on sofa), 100 (D.Hanover), 104 & 106 (W.Hodges/lorry driver), 106 (Kaluzny/Thatcher/college lecturer), 108 (W.Hodges), 110 (T.Garcia/man screaming), 118 (Z.Kaluzny/woman asleep), 119 (I.Murphy/miner), (A.Sacks/ firewoman), 122 (C.Everard/pizza); GettyOne Telegraph pp.8 (D.Luria/family swimming), (J.Giustina/girls playing), 28 (football), (kitchen), (A.Smith/motorway), 31 (D.Felix/men on bus), 81 (K.Chenus/man walking away from caravan), 106 (D.Hallinan/ doctor), 110 (M.Crosby/two women screaming), 119 (V.C.L./ T.Howell/pilot; Hulton Getty Archive pp.6 (Gandhi), (Monroe), (Ford), 89 (boys on pogo sticks), 126 & 130 (Dickens), 130 (Picasso); Katz Pictures pp.58 & 60 (Brown/SABA/REA/elderly woman), 60 (Mark Petersen/SABA/younger woman & two men), 64 (A.North/shopping centre), 102 (G.Trott/commuters), 111 (V.Eckersley/contortionist); Magnum Photos pp.48 & 54–55 (P.Marlow/dealing room), 66 (C.Steele-Perkins/pop.group); Mary Evans Picture Library p.88; Harald Nordbakken p.98; PA Photos pp.6 (EPA/Gates & Pope John Paul II), 26 (S.Dempsey), 30 (B.Batchelor/station), 32–33 (EPA), 36 & 40 (Roslin Institute/Dolly the sheep), 88 (J.Green/Gameboy), (EPA/ skateboarding), 111 (EPA/tightrope stunt); Panos Photos p.20 & 25 (P.Tweedie/man on phone); PhotoDisc pp.14 (computer), 42, 53, 56 (boots), 80 & 82 (boy), 82 (sunglasses), 90–91 (hamburger), 94, 101, 110 & 112 (student cheating), 122 (suitcase), 124 (black cabs), 134 (man); Photofest, NY pp.121 (Tom & Jerry), 135 (Catwoman); The Photographer's Library p.70 (woman listening to music); Photonica pp.81 (M.Persson/woman leaping & woman at computer); Redferns pp.66 (R.Parkin/ballroom dance), (S.Gillet/pop singer), (E.Roberts/ Reggae), T.Wales/Latin salsa), 70 (L.Morris/orchestra); Retna p.48 (A.Gallo); Rex Features pp.6 (C.Sykes/Winfrey), 16 (R.Tang/internet café), 30 (cyclist), 61, 88 (Lego), 89 (rollerskating), 111 (P.Brooker/ cigarettes); Robert Harding Picture Library p.21 (man crossing road); Ronald Grant Archive pp.22 (time of Jesus), 68 (© Sky Movies), 88 & 92 (Braveheart), 92 (Crouching Tiger, Hidden Dragon), (Casablanca), 121 (The Pink Panther), 135 (Cruella Devil © Disney/Clive Coote); Scala p.22 (Renaissance Florence/painting by Maestro del Cassone Adimari, 15th century, Galleria dell'Accademia, Florence); Science Photo Library pp.22 (C.Jegou/Publiphoto/early man), 40 (W.A.Ritchie/Roslyn Institute/cloning), 40 & 41 (A.Pasieka/DNA), 44 & 46 (P.&T.Leeson/crocodile), 62 (T.Craddock); © Siggi Musique/Photo Sophie Bachelier pp.66 & 71; Courtesy of Sony p.14 (CD player, camcorder); Still Pictures pp.74 (Schafer and Hill/inflatable boat), (M.& C.Denis-Huot/safari and lions), 138 (P.Frischmuth/Seattle); Courtesy of Glynn Thomas and his son Dan Thomas p.75; Bo Trond p.127 (sculptured figures in the sea entitled *Another Place* © Antony Gormley 1997); Courtesy of Zanussi p.1

Illustrations by: Stefan Chabluk p.136–137; Rowie Christopher p.22; Matthew Cooper p.50; Emma Dodd pp.11, 54, 97, 132; Melvyn Evans pp.18, 114; Phil Healey pp.77; Ian Jackson pp.34, 85; Sarah Jones p.44; Julian Mosedale p.12

Commissioned photography by: Mark Mason Studios p.38, p.56 (cardigan, cigarette, handkerchief, photo, sandwich, glasses, pullover, remote control); 82–83 (zip, shoe, ticket, rose, pipe, match, duck, biscuit, lipstick, mousetrap, pill, screw)